Important Telephone Numbers

Veterinarian: _____

  Address: _____

  Phone: _____

Emergency Clinic or

  Veterinary Hospital: _____

Poison Control Center: _____

ASPCA (Humane Shelter): _____

Your Cat's Records

Name _____ Breed _____ Breeder_____

                                                                     Tom _____

Birthdate_____Registration number_____Queen _____

	7-14 wks.	6 mos.	1 yr.	2 yrs.	3 yrs.	4 yrs.	5 yrs.	6-15 yrs.
FUR-C-P								
Rabies								
Stool sample								
FLV test								
FIP test								

FUR-C-P Rhinotracheitis, Calicivirus, Panleukopenia (distemper). A kitten series and *yearly* boosters throughout life are needed for protection.

Rabies Vaccination at four to six months and *yearly* boosters are required by state laws.

Stool sample Feces should be checked whenever vaccinations are given. Bring a fresh sample to be examined.

FLV test Feline leukemia virus test, see page 237.

FIP test Feline infectious peritonitis test, see page 134. If you plan to breed your cat or if the illnesses described are present, the FLV and FIP tests should be done.

Surgery		Date			Complications

Problem or illness	Date	Medication used	Doctor was seen	Used home treatment	Resolved without medicine

In heat	Date bred	Mate:_____ FLV = free?	Owner:_____ FIP = free?	Number of kittens	Kitten mortality

Taking Care of Your Cat

Taking Care of Your Cat

A Complete Guide to Your Cat's Medical Care

Sheldon L. Gerstenfeld, V.M.D.

ADDISON-WESLEY PUBLISHING COMPANY

Reading, Massachusetts • Menlo Park, California
Don Mills, Ontario • Wokingham, England • Amsterdam • Sydney
Singapore • Tokyo • Madrid • Bogotá • Santiago • San Juan

Library of Congress Cataloging in Publication Data

Gerstenfeld, Sheldon L   1943-
    Taking care of your cat.

    Includes index.
    1. Cats--Diseases. I. Title.
SF985.G47   636.8'08'9   79-2338
ISBN 0-201-03058-6
ISBN 0-201-03059-4 pbk.

Fifth Printing, April 1986

ISBN 0-201-03059-4-P
ISBN 0-201-03058-6-H
EFGHIJ-DO-89876

To my dear wife, Traudi, whose love and whole being have expanded my creativity and my sensitivity of the world.

To my dear parents, Sidney and Isabelle, who encouraged their son to pursue his dream to be an "animal doctor."

To our dear Pepe, who recently passed on. He brightened our lives for fourteen wonderful years and will always be remembered.

To the Reader

This book can be of great help to you and your cat. Many veterinarians have reviewed each section and have agreed on the medical recommendations for each problem. The recommendations will not work in every case, however, so here are some qualifications:

1. If your cat is under the care of a veterinarian who gives advice contrary to that given in this book, follow your veterinarian's advice. The individual characteristics of your cat can then be taken into account.

2. You know your cat best; do not hesitate to follow your own judgment as to when to seek professional assistance.

3. If your cat has an allergy or a suspected allergy to a medication, check with your veterinarian, at least by phone.

4. If your cat's problem persists beyond a reasonable period, you should make an appointment with your veterinarian.

Acknowledgments

The sincere help and encouragement of many people made the writing of this book a most pleasurable experience.

First and foremost, I thank my wife Traudi for her very helpful comments and patience, and for providing a loving and creative environment.

Ann Dilworth accepted the manuscript with those three little words that mean so much to an author—"We love it!" The raw manuscript evolved into its most effective form thanks to the teamwork of Doe Coover, Martha Drumm, and Tess Palmer. They helped me rearrange, reword, and delete, studying every word and paragraph until they could almost recite the text verbatim! Lois Hammer deserves a lot of credit for turning my "doctor's handwriting" into a typewritten beauty. John Hackmaster did the marvelous medical illustrations, and Beth Anderson finalized my original cartoons.

Five colleagues took time from very busy schedules to review the manuscript and offer suggestions: Dr. Gus Thornton, Dr. Jean Holzworth, Dr. Robert Brodey, Dr. Donald Patterson, and Dr. Al Kissileff. Encouragement and suggestions were also enthusiastically provided by Eleonore Gerstenfeld, Jack Neifert, Bob and Jill Terranova, and Baxter and Betsy Holland.

I also want to thank Dr. Donald Vickery, Dr. James Fries, and Dr. Robert Pantell for laying the groundwork with **Take Care of Yourself** and **Taking Care of Your Child.**

All my patients' owners deserve a great deal of credit for caring so well and so responsibly for their pets. Their hopes, fears, and needs and their development into well-informed pet owners formed the foundation for this book.

Finally, I want to thank my patients themselves for giving me their unquestioning love and trust.

S. L. G.

Contents

Introduction

Owning a cat is a big responsibility. As the owner, your care is instrumental in helping your animal—whether it be a Persian cat of royal breeding or a stray who followed you home one day—live a happy and healthy life. With the information in this book, you will be able to take good care of your pet at home and ensure that professional veterinary care is obtained when it is needed. You will also save time and money.

The writing of this book was a labor of love. I am thankful that I was able to become a veterinarian, to help injured and ill pets, and to be a source of information, comfort, and reassurance for many, many pet owners.

I have been very fortunate in veterinary practice. My pet owners have become *active* partners with me in sharing the responsibility for their pets' well-being and health. **Taking Care of Your Cat** is the result of this wonderful experience.

Your veterinarian is a busy person. A typical day may include reuniting a child with her cat, Jaws, who has mended from serious automobile injuries; watching as an owner gives his diabetic dog its first life-sustaining injection of insulin; performing one or two "Marcus Welby"-type heroics (without a commercial break); giving several well-pet exams, which cover vaccinations and routine tests; and diagnosing and treating illnesses and injuries that require immediate attention. Your veterinarian also sees many minor medical problems that could be called "unnecessary" visits. In human medicine, up to 70 percent of first visits to the doctor have been termed "unnecessary." There is no reason to believe that our pets' illnesses or injuries are any different. You can save money and time and provide the best care for your pet by learning to treat many of your pet's medical problems at home and by learning when it *is* important to visit or telephone your veterinarian. I'm very proud of my pet owners when they handle minor medical problems efficiently at home. They know that I am around if they need reassurance or advice. I'm equally proud when they recognize *early* that their pet's problem requires my help. The step-by-step Decision Charts in **Taking Care of Your Cat** will provide you with enough information to make sound judgments about most of your cat's medical problems.

To help you become an active partner, an aware pet owner, a good consumer, and a constructive critic, the chapters in Part I provide the following useful information:

Selecting a Cat

Taking care of a pet actually starts *before* you choose one (or two). This chapter will help you select and find the proper pet for your life-style, and it emphasizes the *responsibility* of pet ownership.

The Owner's Home Physical Exam: Your Cat's Body and How It Works

You'll be fascinated at the similarities between a person's body and a cat's body. This chapter also shows you how to examine your pet at home.

Keeping Your Cat Healthy, Happy, and Obedient

Many illnesses and injuries are the result of long-term abuse or lack of proper maintenance. Preventive care—grooming, training, good nutrition, annual vaccinations, checking for parasites, and dental care—will keep your pet healthy. The section entitled How Do I Know When My Cat is Sick? describes some general signs that may be the first indication that your pet is not feeling well.

Going to the Veterinarian

Finding a competent and interested veterinarian and being a cooperative, aware, and concerned owner are important for your cat's health. You should understand and appreciate the procedures that may be necessary for your veterinarian to diagnose and properly treat your pet's health problem.

Your Cat's Home Pharmacy

A first aid kit is a must, and this chapter will help you stock it with the most effective medications for minor medical problems. Included are hints on uses, dosages, and possible side effects for a variety of over-the-counter medications.

Part II provides specific guidance for 55 of your cat's most common medical problems. This section is designed for quick and easy reference. First, identify your pet's primary symptom—for instance, coughing, vomiting, or straining to urinate. To find a discussion of the problem, look it up in the Contents or the Index.

Emergency Procedures

Chapter 6 details the best way to approach injured animals and the things you can do during those first vital minutes that could mean the difference between life and death.

Accidents and Injuries

This chapter goes into common injuries sustained by cats, listing any appropriate home treatment and what to expect from your veterinarian.

Common Problems and Diseases

Each of the medical problems in this section includes a general discussion, suggestions for home treatment, and pointers to show you when a telephone call or visit to your veterinarian is needed. Information on what to expect at the veterinarian's office is also given to help you be aware of appropriate care. The Decision Charts that accompany each problem provide step-by-step instructions to help you decide whether to use home treatment or to seek professional advice. No medication suggested in this section should be used without knowledge of its dosage and side effects. Most medicines are discussed in Chapter 5, Your Cat's Home Pharmacy. First aid information for handling the most common cat emergencies is provided. Your handling of the emergency at home and knowing what to expect at the veterinarian's office may combine to save your pet's life. Prevention of injuries is also discussed.

Breeding and Reproduction

Breeding, pregnancy, delivery, and nursing are fully discussed. Step-by-step charts on delivery and nursing will give you easy instructions to follow if your help—or the veterinarian's help—is needed.

Genetics and Hereditary Diseases
Cancer

These two chapters provide you with the latest information on advances in these important health areas.

Euthanasia

In today's world, it is painful to lose the unselfish love and companionship that a pet provides. When that pet is suffering and there is no hope for a cure, euthanasia should be considered an act of love and mercy. It is a very difficult decision to make and should be considered only after discussion with your family and your veterinarian.

I know you will find the book informative and helpful in taking care of your cat. I hope you also find it enjoyable and interesting reading.

Philadelphia, Pennsylvania   S. L. G.

Part I

You and Your Cat

Chapter 1

Selecting a Cat

One of the greatest pleasures human beings can experience is to share their home with a pet. Having a cat or dog can keep you closer to nature. It should also kindle your spirit of reverence for all life on earth, from the ant on your picnic table to your brothers and sisters in every country. Cats and dogs are an unfailing source of companionship during times of sadness or joy. They have a sense of timing, of humor, seen in few human comedians. You'll always remember their body movements, facial expressions, and "one-liners," even after their bodies have departed and their spirits have become part of your memories. A kitten or puppy is a wonderful aid in teaching a child (and even some adults) about responsibility, patience, love, understanding, and self-control.

No other animal on earth has enjoyed such varied public relations as the cat. Cats have been both vilified and deified throughout history. Their association with witchcraft gave them a bad reputation during the seventeenth century, but ancient Egyptians revered them. Many others have had similar feelings. A French philosopher once said that there are only two aesthetically perfect things in the world, the clock and the cat. Lafe Hill (*Town and Country,* March, 1979) quotes Colette:

> [The cat] is the animal to whom the Creator gave the biggest eye, the softest fur, the most supremely delicate nostrils, a mobile ear, an unrivaled paw, a curved claw, borrowed from a rose tree. . . . I am indebted to the cat for a

particular kind of honorable deceit, for a greater control over myself, for a characteristic aversion to brutal sounds, and for the need to keep silent for long periods of time.

JOY AND RESPONSIBILITY

With the joy of owning a cat, however, comes *responsibility*. The lack of responsibility and lack of planning for owning or breeding a pet can be witnessed on the streets and in the humane shelters. Millions upon millions of cats are put to death yearly; the reasons range from "too much trouble" or "too much money" to "the kids went to college" or "the kitten's not cute any more."

Owning a cat takes a commitment of time (as much as ten to fifteen years) and money. You and your family should ask yourselves the following questions before deciding on the new family member:

Do we have time for a cat?
Who will have the responsibility for feeding the cat and caring for its toilet needs? Does the breed need daily grooming?

Can we afford to keep a cat healthy and well nourished?
The purchase price is small change compared to the maintenance fees: food, accessories, veterinary care, boarding, and kitty litter.

Food and accessories	$125 per year
Veterinary care	$50 to $200 per year
Boarding	$2 to $5 per day
Kitty litter (if house cat)	$50 per year

These figures are estimates and will vary in different regions, but they provide a model for figuring your pet's expenses for the year. Be sure that you have a little extra money set aside for unforeseen problems.

Do we have room for a cat?
Will it be convenient to have a house cat? an indoor-outdoor cat?

Do we want a male or a female?
See Breeding and Reproduction, page 215, for a discussion that should help with this decision.

What are our favorite breeds?
Selecting a pedigreed or nonpedigreed cat is a personal choice. Nonpedigreed cats are like us—a product of mixed breeding. For the most part, these unions produce wonderful and beautiful offspring.

Pedigreed cats (the term means that there is a record, a pedigree, of the kitten's ancestors for three or more generations) that are raised by responsible private breeders are excellent specimens of their breed. The good breeder looks for outstanding physical and mental qualities, such as soundness, beauty, and good temperament, and is continually trying to improve the line. Responsible breeders prepare their cats for breeding (see Breeding and Reproduction, page 215) so that healthy and vigorous kittens are produced.

There are thirty-six breeds recognized by cat associations. You can become familiar with the breeds that interest you by attending cat shows or talking to a neighbor who owns the breed that you like. The specialty magazines listed below are another excellent source of information:

Cat Fancy
P.O. Box 24648
Los Angeles, CA 90024

All-Cats
Suite 7
15113 Sunset Boulevard
Pacific Palisades, CA 90272

Cat World
5395 South Miller Street
Littleton, CO 80123

Cats
P.O. Box 83048
Lincoln, NB 68501

Your veterinarian can supply advice on the breeds that interest you and help you to answer the final three questions:

What are the positive and negative characteristics of the breed?

Can such a cat adapt to our family?

What are the hereditary or common problems of the breed?

FINDING THE RIGHT CAT FOR YOU

If you have decided that you can afford the time and money to own a cat (and I hope you can), where can you go to select the new member of your family? If a specific breed appeals to you, ask your veterinarian for a list of reputable breeders in the area. In addition, for $1.50 the Cat Fanciers' Association will send you a directory of the more than 3,000 cat breeders throughout the United States. You can also check the daily newspapers or the specialty magazines.

If you want a pedigreed pet, avoid outlets. The breeding that produces outlet kittens is often indiscriminate, with no regard for good physical and mental characteristics. Crowding, malnutrition, intestinal parasites, and stress make the kittens vulnerable to many viral and bacterial diseases. The most critical period in the formation of a cat's personality is the first sixteen weeks of life. Outlet kittens are given little love and attention during this time—a tragedy that can affect them for the rest of their lives.

Breeders' home-raised kittens are generally healthy and well socialized because reputable breeders usually follow a standard procedure before breeding, during pregnancy, and at nursing that will give the newborns every chance at a healthy and long life. The new kittens are also checked, vaccinated, and wormed (if necessary) by a licensed local veterinarian. Most important, they are handled gently and given lots of love during the critical socialization period.

Breeders' kittens actually cost less, in most cases, than outlet pets, since the breeder does not have high advertising costs and overhead (shipping costs, rent, and employees' salaries). The breeder is not in it for the money but because of a love for fine physical and mental specimens of the breed.

Mixed-breed cats can be found through newspaper ads, through the neighborhood pipeline, through notices on veterinarians' bulletin boards, or at the local humane shelters. There can be drawbacks to getting a nonpedigreed kitten. Since the mother may not have had good prenatal care, the kittens have more "youngster" problems, such as external and internal parasites, and their future temperament is harder to predict unless you can see the home where they were raised and the temperament of the parents. But these are correctable problems, given the help of your veterinarian and a lot of tender loving care and proper training. Remember, "mixed breeds are beautiful!"

The best time to form a human bond with a cat is when the cat is very young, from seven to twelve weeks old. (Anything younger should still be with its mother.) But don't forget that adult cats, especially at humane shelters, are begging for homes, too. That's where "Morris the Cat" of television fame was found.

To help overcome the "They're *all* so cute, which should we take?" syndrome, go through the following checklist:

Is this a good breeder and a good cattery?
Of course, your veterinarian's recommendation is usually adequate, but your own observations are important. A good breeder will keep the kennel clean and orderly. He or she will also be active in cat shows and interested in improving the breed. Do the owners seem to love their cats? Does the breeder want to know about *you*, your family, and your life-style? A good breeder will not sell his cats to just anyone. Visit several breeders. This will give you a "feel" for the breed and more information. Be sure to telephone for an appointment. Private catteries are part of the breeder's home and should be respected.

Can we meet the kitten's parents?
Meeting the mother and father will give you some idea of the eventual size and temperament of the kittens. The cat's parents should be friendly and outgoing, not vicious or shy.

"This is the one we want!"
Select a kitten that seems physically healthy . . .

- no eye or nose discharges
- no black debris in the ears*
- a healthy, glossy coat with no hair loss or reddened, scabby areas
- no fleas* or ticks
- pink gums
- no coughing
- firm bowel movements
- no lump at the belly button (this would indicate an umbilical hernia, which is correctable by surgery or, if small, can be left untreated)

. . . and temperamentally well balanced.

- friendly
- responds to your attention
- doesn't mind being held

BUYING A KITTEN

Besides the new kitten, what else should you receive from the breeder at the time of payment? He or she should ask you to take your new pet to a veterinarian of your choice within two days of purchase. The breeder should also offer to let you return the kitten for a refund if it is not in good health.

Purchase Papers

You should receive a **written bill of sale** stating: (a) the aforementioned privilege of return; (b) the date of purchase and any conditions of sale; (c) the price paid; (d) the registration numbers and names of the parents; (e) the litter or individual registration number of the kitten; and (f) its date of birth and description, including breed, sex, and color.

You should also receive **registration papers.** If the breeder has not yet received the papers (sometimes this happens) be sure that the bill of sale states this fact and indicates that the papers will be sent when they are received by the breeder. You should never be asked to pay extra for the kitten's registration papers—you have a *right* to them.

Note: In some instances, the breeder may indicate that the kitten is not for breeding purposes and will ask you to sign an agreement to this effect. One copy of the agreement goes to the registry. The breeders are within their rights to ask this.

Instructions for Care

The breeder should also give you **written instructions on feeding and care.** Dates of any worming that has taken place, and the type of medicine used, should

---

*The presence of fleas or ear mites doesn't necessarily disqualify a kitten for purchase.

be included. You should also receive a statement, signed by a veterinarian, of all vaccinations given and the date of the next scheduled vaccination.

When you take your new kitten home, be sure that it has plenty of time for rest. Have a litter box, bedding (a blanket or soft pillow), food, and water awaiting your new arrival. Be gentle and patient and always keep in mind your *size*. After all, the kitten has been brought to a strange home to live with "giants," who cannot communicate directly and have new rules. Follow the breeder's instructions for feeding and care until you see your veterinarian. Be sure that you are present when your kitten is with small children. Severe injuries and even death can result from being dropped, hit, or squeezed by a child.

Registries

After the first cat show was held in England in 1871, breeding cats for certain physical and temperamental qualities, and registering the cats produced, became important. There are several registries in this country, and more abroad, each with its own standards and specifications for the breeds.

The Cat Fanciers' Association (C.F.A.), founded in 1906, is the largest registry in the United States. The C.F.A. has registered more than one-half million cats since its inception and sponsors some 200 annual shows across the country. The American Cat Association registers over 10,000 cats a year and sponsors about 75 national cat shows. In addition, there are the Cat Fanciers' Federation, the American Cat Fanciers' Association, the International Cat Fanciers, and United Cat Fanciers. In Canada, the Canadian Cat Association is a major registry. The Federation International Feline d'Europe is a primary European association. Addresses follow.

Cat Fanciers' Association
P.O. Box 430
Red Bank, NJ 07701

Cat Fanciers' Federation
2013 Elizabeth St.
Schenectady, NY 12303

American Cat Association
302-B S. Brand Blvd.
Glendale, CA 91204

Canadian Cat Association
14 Nelson St. W., Suite 5
Brampton, Ontario, Canada

Federation International Feline d'Europe
c/o Madame Claudine Rossi
No. 33, Rue Duquesnoy
Brussels, Belgium

American Cat Fanciers' Association
P.O. Box 203
Point Lookout, MO 65726

Chapter **2**

The Owner's Home Physical Exam:

Your Cat's Body and How It Works

A veterinarian often hears a pet owner's surprised exclamation, "You mean that my pet has [diabetes, jaundice, leukemia, etc.]! Why, I didn't even know that [cats, dogs, parakeets, etc.] had a [pancreas, liver, kidney, etc.]!" Yes, pets *do* have the same organs in the same locations, and those organs can malfuntion. The same diseases are seen in humans, dogs, and cats—and even in birds, guinea pigs, and snakes.

There is nothing more awe-inspiring than the way a body is put together (*anatomy*) and the way the parts function by themselves and in cooperation with the rest of the body (*physiology*). Even that fly or ant that visits your picnic lunch has a heart and intestines. So what does all this have to do with your cat's health? Health (yours and your pet's) is precious. You should know how the body is put together and how it functions so that you can respect it and do your best to prevent illness. For example, giving your cat a ball of string to play with is disrespectful to its stomach and intestines since, if the string is swallowed, it can cause vomiting, bloody diarrhea, or constipation. A more serious, life-threatening complication, such as an intestinal obstruction, can also occur.

You and your cat share more similarities than differences. You have less body hair, no tail, and a thumb, and you walk on two legs; but this is just about where the physical differences end. People do have more complex thinking centers in their brains (which, it seems, they often don't use very well) but cats leave human beings far, far behind in the development of the senses of smell, hearing, and sight. Many people go through life without developing these senses to their greatest ability—and some never use them at all. So who is "smarter" in "feeling" life—you or your cat?

The normal appearance and functions of your pet's body should be studied so that by using the Decision Charts and by doing a brief physical exam, you will be better prepared to know when to treat your cat at home and when to see your veterinarian.

It's a good idea to examine healthy cats about once every six months. If your cat doesn't seem to feel well (see How Do I Know When My Cat Is Sick? page 31), it's advisable to run through it again.

SKIN

A wrapping of fur is not all there is to your cat's skin. It is also a factory for vitamin D production; it protects the internal parts from injury, bacteria, and viruses; and it contains a sensory system that is unsurpassed in efficiency. The network of skin nerve cells goes to work when your cat is cold, has a cut, or receives a pat on the head. In cold weather, the hairs stand erect and form air pockets that will insulate against the cold.

Healthy skin and hair coats are flexible, glossy, and free of excessive oiliness, redness, dandruff, scabs, eruptions, or parasites (see page 159). There should be no areas of hair loss. Each cat has its own shedding cycle, which may change from year to year. Some pets shed a small amount all the time, while others may lose large clumps at various intervals. Don't be concerned unless the skin Decision Chart indicates a problem. Cats may have a normal receding hairline in front of both ears. This is the area of the *temporal gland,* a scent gland thought to be used for marking territory by rubbing the forehead against an object. Run your hand against the hair coat and check for growths or blemishes.

Pets can have freckles, concentrations of cells containing the brown pigment called *melanin.* These can be found anywhere on the skin and even in the mouth. Be sure to check the skin's special alterations: the mammary glands, the footpads, the claws, supracaudal organ (an oil gland located on the top of the tail base), and whiskers.

The *mammary glands* are located on the abdomen. As shown opposite, there are five pairs of nipples. The glands of nursing females enlarge and produce milk tailor-made for their new kittens. Females experiencing a false pregnancy (see page 219) can have enlarged breasts and produce milk. Once your female cat has passed seven years of age, routinely *palpate* (feel gently) each gland to check for lumps (see page 176). See your veterinarian if you find any.

Check your cat's paws. The thick, pigmented, tough *footpads* are excellent shock absorbers. The pads are named for their location. Pets have sweat glands in the footpad area. If your cat gets excited at the veterinarian's office, you may see sweaty pawprints on the exam table. Check the spaces between the digits. Since

Nipple

Umbilicus ("belly button")

Carpal pads

Metacarpal pad

Digit pad

your cat walks barefoot and this is a very moist area, the interdigital area can be easily irritated and infected by briars, stones, foxtail, sand, and salt (for melting snow).

The claws are used for getting traction and digging. A cat is able to retract and extend its nails for use as excellent offensive and defensive weapons. However, your pet's nails should be trimmed (see page 55), since cats keep their nails sharp and mark their territory by scratching. Nail trimming, declawing (see page 152), or supplying your cat with a scratching post can save your furniture.

Some cats develop *stud tail,* formed when the supracaudal organ secretes a greasy, brownish material, which scales, crusts, and mixes with matted hair on the top of the tail base. It is seen most often in confined, uncastrated male cats, hence the name. Treatment consists of clipping the area and washing it with soap and water. Cleaning the area daily with alcohol seems to control the problem, and outdoor romps in the sunshine seem to be beneficial.

Whiskers (*tactile hairs*) are long, stiff hairs located on the muzzle, upper eyelids, cheeks, and legs. They are used as feelers and are especially handy for navigation at night or in dark areas.

Tepetum
lucidum

Retina

Anterior
chamber

Cornea

Pupil — Lens

Optic
nerve

Iris

Vitreous
body

Sclera

EYES

No other organ in your cat's body contains such an intricate and complex mechanism in such a small structure as the eye. Without their eyes, your pet's ancestors would not have been able to avoid predators or to capture their food.

The first parts seen when examining your pet's eyes are the upper and lower eyelids—specialized curtains that protect the eyes. Eyelashes are located primarily on the edges of the upper lids. Examine the eyelids; they should be smooth and sharp. The eye margin should not turn in (*entropion*) or turn out (*ectropion*). Be sure the eyelashes and hairs on the nose (especially of Persian and Himalayan cats) do not rub the eyeball. Sometimes these hairs can be distorted and misdirected and can irritate the eye.

By pulling up on the upper eyelid or pulling down on the lower lid with your thumb, a smooth, pink tissue (the *conjunctiva*) can be seen covering the inner surface of the lids and continuing onto the eyeball. The conjunctiva helps lubricate the eyeball and protect it from infection. The space between the eyelid conjunctiva and the eyeball conjunctiva is the *conjunctival sac*. If the conjunctiva is red and swollen or if there is a green or yellowish discharge, an inflammation of the tissue is present (see page 180).

Cats have a structure called the *third eyelid,* or *nictitating membrane,* that contributes to tear formation and distribution. It is light pink and is located at the inner corner of the eye. In sick pets, and sometimes even in healthy pets, the third eyelid may cover more than half the eye. "My pet's eyeball has disappeared," is sometimes the first thought of an owner who sees the third eyelid covering the eye. Don't worry—the eye is still resting comfortably under the membrane.

The *cornea* is the clear "front window" of the eye that bends the incoming light rays. The cornea can lose its clarity if it becomes inflamed or injured. Hairs and twigs can injure the cornea, especially in pop-eyed cats.

The *sclera* is the fibrous coat that gives the eyeball its ping-pong-ball shape and dull white color (this is often called the "white" of the eye). The sclera frequently takes on a yellow color (*jaundice*) in cats with liver problems.

The *iris* controls the amount of light entering the back of the eye and gives your pet's eye its color. The black hole in the center of the iris is the *pupil*. It *dilates* (gets larger) to let more light enter in dim light and *constricts* (gets smaller) in bright light. Shining a bright light in one eye should constrict both pupils. The pupils should be the same shape and size.

Light rays enter the eye's fluid-filled *anterior chamber,* pass through the pupil, and are further bent by the lens as they continue their journey through the *vitreous body,* a transparent, jelly-like substance that keeps the eyeball firm. The light rays finally hit the "heart" of the eye—the *retina* at the back. This membrane has over 100 million light-sensitive cells, called *rods* and *cones.* These cells set off a flurry of electrochemical activity that transmits the image to your cat's brain by way of the *optic nerve* in about two-thousandths of a second. That's traveling!

Your cat's retina contains a remarkable wedge of reflector tissue, the *tapetum lucidum.* The tapetum makes it possible for your cat to see better than humans in dim light. Light rays are reflected off the tapetum and back to the light-sensitive cells. The bright green eye reflection seen in dim light is the tapetum.

Cataracts, white opacities that block the light's passage through the eye, can be seen by shining a bright light in the pupil of affected pets. A normal aging process called *senile cataracts,* in which the pupil of older pets takes on a blue-white hue, does not interfere with vision. Senile cataracts, or *nuclear sclerosis,* is caused by a rearrangement of the fibers and a loss of water in the older lens.

Tears cover the eye with each blink. They keep the eyes moist and help protect them from foreign objects, bacteria, and viruses. Tears are formed by the secretion of glands located around the inner lids and behind the third eyelid. They drain from the eye through a canal system that runs from the *medial canthus* of the eye to the nostrils. (This is why your nose runs when you cry.) The blockage of these canal openings by debris or by an eyelid turning in (*entropion*) can cause excessive tearing (*ephiphora*) and brown staining of the hair around the eye.

EARS

Not long ago, we came home to a very strange sight. All our cats had gathered around the refrigerator and were completely entranced by its bottom. On moving

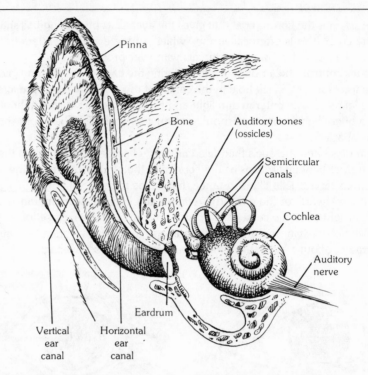

the refrigerator, we found cockroaches! The high-pitched communication of bugs or rodents that falls on our "deaf" ears is music to a cat.

A cat's superb hearing ability begins with the sound-gathering flap called the *pinna*. The inner surface of the pinna and the beginning of the ear canal (which you can see) should be a light pink. You may see a small amount of yellow wax and a few hairs at the canal opening. These act like flypaper, trapping dust, insects, or other potential irritants and guarding against infection. If this area is reddened, foul-smelling, or has a puslike or brown, waxy discharge, an ear infection may be present (see page 182). Your veterinarian can check the rest of the ear with an *otoscope*, a special instrument equipped with a light source and magnifying lens.

The ear canal is L-shaped, going down (*vertical canal*) and then in (*horizontal canal*). The *eardrum* is at the end of the horizontal canal. Sound waves (the cockroach talk, for example) travel down the canal and beat against the eardrum—like a stick beating a drum. The cockroach talk vibrations are amplified in the *middle ear* by three small bones called the *auditory ossicles,* which pass the sound on to the *inner ear's* snail-shaped and fluid-filled *cochlea* via the *oval window* (a vibrating membrane). The waves produced in the cochlea are converted to electrical messages that travel to your pet's brain via the *auditory nerve.* Your cat interprets the message as cockroach talk and sits in front of the refrigerator, patiently waiting for a roach snack.

Above the cochlea are three small, fluid-filled *semicircular canals*. These loops of tubing contribute to your cat's remarkable sense of balance. If your cat starts to fall, fluid in one of the canals is displaced. Hair cells in the canals detect the change and immediately inform the cat's brain, which orders muscles to tighten and keep your cat upright.

THE CIRCULATORY SYSTEM

The hardest worker in your cat's body is the heart. It is a top-of-the-line, four-chambered model (just like the human heart) that actually consists of two pumps. The right side of the heart receives the blue blood (depleted of oxygen) that has already dropped off its cargo of oxygen and nutrients and has returned with waste products, such as carbon dioxide, by way of the veins. This blue blood is pumped through the lungs to receive fresh oxygen and to remove the carbon dioxide. The blood then returns to the left side of the heart and is pumped out through the arteries to the trillions of cells in your pet's body.

The normal heart beats about 120 times per minute in a resting cat. You can feel the heart beat by placing the palm of your hand against your pet's chest, near the left elbow (see Taking Your Cat's Heartbeat, page 20). You may hear the "lub-dup" of the normal heart valves closing by placing your ear there. Panting, breathing, and purring may make it difficult for you to hear even with a stethoscope, which you can purchase at a medical supply store. The heart receives its oxygen by way of two branching *coronary arteries* that are about the width of a

Superior vena cava   Aorta   Pulmonary artery

Right lung

Left lung

Valves

Left atria

Right atria

Left ventricle

Inferior vena cava

Right ventricle

piece of spaghetti. Fortunately, cats do not have heart attacks (sudden blocking of the coronary arteries), but after eight years of age they often develop a problem with the heart *valves* (flaps that control the passage of blood through the heart's chambers): The valves do not close properly, and the heart must work harder to pump the blood. It may even fail unless treated with digitalis-like drugs. Your veterinarian (or even you, by using your stethoscope) will detect a heart *murmur* when the valves are closing improperly. A "zsa" sound may be heard between the "lub-dup" of the regular heart beat: "lub-zsa-dup." The regurgitation of blood around "sick" valves is responsible for the "zsa" sound. Not *all* heart murmurs are serious problems. Your veterinarian is the best judge. *Cardiomyopathy* (a disorder of the heart's muscle tissue) is another typical cat problem.

The *pulse* and *capillary refill time* will give you some indication of how well the heart and blood vessels are working to maintain your pet's blood pressure (see Taking Your Cat's Pulse, below). When you press a finger against your pet's gum and then lift it away, the white area produced should return to the normal pink color in one second. This indicates that the capillaries are refilling with blood.

TAKING YOUR CAT'S HEARTBEAT

- Place your palm over your cat's left chest wall.
- Hold this position for fifteen seconds and count the number of beats felt in that time.
- Multiply the number by four. EXAMPLE: 30 beats in 15 seconds $= 30 \times 4 = 120$ beats per minute.
  Note: A normal cat heart rate should fall in the range between 80 and 175.

TAKING YOUR CAT'S PULSE

- Place your fingers lightly in the middle of your pet's upper inner thigh.
- Hold this position for fifteen seconds and count the number of beats felt in that time.
- The number of pulse beats should equal the number of heartbeats.
  Note: The pulse should be easier to detect if the heart is pumping strongly, and fainter if the heart is pumping weakly (as in shock).

What are the *capillaries?* These microscopic vessels serve as the unloading dock for new goods (oxygen, nutrients, antibodies, hormones) and the loading dock for the waste products, such as carbon dioxide. The capillaries are like tiny streams that connect two large rivers (arteries and veins). The capillaries are so tiny that *red blood cells* (the delivery trucks loaded with oxygen) have to travel single file through them. The *white blood cells,* which are important in preventing and fighting infections, and *platelets,* which are vital to patching leaky blood vessels and initiating the clotting mechanism, also flow through these tiny streams. The fluid that keeps all the cells and other components floating is called *plasma.*

The *lymphatic system* is a great helper to the heart and blood vessels. It filters out invaders and transports to the bloodstream, in a watery substance called *lymph*, the *antibodies* and *lymphocytes* produced in *lymph nodes*. These components protect your pet's body against invaders such as bacteria, viruses, and even cancer cells. Three pairs of lymph nodes that may be examined are the *tonsils*, *prescapular nodes*, and *popliteal nodes*. These may enlarge during infections or in *lymphosarcoma* (*leukemia*, see page 237). They may be difficult to find, so on your next visit ask your veterinarian to show you where they are. The tonsils are housed in pouches—one on each side of the throat entrance. They are the throat's watchdogs (or watchcats!), ready to gobble up any bacteria or viruses with bad intentions. Tonsils rarely have to be removed. Enlargement of the tonsils is usually not a good reason for removing them.

THE RESPIRATORY SYSTEM

Cats, like people, need to gather oxygen from the air and to expel carbon dioxide (a waste product of metabolism). The *respiratory system*, consisting of the nose,

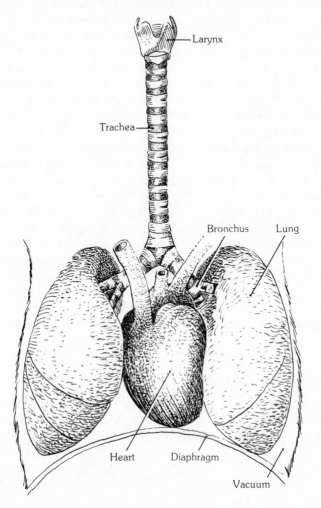

Larynx

Trachea

Bronchus   Lung

Heart   Diaphragm

Vacuum

mouth, larynx, trachea, bronchi, lungs, diaphragm, and chest muscles, makes it all possible.

The normal *rate of respiration* is ten to thirty breaths per minute. *Panting,* an increased respiratory rate (as high as 300 breaths per minute), is the primary way that your cat can sweat and thus lower body temperature. Panting is seen in hot weather, after exercise, with lung disease, and even with pain or excitement. Notice also your pet's respiratory *rhythm.* The chest should expand (*inspiration*) and contract (*expiration*) with no difficulty.

A dry, hot nose or a moist, cold nose is not a reliable way to determine your pet's health, but the discharge, if any, might be an indicator of illness. Normally, there is a slight, clear, watery secretion from your pet's nostrils. A bloody or thick yellowish, white, or greenish nasal discharge is abnormal.

A light pink color to the gums indicates that your pet is getting enough oxygen. A blue or muddy red color to the tongue and gums indicates a serious problem in the respiratory or cardiovascular system. Pale gums may indicate anemia.

The *larynx* (Adam's apple or voice box) can be felt as a hard structure at the top of the windpipe—the same location as the human voice box. The larynx produces your cat's snarls and meows by vibrations of the *vocal chords.* The purr is thought to originate from vibrations of the "false" vocal chords.

Air passes through the larynx into the breathing tubes: the windpipe (*trachea*) and its smaller divisions, the *bronchi.* The air is warmed and filtered of dust, bacteria, and viruses by the microscopic hairs and mucus in these tubes until the air finally reaches its destination—the lungs. Your veterinarian uses a stethoscope to hear the passage of air in the breathing tubes and lungs. *Percussion of the chest* is useful in an examination of the respiratory system.

All that dirty air passing down the breathing tubes must be cleaned. The mucus that traps the dust, bacteria, and viruses is expelled through your pet's *cough reflex.* Occasionally, your cat will cough up some mucus. Although owners frequently confuse this with vomiting (expelling food from the digestive system), it's just normal "housecleaning" (see Coughs, page 188), so don't get alarmed.

The lungs don't have any muscles. They expand only when your cat's chest expands and the *diaphragm* (a muscular divider between the chest and abdomen) moves backward. This creates a slight vacuum in the chest, and air is sucked into the lungs. When your cat exhales, the lungs collapse and blow out the carbon dioxide. If air leaked into the vacuum chamber (a condition called *pneumothorax*), or if a tear in the diaphragm allowed intestines to enter the chest cavity (a condition termed *diaphragmatic hernia*), your pet would have a very difficult time breathing. These conditions happen frequently when pets are hit by cars (see page 104).

THE DIGESTIVE SYSTEM

The most finicky and most delicate part in your pet's body *has* to be the digestive system. Throughout your cat's lifetime it will remind you both that it won't stand for any foolishness. Spicy foods, bones, bad-tasting mice, pieces of wood, and any other garbage will cause a fit of vomiting and/or diarrhea that will send you running to the Decision Charts!

Your cat's digestive system is a food processor par excellence. It puts the Cuisinart® to shame! Not only does the digestive system chop, pulverize, blend, grind, and emulsify food, but it converts carbohydrates, fats, and proteins into easily digested molecules that are then handed over to the bloodstream and lymphatic system for delivery to your cat's cells for energy, growth, and tissue repair.

Digestion begins when food enters your cat's mouth. The tongue positions the food for the shredding and tearing action of the teeth and mixes the food with the saliva to start the digestion of carbohydrates.

Open your cat's mouth as described on page 76. Your cat's tongue, which should be pink, has hard spiny projections similar to those on a wire brush. The tongue, in fact, does act as your cat's own built-in wire brush for pulling out loose hairs. The tongue also has taste buds that are aided by a primitive gland (*vomeronasal gland*) located in back of the upper front teeth. Occasionally, you may see your cat "taste" by first licking (such as when a male cat licks a female's vulva) and then flicking the tongue behind its upper front teeth, thereby distributing the taste to the sensitive vomeronasal gland, which can't be seen.

Your pet's teeth are used for protection and for grasping, cutting, and crushing food. Your kitten doesn't have teeth at birth. The "baby" (*deciduous*) teeth appear between two and five weeks of age. The permanent teeth begin replacing the "baby" teeth at four months of age. Cats have four types of teeth: *incisors, canines, premolars,* and *molars.* The teeth should be white, and the gum line should be pink, not swollen or red (see Mouth Odor, page 192).

Skull (cut)

Adult canine tooth

Deciduous ("baby") canine tooth

Some cats fail to lose all their "baby" teeth (especially an incisor or canine) by eight months of age. In that case, you may see a double tooth. The "baby" tooth should be surgically removed, since it produces a good location for food entrapment and infection and may cause misalignment of the adult teeth.

A normal bite in cats has the upper incisors slightly overlapping the lower incisors. A slight overbite (a more marked overlapping) or an underbite (the lower incisors overlap the upper incisors) doesn't seem to cause any problems.

The rest of the digestive system cannot be seen, but with practice you may be able to palpate some of the organs. Remember, palpate *gently* to avoid injury.

After your cat swallows, the food enters a muscular tube, the *esophagus,* through which it is transported to the stomach by coordinated waves called *peristalsis.* Cats, since they eat odd things and fail to chew, can occasionally get blockages in the esophagus, caused by bones, fish hooks, small toys, etc. Early diagnosis and treatment are a must since a perforation in the esophagus can cause a fatal pneumonia. Persistent gulping, difficulty in swallowing, regurgitating (not vomiting) food ("it just seems to come right back out") and excessive salivation are some early signs.

The stomach is the chief active partner in the digestive system, churning food and making it acceptable for the intestines. When your pet's stomach is full of food (or full of gas) it may feel like a doughy bag (feel behind the last rib on the left side).

Esophagus

Diaphragm

Chest

Liver

Stomach

Left kidney

Spleen

Pancreas

Transverse colon

Right kidney

Small intestine

Ascending colon

Descending colon

Cecum

The kitten's stomach can distend considerably after a meal, and this is not necessarily a sign of disease or worms.

Although the liver is the largest organ in your pet's body, it cannot be palpated well in the normal cat because it nestles under the rib cage, probably because it has hundreds of jobs to do and can't be interrupted. The liver makes the proteins that provide energy for your cat's graceful leaps, manufactures the clotting agents that stop the bleeding of a cut, and is very important in fat and sugar metabolism. In addition, the liver is the "great detoxifier"—purifying toxins and drugs in your cat's system—and it recycles the bodies of dead red blood cells. Some of its products are used to make new red blood cells; others are used to make *bile,* the green digestive juice stored in the *gall bladder* that, at mealtime, is released to the intestine through the bile duct to help break large fat molecules into smaller ones. Liver disease or the rapid destruction of red blood cells will release large amounts of bile into the bloodstream, producing *jaundice* and staining the *eyes, gums,* and *skin* yellow.

The *pancreas* resides behind your cat's stomach and also can't be palpated easily. The first job that the pancreas undertakes is to neutralize the acids in the soupy gruel that the stomach passes on to the intestines. These acids are no laughing matter; they could inflict serious damage to the intestines if not neutralized. Your cat's pancreas also produces an impressive array of enzymes that are important in sugar, fat, and protein digestion. If the pancreas becomes inflamed (*as in pancreatitis*), some of these enzymes leak from the cells into the blood stream. The pancreas is best known, however, for its manufacture of *insulin*, which ensures that all your pet's cells get *glucose*, a simple sugar, for their energy needs.

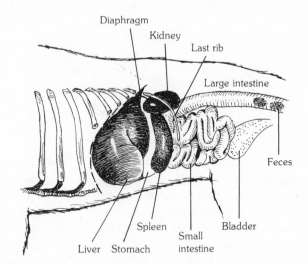

Diaphragm
Kidney
Last rib
Large intestine
Feces
Spleen
Small intestine
Bladder
Liver   Stomach

All nutrients are absorbed in the *small intestine,* which then passes them to the bloodstream and lymphatic systems. By gently grasping the abdomen between the thumb and fingers, you may feel the small intestine as a slippery tube. The last stop on the way is the *large intestine,* where water is extracted for your pet's use and the *feces* (the stool) become firmer. You may be able to feel the large intestine by gently palpating high in the posterior abdomen. Any problems in this organ can produce diarrhea, sometimes mixed with blood or mucus (see page 200).

All indigestible material has to leave the body by way of the *anus*. The entire trip takes about twenty hours. Your pet's normal feces should be firm and brown in color. If the feces are loose, black, clay-colored, bloody, streaked with mucus, have a foul odor, or are extremely large in volume, see the Decision Chart, page 201. Anal sacs are discussed on page 206.

THE UROGENITAL SYSTEM

Your pet's urinary system is the main waste-disposal plant. The paired kidneys clean and filter the blood continuously as it passes through them. It regulates the amount of salt, potassium, and water that is needed in the body. The excess is passed on with the waste products of metabolism through two tiny tubes called *ureters* to the storage tank, the *bladder*. When your pet's bladder fills with enough urine, a signal is sent to the brain for your pet to head for the litter box or ask to be let out. The urine exits to the outside by a thin tube called the *urethra,* located in the vagina of the female and the penis of the male.

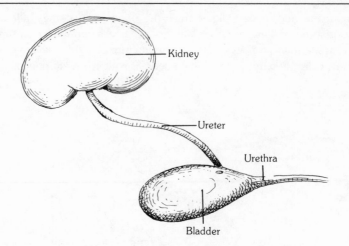

The one important time for you to examine your pet's urinary system at home is if your cat is straining to urinate or has blood in the urine (see page 208). A large bladder accompanied by frequent attempts to urinate is a very serious problem. The bladder is located in the posterior abdomen between the rear legs. Using *very* gentle pressure, with your left hand on the left posterior abdomen and your right hand on the right posterior abdomen, you may feel a firm, round ball that varies in size from a ping-pong ball to an orange. During your next visit, you should ask your veterinarian to show you how to palpate the bladder.

The sperm factories of your male cat are the *testes*. There should be two *testes* located within paired sacs called the *scrotum*. The testicles should be present in the scrotum at birth. If only one testicle is present, your pet is called a *monorchid;* if neither testicle is in the scrotum, your pet is a *cryptorchid.* This condition is hereditary (see page 229) and may be the source of a tumor in later life (see page 228). Pick up your male cat's tail. The scrotum with the paired testicles is located about one-half inch below the anus. They're very sensitive, so handle them gently. The two are generally the same size and shape in the normal male cat. A small lump may be felt on the back end of both testes. This is the *epididymis,* a storehouse for the sperm.

When your male cat ejaculates, millions of sperm (enough to repopulate the whole world) travel through the *vas deferens* to the urethra, where a very special fluid from the *prostate* and the *bulbourethral glands* mixes with the sperm. This special fluid contains proteins, fats, sugars, and enzymes to nourish and protect the fragile sperm on their hazardous journey out of the penis and up the female's reproductive system to meet the egg.

The penis and vagina serve both urinary and reproductive systems. Your male cat's penis can be examined, but first you must find it. It lies within a fold of skin called the *prepuce,* or sheath, located just below the scrotum. Push forward on the prepuce and out pops a pink penis with small barbs, or *papillae,* on the tip. These papillae are thought to stimulate the female and to initiate ovulation. They are probably responsible for the ear-piercing howls of the female while mating and for her swat at the male at its conclusion.

The only readily visible portions of the female cat's reproductive system are the soft, pliable *labia* (lips of the *vulva*) that form a vertical slit a few inches below the anus. By gently separating the lips, the pink *vestibule* of the vagina is seen. Urine exits through the urethral orifice located inside the vestibule.

Again, the internal parts of the female cat's reproductive system are the same as in the human: ovaries, fallopian tubes (or *oviducts*), uterus, cervix, and vagina. The paired ovaries produce eggs and female hormones. The eggs are delivered to the thick-walled uterus through the small, coiled fallopian tubes. After ejaculation, the male's tadpole-like microscopic sperm, their tails whipping furiously, must swim a long distance (equivalent to humans swimming about thirty miles), up the vagina and through the opening of the muscular cervix. Once in the uterus, there is no guarantee of making contact with the eggs waiting there.

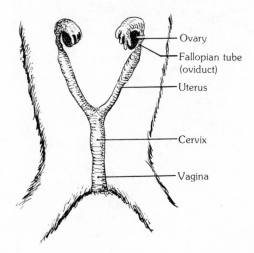

- Ovary
- Fallopian tube (oviduct)
- Uterus
- Cervix
- Vagina

THE MUSCULOSKELETAL SYSTEM

Without the support and protection of bones, your cat would collapse into a pile of fur and skin. Most of the two essential minerals calcium and phosphorus are stored in, inventoried by, and distributed when needed from the bones. Without calcium, your pet's heart could not beat, nor could the nerves conduct messages. When your cat is pregnant or nursing, the need for both these minerals is at a peak, to aid in the growth of the fetuses and in milk production (see page 38). Also, old, tired red and white blood cells must be "retired," so replacements are constantly and enthusiastically manufactured by the bones' spongy marrow and sent out into the bloodstream.

The grouping of the 250-or-so bones and the joints, under command of the nervous and muscular systems, makes it possible for your cat to climb, jump, and scratch its fleas. The joints connecting the *cervical* (neck) bones are so flexible that your cat can lick itself everywhere but the back of the head.

Cats walk on their "finger tips" and "tiptoes." If you got down in this position, you would find that almost all your bones, muscles, tendons, and ligaments are in

Tibia

Heel bones

Foot (metatarsal bones)

Toes

Human

Tibia

Heel bones (tarsals)

Foot (metatarsal bones)

Digits (toes)

the same positions as your pet's. For example, in this position, your heel would be sticking up in the air. Well, so does the "heel" of your cat's rear legs.

The most important time to examine your pet's musculoskeletal system is when you see a lameness (see page 156). If your pet has a lame front leg, its head will bob up when that leg touches the ground; the head will bob down when a sore rear leg touches the ground. A shorter stride and lighter touch are usually seen in the sore leg.

If you notice a lame leg, take the cat's temperature first, since in cats the cause is often a bite wound that has formed an abscess. In that case a fever of 104° to 105° may be seen (see page 174). If the temperature is normal, start the exam. You will be looking for swelling or pain by gently pressing on the bones with your finger or moving a joint. Your pet will exhibit pain by crying or pulling the leg away. If you think you've found a painful area, repeat that part of the exam again to see if you get the same reaction.

To examine the individual areas of your cat's skeletal system, you may find it helpful to locate your own corresponding bones and/or joints first. The chart on the following page is a handy guide to follow. Remember to be gentle.

To be checked	Human equivalent	How to examine
Digits, pads, and spaces between	Toes and fingers	Press on each bone and move each joint
Metacarpal bones and *metatarsal* bones	Bones between the fingers and wrist and between the toes and ankle	Press the length of each bone
Carpal bones and *tarsal* bones	Wrist and ankle	Press on each bone and move each joint
Achilles tendon	Attached between heel bone and muscle	Make sure the tendon is taut
Radius, ulna, tibia, and *fibula*	Forearm bones and lower leg bones	Press the length of each bone
Elbow joint	Same	Press on each bone and move each joint
Patella	Knee cap	Press each bone and move the joint
Humerus and *femur*	Upper arm bone and upper leg bone	Press the length of each bone
Shoulder joint and hip joint	Same	Move the humerus and femur back and forth in their respective joints
Scapula	Shoulder blade	Press on each bone
Cervical bones	Neck	Press each bone and move the neck up and down
Spine	Same	Press the length of the spine and all projections (*dorsal spines*)

That finishes the skeletal system exam. If your cat exhibits pain at any point, by crying out and/or pulling away, repeat that step of the exam to double-check the reaction.

The muscles, after receiving messages from the nerves, move the bones, blink the eyes, and twitch the tail. These are the skeletal muscles that your cat can consciously move. Two special types of muscles work day and night involuntarily. The heart (*cardiac*) muscle contracts with less than one-half-second rest between beats throughout your cat's life. Smooth muscle tissue, which moves food along the digestive tract day and night, is also primarily involuntary.

THE NERVOUS SYSTEM

Your cat's brain, the "central computer," coordinates the heavy traffic of messages received from inside and outside the body with the activities the body can perform, via the network of nerves and the spinal cord. The brain is the "top cat." In fact, it *is* your cat. The nervous system, one of the primary controllers of the body's activities, can adjust your pet's body very quickly to environmental and internal changes.

THE ENDOCRINE SYSTEM

People's and cats' bodies alike contain small chemical factories tucked away in obscure corners. These are the *endocrine glands,* whose specialty products are *hormones* (from the Greek word meaning "to arouse to activity"). Hormones regulate chemical reactions. The endocrine system primarily regulates processes of long duration, such as growth and reproduction.

Malfunctions of endocrine glands, such as *diabetes* (see page 146), *hypothyroidism* (see page 148), and *Cushing's syndrome* are seen frequently in pets. *Note:* Continuous, long-term corticosteroid therapy can cause serious problems, including Cushing's syndrome. Many disorders cause characteristic skin changes. See your veterinarian if your cat is over eight years of age and has symmetrical hair loss or bald spots but does not scratch. The skin in these areas often becomes brown. Most endocrine disorders are treatable. Your veterinarian will have to perform blood tests and a urinalysis to make the specific diagnosis.

HOW DO I KNOW WHEN MY CAT IS SICK?

The following signs should indicate to you that something is not right:

- Your cat's behavior changes—it becomes less active and withdrawn.
- Your cat exhibits a change in appetite that lasts for a few days. Loss of appetite (*anorexia*) or increased appetite (*polyphagia*) may indicate disease.
- Your cat is urinating more or less than normal.
- Your cat exhibits either vomiting or diarrhea for an extended period. Fluid is lost during vomiting and diarrhea, and *dehydration* (depletion of body water), a serious situation, can result.

Is Your Cat Dehydrated?

Pick up a fold of skin in the middle back area. If it snaps back rapidly, your pet is not dehydrated. If it stays up or returns slowly, dehydration is present. Do not test the skin in the neck area; this is normally loose in many animals and will give you false results. If dehydration is present, your doctor will find the underlying cause and will give fluids *intravenously* (in the blood vessel) or *subcutaneously* (under the skin) to replace the water lost.

Is Your Cat in Pain?

Lameness, a stiff neck, reluctance to get up or lie down, or tense abdominal muscles are indicators that your pet is in pain.

What Is Your Cat's Temperature?

A normal temperature is from 101.0°F to 102.5°F. Anything higher indicates a problem that needs professional attention (see Fever, page 134, for more information). To use a thermometer, follow these steps:

TAKING YOUR CAT'S TEMPERATURE

- To take your cat's temperature, use a *rectal* thermometer, which has a rounded, stubby tip. Shake it down first by holding it between your thumb and index finger and snapping your wrist.
- Apply vaseline or mineral oil to the bulb.
- Restrain the cat (see page 83). *Note:* It is advisable to have someone hold the back end of your pet while you hold the tail and the thermometer, so that your pet cannot move from side to side or up and down and break the thermometer.
- Lift the tail, gently slide the thermometer into the anus, and leave it in for three minutes.
- Remove the thermometer and read the mercury level.

Chapter 3

Keeping Your Cat Healthy, Happy, and Obedient

A cat that is groomed regularly, fed properly, trained well, travels nicely, and sees its veterinarian on schedule for vaccinations, parasite control, and dental care should have a happy and healthy life.

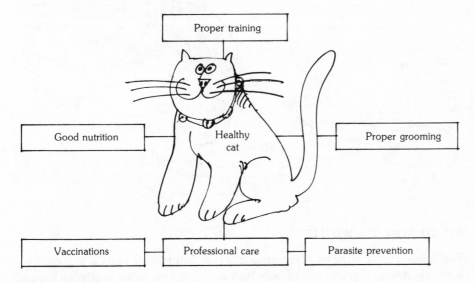

Proper training

Good nutrition

Healthy cat

Proper grooming

Vaccinations

Professional care

Parasite prevention

NUTRITION

What is good nutrition and why is it so important? Nutrition is the process of using or transforming food into living tissue. Without a complete and balanced diet, your cat will not grow properly, reproduce, maintain the health of all its body tissues, or fight infection.

The "Great Food Hunt"

Your cat's hunt for a complete and balanced daily food intake is made much easier than its ancestor's hunt of thousands of years ago, thanks to commercial pet foods. The sound of the can opener or the jumbling of the dry food in the box will awaken the beast inside your cat—it will run from the comfy carpet near the fireplace to the kitchen to devour its neatly packaged and completely nutritious "prey." Your cat's ancestors had to go "shopping." The game they caught provided everything: Protein came from muscle tissue; fats, vitamins, and minerals from organs and bones; carbohydrates were extracted from the vegetable and cereal matter left in the game's digestive tract. Vegetables and cereal starches aren't required by cats, but they do provide calories and bulk.

Years of research and development by the major pet food companies have produced complete and balanced foods for your modern cat. These products, which are excellent from weaning to old age, eliminate the need for homemade diets that are time-consuming and expensive to prepare and may lack important nutritional requirements. The following discussion will focus on (a) the composition of food, (b) the types of pet foods, (c) how much to feed at different stages of your cat's life, and (d) the advantages and disadvantages of each type of commercial pet food.

FOOD FOR THOUGHT

Fuel needed to keep the heart pumping, the chest expanding, and the legs climbing is provided by the breakdown of carbohydrates, fats, and proteins. The amount of energy provided by molecules is measured in *kilocalories* (or *calories*). Fats provide the most energy per unit molecule. Carbohydrates, proteins, fats, vitamins, minerals, and water must be supplied in adequate and balanced amounts. Pregnant or lactating cats, growing kittens, and all heavily-exercised pets may require up to twice as much energy as the inactive pet.

Carbohydrates

Use	For energy
	For bulk (indigestible cellulose)
	Fiber absorbs water; this bulk stimulates intestinal movements and can prevent constipation
	Spares proteins; since carbohydrate is used for quick energy, protein can be used for body growth and repair
Sources	Primarily well-cooked cereal grains, cellulose, starch, sugars
Amount needed	No more than 30 percent (on a dry weight basis)

Note: The milk sugar *lactose* may cause diarrhea in many kittens and adult cats, since the amount of *lactase,* an enzyme that breaks up the sugar molecule, may be low

The large lactose molecule pulls water into the intestines and causes diarrhea

Remedy: Use little or no milk or milk products if diarrhea develops

Try yogurt, which has a lower lactose content

Proteins

Proteins are composed of *amino acids,* some of which (*essential* amino acids), cannot be manufactured by the body and must be supplied in the food. Eggs, soybeans, milk, fish meal, and muscle meat contain all the essential amino acids and are therefore said to be of high biological value.

Use	For growth
	Healthy tissue repair and maintenance
	Formation of antibodies that fight infection
	Formation of enzymes and hormones that help in body's chemical reactions
Sources	Meat, eggs, fish, vegetables (especially soybeans), milk and milk products, yeast
Amount needed	About 25 to 30 percent (on a dry weight basis); kittens need 35 to 40 percent

Note: Do not feed raw white of egg

This binds up *biotin* (a B vitamin), which is necessary for growth, but cooked eggs or raw yolk are very good protein sources

Do not feed raw fish

Raw fish (especially freshwater, such as carp) contains *thiaminase,* an enzyme that destroys the B vitamin, *thiamine*

Thiamine deficiency causes a serious nervous system disorder

Fats

Use	Provide more than twice as much energy per unit molecule than carbohydrates or protein (9.1 calories per gram)
	Transport vitamins A, D, E, K (the fat-soluble vitamins)
	Provide fatty acids (e.g., linoleic) for a healthy skin and hair coat
	An important taste factor (such as marbling in steak)
Sources	Commercial cat food has generally adequate amounts
Amount needed	About 25 to 30 percent

Note: If your cat has a dry, lusterless hair coat and scaly skin, consult your doctor

Sometimes the addition of vegetable oil (corn or safflower) is beneficial, but excess oil in the diet can decrease the food intake and retard growth

Consult your doctor before starting supplements

Note: Do not use cod liver oil as a routine supplement

Vitamins

Chemically known as *coenzymes*, vitamins are essential for life but are needed in very small quantities. A balanced diet should not let a deficiency develop.

Use	For normal body functioning
Sources	Supplemented commercial pet food has generally adequate amounts

Note: Be sure that the food is supplemented with all vitamins, especially A, B (thiamine), and E

A deficiency of vitamin A (a problem with cats fed dog food, which is too low in many components) is thought to start degeneration in the cat's eye

Thiamine deficiency can result from feeding raw fish or unsupplemented cat foods

Vitamin E deficiency causes *pansteatitis* (a painful inflammation of the fatty tissue; it was seen in cats fed red meat tuna with no vitamin E supplementation)

Prolonged diarrhea or vomiting can cause a loss of water *and* water soluble vitamins (such as the B vitamins), which should be replaced with supplements

Minerals

Use	For normal body functioning
	For bone development
Sources	Commercial cat foods have adequate amounts of sodium, potassium, iron, and calcium

Note: Do not use unprescribed calcium-phosphorus preparations

If the calcium-to-phosphorus ratio is altered by unneeded supplements or by an all-meat diet (too high in phosphorus), severe skeletal problems result

Water

Water is essential. It is obtained from the process of *metabolism* (especially of fats) of the food and liquids that your cat ingests. Your cat also needs constant access to clean, fresh drinking water.

Cats need about 30 ml. (1 oz.) per pound of body weight daily. Lactation, fever, hot weather, exercise, and water loss from vomiting or diarrhea will increase your pet's need. Dry foods (only 10 percent moisture) will increase your pet's water intake, while canned foods (75 percent moisture) will decrease the amount of water it drinks. *Note: Do not* allow your pet to drink water from unsanitary sources, such as stagnant pools or streams and toilet bowls.

YOUR CAT'S FOOD

	Dry	Semimoist	Moist (canned)
Advantages	Most economical	Convenient to feed	Very palatable
	Easy to feed	Very palatable	
	Excellent for self-feeding (see below)	Easily stored	
	Easily stored	No refrigeration needed	
	No refrigeration needed	Convenient to use when traveling	
Disadvantages	None	Expensive	Expensive
		Good taste may lead to overeating	Must refrigerate leftovers
			Spoils if left in bowl all day
			Good taste may lead to overeating
How to feed	Self-feeding—leave daily ration in bowl; cat will eat whenever hungry	Divide daily ration into two equal feedings for less chance of digestive upset	Divide daily ration into two equal feedings
	May be moistened with water or with semimoist or canned food		May be mixed with dry food (up to 25 percent of total daily intake)

Feeding Your Kitten

A kitten's caloric needs are twice as much as an adult cat's requirements. The protein requirement is about 50 percent greater. The major pet food companies have special kitten foods that meet these standards. If you cannot obtain the kitten foods, the adult maintenance foods should be supplemented with proteins of high biological value (cooked eggs, yogurt, cooked liver, milk and milk products). If the milk and milk products cause diarrhea, discontinue their use.

Feeding Your Adult Cat

Adult cats need about 40 calories per pound every day.

Weight (in pounds)	Calories needed	Daily feeding (in ounces)		
		Dry	Semimoist	Moist (canned)
4	160	1½	1½	5
6	240	2½	2½	8
8	320	3⅓	3⅓	10
10	400	4	4	13
12	480	5	5	16
14	560	6	6	18

The above feeding recommendations are estimates that will vary according to your cat's activity, metabolic rate and growth. Even the environmental temperature is a factor. An alert active cat that is neither fat nor thin and has a glossy haircoat is being fed properly.

Feeding Your Pregnant Cat

The pregnant cat's nutritional needs (energy and protein requirements) will not increase drastically until the last trimester of pregnancy, which begins on the thirty-fifth day. The fastest growth and calcification of the fetus occurs during this period.

At two weeks, start to increase its food intake by 20 percent. Supplements of cooked eggs, cooked liver, cooked muscle meat, milk, and yogurt are good. At delivery time, the food intake will be 50 to 60 percent higher than the maintenance level.

A high-protein commercial food or supplemental proteins of high biological value (cooked eggs, cooked liver and meats, milk, or yogurt) are very important in late pregnancy to assure a good milk supply.

As pregnancy progresses, the fetuses occupy a large area of the abdomen. The mother's digestive tract will be able to handle only smaller, more frequent feedings.

Feeding Your Lactating Cat

A well-balanced commercial cat food should supply adequate nutrients. Your cat's appearance and milk production are the best indicators of nutritional status; if you notice any change, try supplementing the diet with high protein foods such as milk products and cooked eggs. *Note:* Supplements of vitamins and minerals *should* be given to heavily lactating cats with large litters.

Although the content of the mother cat's diet won't alter much, the amounts eaten will. A general rule is to feed an additional 100 calories per pound of kitten (you can weigh the babies on an ounce or gram scale). By the end of the nursing period, the mother may be eating three times the prebreeding level (see Nursing Period, page 223).

Feeding Your Old Cat

Time passes very quickly. Soon you'll find that the little ball of fur you played with on the livingroom rug twelve years ago is slow in getting around and stays close by your side as if every minute counted. In old age, everything in the cat's system becomes less efficient. Fewer calories are needed because your old pal is less active and the metabolic rate is slower. The digestive process and absorption of food take longer. If your cat is getting fat, too many calories are being fed, so decrease the daily ration. Unless your cat is a self-feeder, smaller, more frequent feedings will help the old cat digest and absorb the food better.

VACCINATIONS

In 1879, Louis Pasteur coined the word "vaccination" (from the Latin word for cow), when he realized that his research was based on the same principle that Edward Jenner, an English physician, had observed almost 100 years previously. Dr. Jenner found that cowpox could be used to protect humans against smallpox. Pasteur went on to develop a rabies *vaccine* by drying the spinal cords (thus making the virus noninfectious) of rabbits infected with the rabies virus.

Years later it was discovered that the invading agents, viruses and bacteria (also called *antigens*), cause the body's lymphocytes to produce *antibodies* that

Antigen

Frightened antigen

Antibodies (Ab) attack the antigen

Lymphocyte— a factory for antibodies

The captured antigen is "eaten" by various body cells called phagocytes

Captured antigen bodies

fight these foreign invaders. It was also discovered that antigens could be chemically modified to lose their disease-producing quality while still triggering the production of antibodies to fight the disease. The chemically modified antigens together are called an *attenuated vaccine,* and this is what your pet receives in the injections from the veterinarian.

The body's *amnestic response* ("memory") is the basis for the series of vaccinations given to kittens and for the yearly boosters. Each time a vaccination is given, the body "remembers" its prior experience with these antigens and therefore produces a successively higher number of antibodies (thus affording more protection). Boosters, usually at yearly intervals, are essential to keep the "memory" (and the antibodies) at peak level.

Your pet's immune system must be in good working order to respond to the vaccine. Any stress, such as the presence of external or internal parasites or malnutrition, can decrease your cat's manufacture of antibodies. Treating the parasites (see page 44) and correcting the malnutrition (see page 34) are essential for successful vaccinations.

Kittens receive actual antibodies (*passive immunity*) to *panleukopenia* (destruction of the white blood cells) while still in the uterus and from the "first milk." These antibodies help protect your kitten for six to twelve weeks after birth. Although they can sometimes interfere with the vaccine, the kitten series of vaccinations should still be initiated at an early age. The last shot should be given at twelve to sixteen weeks.

On rare occasions a kitten can get the disease while still receiving the series. It is usually a result of the virus infecting the kitten before the vaccine becomes effective. In some instances (also véry rare) the kitten is genetically incapable of producing the necessary antibodies.

The vaccinations should be given only by a *licensed* veterinarian. He or she will use vaccines approved by the Animal Health Inspection Service of the U.S. Department of Agriculture (in Canada and England, by their equivalent departments). All the vaccines are tested for safety and potency. If your veterinarian gives the vaccination, you can be assured that the vaccine was manufactured by a reputable company, that it was refrigerated properly during and after delivery, and that it will be administered to your pet with proper care. *Note:* It is a good idea to sit in the reception area of the hospital for five to ten minutes after the second and third shots, since occasionally a kitten may suffer a *severe allergic reaction* (collapse and shock). If this happens, an emergency intravenous injection of *epinephrine* (and possibly oxygen) is necessary.

Calicivirus

What is the nature of the illness?	A virus that primarily attacks the mouth and lungs Infects only cats
What are the signs?	Fever Weakness Loss of appetite

What are the signs? (cont.)	Ulcers on the tongue, nostrils, or roof of mouth (*hard palate*) Heavy breathing Watery discharge from eyes and nose Sneezing Drooling
How is it spread?	Airborne transmission Direct contact
What is the treatment?	Antibiotics, fluids, vitamins, and forced feeding are usually necessary Inhalation therapy may loosen the nasal and tracheal congestion and increase the cat's appetite Good nursing and supportive therpay are very important
How is it prevented by vaccination?	An attenuated vaccine usually given in the same innoculation with the rhinotracheitis vaccine Boosters are necessary every six to twelve months *Note:* If the drops are used, sneezing may be noticed in four to seven days after innoculation; no treatment is necessary

Panleukopenia
(Feline distemper, "cat plague," infectious enteritis)

What is the nature of the illness?	A virus that primarily attacks the bone marrow and intestines (it does not cause "bad temper") *Note:* Highly contagious The death rate in infected, unvaccinated young cats is over 90 percent Seen in all members of the cat family, from lions to house cats
What are the signs?	High fever (104° to 105°F) Loss of appetite Weakness Vomiting Diarrhea (sometimes bloody) *Note:* Some kittens may die suddenly with no outward signs of illness

How is it spread?	Direct contact with the saliva, urine, feces, or vomit of an infected cat
	Infected fleas and flies harbor the virus and contaminate surfaces
What is the treatment?	Antibiotics, fluids, vitamins, blood transfusions, antivomiting and antidiarrheal medications, and forced feeding are all generally essential for maintaining life
	A disinfected environment is essential to avoid recontamination
How is it prevented by vaccination?	An attenuated vaccine first given at seven to nine weeks of age; the last after twelve weeks (kitten series)
	Boosters are necessary every twelve months

Pneumonitis

What is the nature of the illness?	A bacteria that primarily attacks the eye lining (conjunctiva) and the lining of the nose
	Infects only cats; fairly rare
What are the signs?	*Conjunctivitis* (inflammation of the eye lining)
	Sneezing
	Watery or puslike discharge from the eyes and nose
How is it spread?	Airborne transmission
	Direct contact
What is the treatment?	Antibiotics, fluids, vitamins, and forced feeding are usually necessary
	Inhalation therapy may loosen the nasal and tracheal congestion and increase the cat's appetite
	Good nursing and supportive therapy are very important
How is it prevented by vaccination?	Vaccination is not very effective because it does not produce a high level of antibodies and the antibody level is elevated for only a short time

Rabies

What is the nature of the illness?	A viral disease that attacks the brain
	Seen in all warm-blooded animals, especially skunks, raccoons, foxes, bats, coyotes, dogs, and cats
	Note: Infectious to humans

What are the signs?	Change in behavior
	Extreme restlessness
	Dilated pupils
	Extreme shyness or aggressiveness
	Tendency to bite anything in its way
	Paralysis of throat, causing voice changes, salivation, and an inability to eat and drink
	Paralysis of the lower jaw
	Generalized paralysis, coma, and death
How is it spread?	The bite of a rabid animal (virus-laden saliva enters the wound)
	Airborne transmission in caves inhabited by bats has been reported
What is the treatment?	Animals are not treated because of the public health danger and the high (almost 100 percent) mortality rate
	A few humans have reportedly been cured by intensive supportive therapy
How is it prevented by vaccination?	Attenuated vaccines are used
	The first vaccination is given between three and six months of age; boosters at one year and annually thereafter

Rhinotracheitis

What is the nature of the illness?	A herpes virus that primarily attacks the eye lining (conjunctiva) and upper breathing tubes (trachea)
	Infects only cats
What are the signs?	Fever
	Loss of appetite
	Watery or pus-like discharge from eyes and nose
	Weakness
	Sneezing
	Coughing
	Drooling
	Breathing through the mouth (nose is stuffed up)
	Note: Pregnant cats may abort
How is it spread?	Airborne transmission
	Direct contact

What is the treatment?

The virus is inactivated easily by disinfection or a dry environment

Antibiotics, fluids, vitamins, and forced feeding are usually necessary

Inhalation therapy may loosen the nasal and tracheal congestion and increase the cat's appetite

Good nursing and supportive therapy are very important

How is it prevented by vaccination?

An attenuated vaccine given by injection or in eye drops

Two inoculations are necessary in kittens, the last given after twelve weeks of age

Boosters are necessary every six to twelve months

Note: If the drops are used, sneezing may be noticed about four to seven days after inoculation; no treatment is necessary

PARASITES

A parasite obtains its nutrition from your pet and gives nothing in return except possible illness. This one-sided relationship has been under attack by concerned pet owners, veterinarians, pet food manufacturers, and pharmaceutical companies.

As a concerned pet owner, reading this section and the Decision Charts will make you aware of your cat's parasite problem (if any), whether you can treat it at home or need to visit your veterinarian, and how to prevent the parasite from finding a home on or in your pet's body. First, let me dispel a few old wives' tales:

1. Garlic does *not* cure worms
2. Cats do *not* transmit pinworms to children
3. Candy does *not* cause worms
4. Worms do *not* always cause disease (many pets live nicely with their parasites)
5. A thin or always-hungry cat does *not* always indicate worm problems

The worm medicine sold in pet stores and grocery stores should *not* be used unless your pet has roundworms and your veterinarian has advised you to use it. Since other intestinal parasites may be present, it is wiser to have your doctor check for other worms with a fecal sample. In most cases, the adult cat has developed an immunity to the worms (*ascarids*) killed by this medication, so once-a-month worming is not necessary. One stool sample that is negative for worm eggs does *not* mean that your pet has no worms—the worms may not be shedding their eggs at test time.

Veterinary medicine, the pharmaceutical companies, the pet food companies, and concerned pet owners, through good diagnostic methods, specific medicines, and sound hygiene and nutrition, have made it possible for today's pets to live almost free of parasites on or in their bodies.

Heartworms
(Dirofilaria)

Who gets them?	Dogs, foxes, and wolves; cats only rarely
	Note: Human infections have been reported but are rare
	Humans seem immune to the dog heartworm
	A worldwide problem, heartworms are prevalent in warm and tropical areas and in any heavily mosquito-infested areas
What do they look like?	Slender, white roundworms that are five to twelve inches long
How are they spread?	Transmitted by the mosquito
What is their life cycle?	After biting an infected animal, the mosquito hosts the *microfilaria* (noninfective larvae) in its sucking apparatus, where they become infective in two weeks
	A subsequent bite injects the larvae (baby worms) into the skin of another animal
	The larvae migrate through the body and grow into mature worms in the right heart chambers
	The worms produce new microfilaria and release them into the bloodstream, where another mosquito picks them up
Are there any signs to look for?	Weight loss despite a healthy appetite
	Anemia
	Coughing
	Heavy breathing
	Tires easily
	Swollen abdomen and legs
	Severe heart, lung, and liver damage leading to death

How are they diagnosed?	A blood test is necessary
	Note: The rarity of heartworm infections in cats makes this test unnecessary
What is the treatment?	Intravenous injections of *thiacetarsamide* kill the adult worms in the heart
	Your veterinarian may take chest X rays and perform an electrocardiogram to see the health of the lungs and heart before treatment
	The liver and kidney will be checked by blood tests before, during, and after treatment, since the chemical can damage these organs and the dead worms can lodge there
	Careful monitoring during hospitalization will minimize the chance of complications
	If everything has gone well, another drug is given about two months later to kill the microfilaria in the bloodstream
Can they be prevented?	Avoid mosquito-infested areas
	Keep your pet screened from mosquitos at night
	Diethylcarbamazine works well to prevent the maturation of larvae into adult worms (a blood test is a prerequisite for this treatment)
	Note: In general, heartworms are not a feline parasite

Hookworms

Who gets them?	Cats and dogs; cats and kittens seem more resistant, however
	Note: A few cases of development to the adult stage in the human intestine have been reported
What do they look like?	They are usually too small to be seen with the naked eye
How are they spread?	The larvae penetrate the skin or are swallowed
	Kittens can be infected while in the uterus or by larvae passing in the mother's milk
Are there any signs to look for?	Severe anemia
	Weakness
	Bloody diarrhea
How are they diagnosed?	Check successive stool samples
What is the treatment?	Medication is necessary

What is the treatment? (cont.)	*Note:* Medication kills only the adults in the intestine, not the larvae migrating through the body, so two or more wormings are necessary to kill all the parasites.
	Recent finding: Hookworm larvae can encyst (form cysts) in the muscles and survive for long periods of time, and medication is not effective against this stage.
Can they be prevented?	Keep environment sanitary
	Remove feces from your yard
	Wash concrete runs often, with salt or sodium borate (borax), if possible, which may be helpful in killing the eggs and larvae.
	Note: These chemicals can damage or kill grass and other vegetation

Protozoan-Coccidia

Who gets them?	Cats and dogs
	Note: Mature animals usually build up immunity to this parasite
What do they look like?	They are too small to be seen with the naked eye
How are they spread?	Infected animals shed the parasite in their feces
Are there any signs to look for?	Bloody diarrhea
How are they diagnosed?	Check successive stool samples
What is the treatment?	Sulfa drugs are effective
	Time (allows immunity to develop)
Can they be prevented?	Good sanitation is essential

Protozoan-Toxoplasmosis

Who gets them?	Cats and dogs
	Note: Highly infectious to humans, and birth defects can result from infection
What do they look like?	They are too small to be seen with the naked eye
How are they spread?	The *oocysts* ("egg-sac" stage) are introduced by eating infected raw meat, rodents, or birds, or by handling the feces of infected animals
What is their life cycle?	The parasite multiplies in the wall of the intestine
	Sometimes the parasite will spread to other parts of the body

Are there any signs to look for?

Fever

Loss of appetite

Weight loss

Weakness

Vomiting

Diarrhea

Breathing difficulties

Coughing

Anemia

Jaundice

Note: Most infections do not develop signs or else the signs are very mild

Note: Pregnant cats may abort

How are they diagnosed?

Special stool and antibody tests

What is the treatment?

Sulfa drugs are effective

Can they be prevented?

Do not feed your cat raw or undercooked meat

Keep your cat indoors

Clean the litter box daily using a 7 percent ammonia solution

Pregnant women should wear gloves when changing cat litter or gardening where a cat may defecate

Wash hands well after handling raw meat

Roundworms
(Ascarids)

Who gets them?

Cats and dogs

Note: Young children (especially under age four) may become infected with the larvae (a rare disease, called *visceral larva migrans*), which can move to the eye, liver, lungs, or brain, causing blindness, pneumonia, or other problems

What do they look like?

White, round worms, coiled into disks that may grow three to four inches long

They may appear in the stool or in vomit

How are they spread?

The worm eggs are introduced by licking infected ground or eating infected insects or mice

Kittens can be infected by larvae passed in the mother's milk

What is their life cycle?	The larvae migrate through the liver, lungs, and trachea on their way to the small intestine
	About a month after being swallowed, they reach sexual maturity and start reproducing
Are there any signs to look for?	Potbelly
	Thinness
	Dry hair coat
	Vomiting
	Diarrhea
	Coughing (as the larvae migrate through the lungs and breathing tubes)
	Note: Adult animals can develop an immunity and show no signs of infection
How are they diagnosed?	Check successive stool samples
What is the treatment?	Medication is necessary
	Note: Medication kills only the adults in the intestine, not the larvae migrating through the body, so two or more wormings are necessary to kill all the parasites
Can they be prevented?	Keep environment sanitary
	Remove feces from your yard
	Wash concrete runs often
	Control mice and cockroaches
	Keep your cat indoors
	Have your veterinarian check at least two or three successive stool samples of a new pet and worm your pet, if necessary

Strongyloides

Who gets them?	Cats (rarely) and dogs
	Note: This parasite can penetrate the skin of humans and cause intestinal problems
What do they look like?	They are too small to be seen with the naked eye
How are they spread?	The free-living parasites burrow through the skin
What is their life cycle?	They migrate through the internal organs on their way to the small intestine
	Strongyloides attach to the wall of the small intestine and when sexually mature, shed larvae in the feces

Are there any signs to look for?	Loss of appetite
	Pneumonia
	Bloody diarrhea
	Weight loss
	Weakness
	Skin infections can also occur from skin invasion
	Note: Younger pets have the more serious signs
How are they diagnosed?	Check successive stool samples for the larvae
	Note: When getting a stool sample, be sure not to include any soil, which has free-living worms that look like strongyloides but don't cause disease
What is the treatment?	A drug called *thiabendazole* is effective
Can they be prevented?	Keep environment sanitary
	Remove feces from your yard
	Wash concrete runs often, with salt or sodium borate (borax), if possible, which may be helpful in killing the eggs and larvae
	Note: These chemicals can damage or kill grass and other vegetation

Tapeworms

Who gets them?	Cats and dogs
	Note: There have been a few reported cases of children getting tapeworms from swallowing infected fleas
What do they look like?	Live tapeworm segments are off-white and flat and move in a back-and-forth motion
	They may be seen attached to the hair around the anus, in the stool, or on bedding
	The dried-out segments look like rice granules or sesame seeds
How are they spread?	The larvae are introduced by eating infected insects (fleas) or mammals (rats and mice, rabbits, or raw fish, beef, or pork)
What is their life cycle?	The tapeworm matures in the intestine
	When sexually mature, the segments, loaded with eggs, detach and pass out the anus
Are there any signs to look for?	Weight loss
	Occasional diarrhea

How are they diagnosed?   Check successive stool samples

Note: Examination of a segment can reveal the *source* of infection

Can they be prevented?   Control flea infestation

Keep your cat away from rodents

Do not feed your pet raw meat or fish

TRAINING YOUR CAT

In all the time man has spent on making a civilized world, the cat has been able to bridge the civilized, uncivilized, and "other" worlds with grace and beauty. The cat, some feel, lives among energy fields that we are just beginning to investigate. For instance, a cat's time sense, such as lying by the door in anticipation of its owner's arrival, its psi-trailing (the ability to find its way home for hundreds of miles), and its empathic responses, such as lying near you when you are depressed, are incredible phenomena.

If you can understand your cat's ancient behavior and language, it will make your life together richer and more pleasurable. In addition, it will make the process of training a happy experience. You may find these books helpful in getting to know your cat:

1. *Cat People,* by Bill Hayward (Garden City, N.Y.: Doubleday/Dolphin Books, 1978)
2. *Understanding Your Cat,* by Dr. M. W. Fox (New York: Coward McCann and Geoghegan, Inc., 1974)

Your Cat's Language

A cat uses facial expressions and its tail as well as its voice for communication. Therefore, be observant and watch for these indicators:

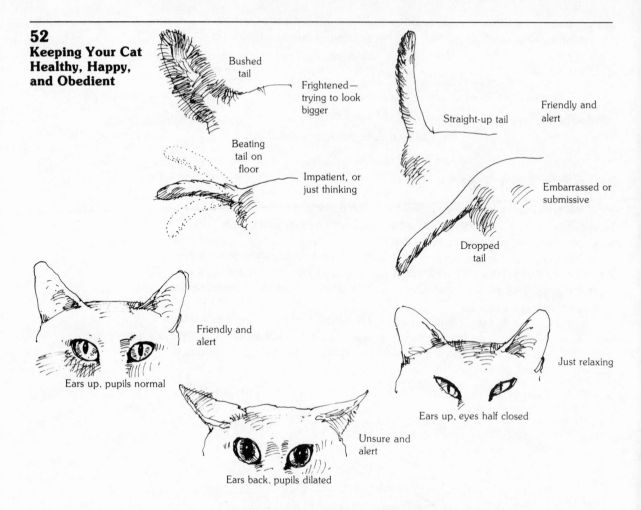

Bushed tail

Frightened—trying to look bigger

Beating tail on floor

Impatient, or just thinking

Straight-up tail

Friendly and alert

Embarrassed or submissive

Dropped tail

Friendly and alert

Ears up, pupils normal

Just relaxing

Ears up, eyes half closed

Unsure and alert

Ears back, pupils dilated

Recognizing these signs will give you an advantage.

In training, it's important to keep your cat's nature in mind. Specifically, a cat is more tuned to high-pitched sounds (remember the cockroach "talk") and to certain behaviors from its mother that should therefore be incorporated into your training procedures.

Touch is your cat's way of demonstrating and receiving love. Give your kittens a lot of cuddling and stroking, and let others do it, too. Cats prefer to be stroked *with,* not against, the hair coat, by the way—start at the neck and stroke to the tail. Speak in a soft voice while cuddling your kitten because loud voices will frighten it. Kittens love to be rubbed on the cheeks and under the chin; in appreciation, they will lift their tails and rub their bodies (especially their cheeks or chins) against you. This is a good time to start talking to your pet, to teach it its name.

When calling your cat, speak in a high falsetto. This will help your pet learn its name faster. Maintain the falsetto during training, feeding, and playing and that tone will then be associated with "good," as will its name. *Never* call your cat and then scold it.

A mother cat scolds kittens by growling and shaking the scruff of their necks. A stern, deep-voiced "No!" from you, along with a similar shake, should be pretty effective. Squirting the cat with water works fairly well, too, but you must do it while the "crime" is in progress.

Housebreaking

Cats in the wild bury their waste in their territory. Tame cats learn to use a litter box by watching their mother use it. If your kitten misses, put the stool in the litter box. That should tell your kitten that this is the proper place and should correct the situation.

A few hygienic practices on *your* part will also help:

1. Use absorbent clay litters.
2. Remove feces daily, using a slotted spoon that is *only* for this practice.
3. Use litter pan liners (newspaper will do) or disposable pans.
4. Replace the litter every third day, washing the pan with hot water, soap, and chlorine bleach; dry the pan thoroughly before refilling.

   Note: Do *not* use phenol, cresol, or resorcinol disinfectants.
5. Do *not* change the type of litter you use once your cat is used to it.

Eating Plants

Wild cats eat both meat and vegetation, so the instinct is there. Eating your house-plants, however, can be dangerous to the cat as well as nerve-wracking to you. For-tunately, grass is a safe substitute. An indoor cat can be let out on a leash to eat its fill—as long as there is no weed killer around. Otherwise, plant some grass seed or wild bird seed in a low pot. And don't forget catnip!

"Hunting"—The Ultimate Game

Naturally, the hunting urge is very strong in even the youngest kitten. This instinct and its appropriate behaviors (stalking, crouching, chasing, pouncing, and killing) are reinforced in infancy by the kitten's mother. Both visual and auditory stimuli will excite your cat. A ball of noisy, crinkly, and shiny tinfoil makes an excellent toy for your kitten. If you attach a piece of string, you can flip the ball into the air, making a flying prey. Then watch your pet's graceful attempts to catch it! Remember to put toys like this safely out of reach when playtime is over: Cats can swallow string and thread, causing serious intestinal obstructions.

Some other ideas for toys are empty boxes and paper bags, empty thread spools, and commercial catnip toys. Make sure that the toys do not shred and that they are too large to swallow.

GROOMING

Regular grooming of your cat consists of hair treatment, bathing, nail trimming, and ear cleaning.

Hair Treatment

Different coats need different strokes: The combing or brushing needs vary according to the length and coat type. Longer coats need bristle brushes, wire, or card brushes, and pet combs with rounded teeth that avoid irritating the skin. Brush short-haired cats weekly with a grooming glove. Use a bristle, wire, or card brush and a metal comb on long-haired cats. This will decrease the chance of hair balls (page 73).

Long-haired cats often have matted hair (from infrequent brushing and combing) behind their ears and under their legs. This should be pulled gently apart and combed out.

Many breeds of cats need regular clipping and stripping. You can learn to do it at home or find a professional groomer, who should be gentle and have a clean odorless establishment. Ask your neighbors and friends for recommendations.

Start the brushing and combing early (about twelve weeks of age) and keep gentle and patient, and this will be an enjoyable and healthy experience for you and your pet.

Bathing

Cats need baths just as humans do, because tongues are *not* adequate cleansing tools. Since the oils come back in the hair and skin within twenty-four hours, bathing could be done as often as necessary, but once every month or two is adequate.

Start bathing your kitten at fourteen weeks of age (sooner if it gets very dirty—just avoid chilling it) so that it will be accustomed to regular baths. The *best* way to bathe is to make your pet comfortable and to make it a game. No noise and slow motions will ease your job. Before placing your pet in the sink or bathtub, fill it with a small amount of warm water (running water will only scare your pet). While talking quietly and stroking and petting your kitten, place it in the warm water. Continue the petting motion and wet your pet with a soft spray hose attached to the faucet or use the water in the tub. The same petting and stroking can be used to lather the shampoo (preferably a good pet shampoo or "no tear" baby shampoo) into the hair coat. It is a good idea to first protect the eyes with a few drops of cod-liver oil or ophthalmic ointment and the ears with a small wad of cotton. Rinse with a soft spray hose attached to the faucet, still stroking, petting and talking to your pet. Rinse thoroughly since dried soap can irritate the skin. A creme rinse or hair conditioner can then be used to make the hair softer and more manageable for combing out. Don't forget to remove the cotton from the ears!

Towel dry your pet and continue all the ploys you used for the bath. The noise of a hair blow-dryer disturbs most animals, but you can try it later—*after* your pet is accustomed to baths. Make the whole experience pleasant and playful. A cat treat would definitely be in order after a successful bath. My cats are easy to bathe, although each needs special care. One has to continually walk around in the water while we lather him; another must be rubbed on the cheek and talked to while being bathed.

If your cat doesn't take to bathing, try placing a window screen angled in the tub. The cat can cling to the screen, making bathing easier. Holding the cat by the scruff of the neck is also helpful.

Nail Trimming

Start trimming the nails at twelve weeks of age to accustom your pet to this important grooming practice. Long nails can get caught in carpeting, grow into the foot-pad, or cause your pet to stand improperly. The dewclaw (equivalent to the thumb) does not touch the ground and needs more frequent trimming.

You can trim your cat's claws with a "human" nail clipper, a "Resco," or a "White" nail clipper. Trim just in front of the pink area, or *dermis*, which contains nerves and blood vessels. If the nail is dark and the pink area cannot be seen easily, shine a bright penlight through the nail to see where the dermis begins. Otherwise, just trim the nail as it curves down.

A nail trimmed too short will bleed. A styptic pencil or direct pressure with gauze or a clean cloth will stop the bleeding.

Pink area

Resco nail clipper

Ear Cleaning

Many owners neglect proper ear care and are made aware of its importance only when their cat "smells funny." Then they look in the ear and discover an infection (see Ear Discharges, page 182).

The wax in the ears should be cleaned once a month (more often if your cat has a history of ear problems). Clean only that part of the ear canal that you can see; otherwise, you may damage the eardrum. Use a cotton swab soaked in mineral oil or alcohol. Wax protects the ear canal, so a small amount left behind is beneficial.

The hair in the ears should not be plucked unless there is so much hair that it impedes air circulation. If your doctor feels this is necessary, use your fingers to remove only the hairs that come out easily. Plucking can expose the hair follicle to bacteria, so be careful. Some doctors recommend an antibiotic ointment after plucking to prevent infection.

TRAVELING WITH YOUR CAT

Cats travel well if you plan ahead. If you start them traveling while they are still kittens, they'll grow into well-adjusted adult travelers.

First of all, get your pet accustomed to the carrier beforehand. (Sturdy carriers can be purchased at pet stores.) At home, play with your kitten and feed it in the carrier until your pet is used to being in it. The next step is to take frequent short trips in the car, with the kitten in the carrier. Soothing talk, loving strokes, and gentle playing will help give your pet confidence that nothing terrible will happen.

Be sure your cat always has an identification tag on its collar or harness when traveling. For extra assurance, your pet can also be safely tattooed with identification marks. In addition, your cat should be in good health, with all vaccinations up to date.

One more general rule: Try to make reservations at hotels or motels that allow pets.

By Car

Do *not* feed your cat for six hours before the trip, and if carsickness is usually a problem, remove access to drinking water two hours before departure. (If needed, *Bonine®* or a medication prescribed by your veterinarian can be used to counteract motion sickness.) Always let your pet urinate and move its bowels before you start out. On long trips, plan for regularly scheduled exercise and water breaks. Feeding should be done at the final stop.

Take your cat's favorite food and bedding along. If feasible, take water from home as well, since the different mineral contents of water in new locations can give your pet diarrhea. Take along a litter box and litter, too.

Note: Do *not* keep a leash on your pet in the car. The leash can get caught on door handles and other projections and cause serious injury. If you leave your cat in the car in hot weather, be sure that at least one window is open a crack for good ventilation (see Heatstroke, page 118).

By Plane

When traveling by air, prior coordination with the airline will smooth things considerably. Each company has different procedures, so call in advance to find out what you need to do. In any case, follow the feeding, water, and motion sickness guidelines listed for travel by car. If traveling to a foreign country, contact the nation's nearest consular office to get any further instructions.

Generally, the airline will request (a) to see a health certificate for your cat; (b) that the cat travel in an approved carrier (available from the airline or from a pet store); (c) that both animal and carrier have proper identification tags, showing your name, address, and telephone number and your cat's name; and (d) that you check in at least one hour before departure. Some airlines will allow the carrier to travel with the passengers, under your seat.

BOARDING YOUR CAT

A good boarding cattery should be clean, relatively quiet, and well ventilated. The staff should treat boarders gently. Your veterinarian will be able to recommend a good place, if he or she does not have boarding facilities.

In general, you should call for reservations at least one or two weeks in advance (allow more time around holidays). Your cat must be healthy—all vaccinations up to date—and it should have an identification tag or tattoo. The staff should also ask for your veterinarian's name and telephone number and for a way to reach you in case of emergency.

If, on your return, you find that your cat has diarrhea, you might request that the cattery feed its regular, at-home diet the next time you board there. Also, a mild tranquilizer might be helpful—but first discuss this with your veterinarian.

Chapter **4**
Going to the Veterinarian

Throughout your cat's life, veterinary attention—from vaccinations to laboratory tests, from radiology (X rays) to surgery—will be needed. In this chapter, I will discuss some of the encounters that your pet will have with the veterinarian. Guidelines will be provided to help you choose a veterinarian to meet your cat's needs.

THE "G.P." AND SPECIALISTS

A local professional will probably be able to handle all your cat's health needs throughout its lifetime. This person will be your cat's family doctor or general practitioner, although sometimes he or she will have an advanced degree in a veterinary specialty, such as internal medicine. It takes four years of premedical or preveterinary education and four years of veterinary school for a person to become a veterinarian. Recently, internships and advanced degrees in over twenty specialties have become available to the twenty-two veterinary schools in the United States.

Solo Practice

The typical local veterinarian works very hard and is usually available when needed—like the physician in "the good old days"—although of course he or she

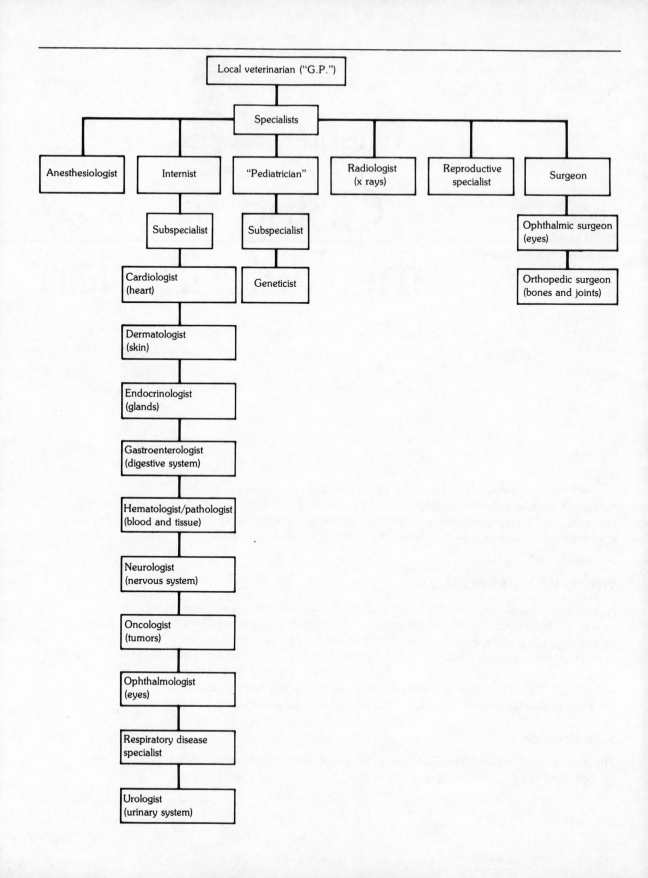

takes time off for personal activities and to attend veterinary meetings. However, if your local veterinarian is a "solo practitioner"—a veterinarian without partners —you may not always be able to see him. Upon reaching your veterinarian's answering service, you may be referred to another professional who is "on call" for the emergency group.

Group Practice

Veterinary group practice—a few doctors practicing in one building, or a central hospital with satellite out-patient clinics—has become a popular arrangement for veterinary care in the last few years. The sharing of night calls and weekend coverage, the reduction of office costs by shared expense, the availability of consultation, and a more medically stimulating environment for the veterinarian all contribute to its increased popularity. The larger group practices may have a few specialists associated with them.

Referrals

Veterinary medicine is just like human medical care: Sometimes the local doctor needs a specialist's expert help. If your local veterinarian feels that your cat has an especially serious or puzzling medical or surgical problem, you and your cat will be referred to a specialist in the area. Most specialists are found in group referral practices—for example, a cardiologist, an orthopedic surgeon, and a neurologist working together—or at veterinary schools. Most specialists complete three or more years of training after graduation from basic veterinary school. If your cat needs to see a specialist, your veterinarian will write a letter of introduction for you and provide a copy of your cat's complete medical and surgical history.

The types of veterinarians available for your cat's care can be grouped as shown on the opposite page.

EVALUATING THE VETERINARIAN

Selecting a veterinarian deserves the same consideration as choosing your own family physician. Ask your neighbors, friends, local cat breeders and groomers, or even your own general practitioner for a recommendation.

The most important factor in the selection is your confidence in that person. To help you select and evaluate your veterinarian, consider the following points:

1. **Is the office clean and well equipped?**
2. **Is the doctor on an appointment system?**

This reduces your waiting time considerably, makes the reception area less crowded, and makes your doctor less rushed.

3. **Can you take a tour of the clinic at a convenient time for the doctor or the staff?**

Most veterinarians will be proud to show you their facilities.

4. Does the veterinarian take an appropriate medical history?

All veterinarians have been trained to organize background information in a logical, concise, and accurate way. This is called "taking the medical history," and it is extremely important to good veterinary care. A history is divided into the major problem(s), the present illness, a review of the systems, and the past medical history. Emergencies (such as injuries), simple problems, and well-pet exams (vaccinations) may not require many questions by the doctor.

The Major Medical Problem(s)   Before your visit, write down all the problems that your cat is having so that you won't leave out an important detail. The major medical problem should be expressed as the *title* of your story:

"Ralph has been urinating more than usual and drinking a lot more water."

Identify each problem without unnecessary details and let the doctor pick up from there.

The Present Illness   Your veterinarian will want to establish the progression of the present illness. This means that you must observe your pet very carefully at home so that you can provide all the relevant information. Again, organize your thoughts so that all the important facts are given:

"Three days ago, Ralph began drinking a lot more water. In fact, I had to fill up a 5 oz. bowl three times during the day. Now Ralph [yes, I *do* see female pets with "male" names] is drinking six bowls of water daily. Her appetite is unsatisfied, though, and she keeps begging for food. She asks to go out to urinate every half hour, even during the night. She also began wetting on the kitchen floor. I didn't see any blood in the urine. I took her temperature when all this started, and it was normal."

Other information that may be useful is any medication that your pet took before and during the present illness. Bring the medications (or their names) with you. If X rays or laboratory tests had been performed for past illnesses or for the present illness at another veterinarian's office, have the results phoned or sent to your present veterinarian. If your cat is allergic to any medication, make sure the doctor knows this.

The Review of Systems   Your veterinarian will ask you specific questions related to the skin, heart, lungs, stomach, intestines, urinary system, muscles, bones, nervous system, eyes, ears, nose, and throat. These questions will help your doctor determine which systems are involved in the present illness.

The Past Medical History   In many cases, previous illnesses, injuries, surgical procedures, or medications are related to the present illness. Be sure that you keep *complete* records. "She had little blue pills," does not tell your doctor anything, so be sure all medications are *named* when dispensed, and write the name in your pet's home health record. Dates of illnesses (both those treated and those not requiring a visit), dates of and reasons for hospitalization (with a *complete* list of all lab tests, X rays, and drugs administered), and surgical procedures (including the anesthesia used) should be recorded. You would be surprised how many times this information is relevant to the present illness. (See the sample home health chart, Your Cat's Records, on pages ii and iii.)

5. Does your veterinarian do a complete physical examination?

Your pet deserves a *complete* physical examination even during well-pet visits, such as for vaccinations. Many early problems can be picked up at these semi-annual or annual visits. A thorough medical history and physical examination will probably suggest the diagnosis to most competent veterinarians.

Each doctor has his or her own order in the physical exam. Some start by taking the temperature; others may examine the head or hair coat. A good physical exam can be very rewarding. Please do not talk to your doctor at this time unless a question is asked of you, since complete concentration is required.

The veterinarian will follow the same basic physical outlined in Chapter 2. Palpation will determine pain, size, shape, or consistency of the tissues and organs. Sharp taps with the fingers on the abdomen or chest wall will tell your doctor the hollowness or solidness of the body part examined. For example, an area that should sound hollow but sounds solid may indicate a mass that does not belong there. Using a stethoscope for *auscultation* allows the sounds of body functions (heartbeats, and lung and intestinal sounds) to be amplified. A visual inspection of your pet's gait, posture, hair coat, gum color, and other visible parts is also a feature of a complete physical. An *otoscope* will be used to look in your pet's ear canal; an *ophthalmoscope* will magnify the eye and its inner structure. An examination of your pet's retina (the back of the inner eye) is part of a thorough physical exam because the presence of certain systemic or local diseases can be discovered by checking the retina.

Certain diseases of the skin, mouth, ears, or internal organs have characteristic odors (for example, a sweet breath may indicate diabetes), so your veterinarian's sense of smell will also be brought into play. *Note:* A rectal exam is *not* a routine part of a cat's physical.

6. Does your veterinarian encourage you to ask questions?

All your questions should be answered in a clear, concise way and in language that you understand—not in medical jargon. Diagrams or simple line drawings are helpful, too.

7. Is your veterinarian gentle with your pet?

Sometimes a little calm talk or a few strokes is all that is needed to make the exam easier.

8. Does your veterinarian have any pets of his own?

9. Is your veterinarian careful with a biting or scratching pet?

Your veterinarian should explain that your pet will be gently but firmly restrained so that nobody gets hurt. Most doctors will use a veterinary assistant, a towel, or a muzzle.

10. If you are a new pet owner, does the veterinarian give you literature on good health maintenance and training, or does he or she explain it to you?

11. Will your doctor refer you to a veterinary specialist if needed?

A good veterinarian knows his limitations.

12. Is your veterinarian a member of an emergency group, or is there another doctor on call when your veterinarian is not available?

13. Are all rates and fees explained to you?

If your doctor does not take the initiative, be sure to ask what the fees will be for vaccinations, lab tests, radiographs, surgery, hospitalization, and treatment. Sometimes it is impossible to give you an exact figure, but high and low estimates are feasible, unless your pet's condition is so unpredictable that the treatment may change. If your pet will be hospitalized for a few days, you could ask your doctor to keep you informed daily of your pet's accumulated tab. Many veterinary hospitals are nearly as well-equipped as human hospitals, and the care is also equivalent—sometimes even better! At the moment there is no national pet care insurance to take the sting out of paying those bills, but knowing the daily financial picture as well as the health picture can be comforting.

14. Does your veterinarian use laboratory tests and radiographs (X rays) discriminately, to confirm a diagnosis?

Your doctor should explain to you in simple language why each test or series of radiographs is being done:

> "I'm going to *catheterize* Ralph—that is, place a sterile tube into the bladder. She'll be tranquilized so it won't be uncomfortable. The urine collected will be checked to see if she has a bladder infection. A *culture* will be taken to isolate, identify, and count the bacteria. The appropriate antibiotic for killing the bacteria will be determined by exposing the bacteria to various antibiotics in an antibiotic *sensitivity test*. I'll take radiographs of the bladder to rule out bladder stones or bladder tumors."

15. Does your veterinarian hospitalize only for serious problems?

Many pets' problems don't need hospitalization, and in fact, pets seem to fare better in the home environment. Being treated by their owners, in close cooperation with the veterinarian, is a very comfortable situation. Most treatment and lab tests can be done on an outpatient basis. Besides, hospitalization can be expensive.

16. Is your veterinarian's hospital well equipped?

This may be difficult for you to evaluate, but up-to-date veterinary hospitals do have modern radiograph equipment, surgical facilities, and laboratories.

If your answers are positive, you have a wonderful veterinarian. Congratulations! If you cannot give a positive answer to most of these questions, or if you are not comfortable with your veterinarian's diagnosis or treatment, seek another doctor or another opinion.

A happy veterinarian-owner relationship also requires a cooperative, aware, and concerned owner. You can have the best veterinarian in the whole world but if you do not follow instructions, or do not understand the instructions, your relationship—and your pet's health—can deteriorate rapidly. Because you live intimately with your pet and know its habits and routine, you can often pick up very early and subtle changes that may go unnoticed by your doctor. The concerned and aware owner will use this book to best advantage by checking the Decision Charts and other chapters whenever necessary.

When a visit is necessary, bring paper and pen and write down (or have your veterinarian write down) *all* important instructions. Trying to remember everything is usually a waste of your time and money and may cause your pet's medical problem to persist, return, or get worse. In many cases, this situation leads to the denouncement "That vet is no good!" If you do not understand why a medication was prescribed, its side effects, or how long it should be given, or the importance, expectations, or limitations of a treatment or surgical procedure, ask your veterinarian to *make* it understandable. Lack of communication, not poor professional care, is the most frequent problem in the veterinarian-owner relationship.

For example, do *not* "double-up" on the medication at night if you were too rushed in the morning to give your cat its medicine. Excess doses can be worse than none at all. Let your doctor demonstrate the best method to administer the medicine if you feel that you will have problems. And do *not* stop the medication just because Ralph seems better. Follow your doctor's instructions. Stopping medication too early can cause an even more serious problem. If your pet experiences side effects from the medication, phone your veterinarian. A change in dosage or in the interval between doses—or a new drug altogether—may be recommended. If your doctor wants a follow-up exam, follow up!

One final word: Thank your doctor when he or she does a good job and is interested in your pet's health. Everyone, including your veterinarian, likes to be appreciated.

LABORATORY TESTS

Tests are often needed to confirm a diagnosis or to determine the best mode or the effectiveness of treatment. Some of the most common tests that may be requested are stool sample, skin scrapings (for skin parasites or fungus), complete blood count, blood chemistry, urinalysis, bacteriology, and tissue biopsy.

Stool Sample

Since cats like to examine their surroundings by licking both the ground and their peers' private areas, and since they walk bare-footed and eat things they shouldn't (such as rodents), a stool sample should be checked once or twice a year. Most doctors will recommend that you bring it with you at vaccination time. A little is all that is needed, and it's OK if the sample has kitty litter on it. If you are gathering an outdoor sample, try not to include any soil, since it contains some worms (harmless "soil" strongyloides) that may confuse the examiner.

Skin Scrapings

Confirming a fungus infection (see Ringworm, page 172) involves transferring a skin scraping of the lesion to a container that contains "fungus food." Confirmation may take one to two weeks. As the fungus grows and uses the "food," the media in the container changes color—from yellow to red. If there is a suspicion of a fungus infection, treatment will begin at the time of the scraping.

Complete Blood Count

If firemen are in a smoking building, you assume that there is a fire and that it will soon be under control. If there are smoke and flames and no firemen, the building may burn to the ground. Your cat's body has a remarkable "fire department" that consists of specialized cells, floating through miles and miles of blood vessels. Some carry oxygen (red blood cells), giving the blood its red color. Others can be mobilized to defend areas of tissue injury (from bacteria, trauma, chemicals, or heat, for instance) and inflammation by "eating up" the particles that invaded your pet's body (white blood cells). These "firemen" consist of *erythrocytes* (red) and *leukocytes* (white). The white blood cells are divided into *neutrophils, lymphocytes, monocytes, eosinophils,* and *basophils.* The bone marrow produces all red blood cells and the neutrophils, eosinophils, and basophils. Lymphocytes and monocytes are produced in the lymph nodes, the spleen, the tonsils, and the lymphoid cells of the intestine.

The number and type of "firemen" may help your doctor determine the type of disease present. For example, the panleukopenia virus can stop a cat's bone marrow from making neutrophils. The blood count for neutrophils and the total white blood count will then be very low. Therefore, a kitten or unvaccinated cat with the signs of panleukopenia (page 136), with a very low total white blood count, and with few neutrophils probably has the disease. The cat's "firemen" are not available, and its "building" (its body) is in grave danger. Parasites that attack the red blood cells, such as *hemobartonella,* can be identified by staining a blood smear and then looking for the parasite in the red blood cells.

The neck (*jugular*) and front leg (*cephalic*) veins are the two most common sites for *venipuncture* (literally, puncturing the vein) to obtain blood for tests. Gentle restraint and a sterile needle and syringe are used, and most pets tolerate the procedure very well. However, fat or hyperactive cats and those with rolling or unusual veins may make it difficult to get a blood sample on the first try. Every veterinarian and technician has dealt with "problem veins." Reactions from the owner such as, "You mean you have to stick poor Ralph *again*?" will just add more stress to the job—so quiet, please!

Blood Chemistry

The health of your cat's body depends on the health of all its parts, and an unhealthy organ will eventually affect the other organs. In order to confirm a diagnosis or to monitor your pet's return to health or its setbacks, various enzymes and products of metabolism found in the blood should be measured. An increase or decrease in their levels can identify and monitor the organ (or organs) that is sick and the proper treatment can begin. A blood test alone is *not* a substitute for a physical examination, but veterinary recognition of the importance of blood chemistries has made this commonplace for good veterinary care.

Most veterinarians are taking advantage of a new development in the field: using a reliable commercial laboratory that provides accurate results at a reasonable price. However, veterinarians may perform certain tests, such as kidney function or blood sugar, in their own clinics, since the results from commercial labs may not be available for twenty-four to forty-eight hours. Pets that are very ill also need immediate results. Even so, the tests require time. In fact, your veterinarian may have to institute basic treatment before the final analysis is known. (In serious cases, life support care, such as antibiotics, fluids, oxygen, and any other treatment thought necessary, *will* be started before all the test results have come back.) If you call the office the day after your cat has been examined to find out what exactly is wrong, your doctor still may not be sure of the complete picture.

The commercial laboratories may run as many as fifteen or twenty different tests on your cat's blood sample. This is called a *biochemical profile*. A few of the most common blood chemistries and other tests in a profile are briefly explained in the next section.

Biochemical profile

Blood Sugar (glucose)   Your doctor will run this test if diabetes is suspected (see pages 140 and 146).

Blood Urea Nitrogen (BUN) and Creatinine   Urea and creatinine are end-products of metabolism that are normally eliminated by the kidney in the urine. If the kidneys are not functioning properly, these products will be increased in the blood. This will not tell your doctor the *cause* of the kidney problem, just that the kidneys are involved. Special radiographs, urinalysis, and even a biopsy may be needed to define the disease process.

Amylase and Lipase   More cases of acute *pancreatitis* (inflammation of the pancreas) are being diagnosed and treated properly, thanks to the availability of these tests. If your pet has abdominal pain and sudden and severe vomiting and is very weak and depressed, these tests may be beneficial. The cells of an inflamed pancreas release the amylase and lipase enzymes into the blood stream, so their number is markedly elevated.

Liver Profile Tests   The liver has so many functions that to see how it is functioning overall, a liver profile has to be done. The blood tests include *bilirubin, protein, SGPT, SGOT, cholesterol,* and *alkaline phosphatase.* Sometimes this still is not enough to tell your doctor the *cause* of the liver problem, so other tests, such as a liver biopsy, may be necessary.

Urinalysis   This is an extremely helpful test for diagnosing diseases of the urinary tract and other problems, such as *diabetes mellitus* and liver disease. Your doctor will check to see if your pet is concentrating its urine (specific gravity) and will study the chemical analysis for such abnormalities as sugar in the urine, which may indicate diabetes or a kidney defect. Microscopic examination of the urine can spot cells that may indicate inflammation, infection, or degeneration anywhere along the urinary tract.

Bacteriology   Bacterial infections are very common in bite-wounds (*abscesses*) and in problems involving the ear, eye, and urinary tract. Your doctor may suggest culture and sensitivity tests, which involve transferring a small amount of the infected material to a container filled with "food" in which the bacteria can flourish. Small paper disks, each containing a different antibiotic, are placed in the container at even intervals. The antibiotics that are effective against the bacteria will produce *zones of inhibition* — areas around the disks where no bacteria will grow. The bacteria will also be identified by its growth pattern and microscopic features. Using a general antibiotic may cure the infection, but performing culture and sensitivity tests — especially in chronic infections — is better practice and may be cheaper in the long run.

Zone of inhibition

Tissue Biopsy

Removing a tissue section for microscopic examination is often an excellent way to make a proper diagnosis, determine if the disease process can be reversed, and suggest the best therapy. Of course, biopsy of the internal organs is more difficult and has more risks than biopsy of the skin, but in skilled hands and with the proper instruments, tissue can be studied from the kidney, prostate, liver, or any other organ. Often, a local anesthetic and the appropriate biopsy instrument are all that is needed to obtain the sample. Biopsy is a good tool for determining the chance for your cat's recovery and the type and cost of the best therapy.

Radiographs (X rays)

Radiographs have become another important tool for diagnosis. The radiographic equipment in many veterinary hospitals is equivalent to that in human hospitals — and just as expensive. Modern X-ray equipment provides excellent "pictures" of the bones and internal organs and the spaces between them. The procedure of taking X rays is painless and relatively harmless, but your pet may be sedated because any movement may cause blurring. Two or more views are needed to get a three-dimensional "picture" of the area under investigation.

To get the "picture," X rays are directed through your cat's body. They travel very rapidly and then penetrate a plate containing film. X rays pass through air easily, but solid masses, such as internal organs and bones, will stop some of them. Those that hit the film turn it black when it is developed. The areas on the film not touched by the rays remain white. So a chest X ray has white areas (such as the heart, backbones, and ribs) and black areas (lung tissue, containing air). Your doctor will study the X rays under a bright light, looking for changes in the normal shape, size, and density of the organs.

Electrocardiogram

An electrocardiogram (ECG) is a graphic measure of the electrical activity of the heart. It is an inexpensive, safe, and painless technique for determining if your pet has heart disease. It is also helpful for diagnosing and monitoring treatments of illnesses not originating in the heart, such as urinary obstructions and Addison's disease. To obtain the ECG, your pet is placed on its right side and *leads* are attached to its legs and body using clips. Cats rarely need to be sedated. The various leads are recorded and the heart rate and rhythm and changes in the heart size are evaluated.

Chapter 5

Your Cat's Home Pharmacy

Home medical care of your cat's minor illnesses and injuries may require medication—*sometimes. Sometimes,* because many of your pet's medical problems, such as a minor abrasion, a sprain, or occasional vomiting or diarrhea, resolve themselves without medication. Feline bodies have a remarkable capability for healing themselves, but we are a drug-oriented society: We feel that an injection of this or a tablet of that will do the job. In reality, a little time and knowledge are often all that are needed, and they may well be the most effective (and the cheapest!) treatment. This should not be abused, however. If the Decision Charts recommend seeing a veterinarian or trying drug or non-drug treatments, such as cleaning and soaking a wound or encouraging fluid intake, follow the instructions.

Veterinarians are occasionally confronted with an injury or minor illness that has healed itself even when the owner did not use the medication or follow the instructions. The owner calls a week later to say that the ear infection is completely healed or the diarrhea has disappeared. This does *not* mean that you should not follow your doctor's instructions!

BASIC NECESSITIES

Below is a list of medications that are good to have on hand, as well as the ailments they treat. Items in bold print are essentials; the other preparations are not so vital. *Remember:* Keep all medicines out of the reach of children. The when and why of using medications, including dosage and side effects, are discussed afterward.

Medication	Ailment
*Milk of magnesia Bulk laxatives mineral oil Fleet® enema	Constipation
Guaifenesin (Glyceryl guaiacolate)	Coughs
Kaopectate®	Diarrhea
Antibiotic ophthalmic ointments	Eye irritations
Tinactin®	Fungus
Petroleum jelly Commercial hair ball medicine	Hair balls
*Bonine®	Motion sickness
Nothing safe	Pain and fever
	Poisoning
Hydrogen peroxide (3 percent) **Activated charcoal** Milk of magnesia	• to induce vomiting • to absorb poison • to speed passage through the digestive tract
A and D Ointment® **Antibiotic ointment** Betadine® Domeboro® solution **Hydrogen peroxide (3 percent)**	Skin irritations
Tomato juice Cranberry juice Vitamin C	Urinary infections
Kaopectate® *Maalox® *Mylanta® **Pepto Bismol®**	Vomiting and stomach upsets

*Do *not* give to kittens without your veterinarian's approval.

Constipation

Laxatives should *not* be used on a regular basis unless recommended by your veterinarian. Safe laxatives are made from *psyllium* (see below). Alternative laxatives are milk of magnesia or mineral oil. If an enema is needed, use warm water (best) or a Fleet® enema.

Bulk laxatives

Products such as Metamucil® and Mucilose® are refined from the psyllium seed. It is not absorbed by the digestive tract; it only passes through. Thus, it is a natural product and one with essentially no contraindications and no side effects. It provides bulk by drawing water into the stool. *Note:* If you think your cat has an intestinal obstruction or impacted feces, do *not* use a laxative.

Dosage   ½ to 1 teaspoon mixed in the food once or twice daily. Be sure to mix water into the food and supply drinking water at all times.

Milk of magnesia

The active ingredient, *magnesium,* causes fluid to be retained within the bowel and in the feces. It is also helpful in speeding passage of any poisons through the digestive tract.

Dosage   1 teaspoon per five pounds of body weight once daily. (One dose should do the job.)

Side Effects   Milk of magnesia is nonabsorbable but it does contain magnesium and some salt and should *not* be used if your pet has kidney or heart disease.

Mineral oil

This is the cheapest and most effective laxative, but it can be dangerous if administered improperly or given for a long period of time. Mineral oil should *never* be given directly in the mouth because it is bland and may enter the breathing tubes and lungs before your pet can cough. Mineral oil in the lungs will cause a severe pneumonia. Instead, mix it in the food. If mineral oil is given for a long period of time, it can cause deficiencies of the fat soluble vitamins A, D, E, and K.

Dosage   1 teaspoon per ten pounds of body weight, mixed in the food once daily, for two days at the maximum.

Side Effects   Pneumonia or vitamin deficiency if administered improperly.

Fleet® enema

If your pet has *obstipation* (impacted or hard feces in the lower intestine and rectum), you should see your doctor. If you must give the enema, use the Fleet® pediatric enema. This may lubricate and soften the hard feces (see Constipation, page 202).

Dosage   The lubricated nozzle is inserted into the rectum and one ounce of the solution is gently administered. Another enema can be given half an hour later, if necessary.

Side Effects   *Note:* Severe complications can result if used when fever, nausea, vomiting, or abdominal pain is present. Do *not* use in cats that are dehydrated or have known kidney disease.

Coughs

The only safe cough medicine I recommend for use without veterinary consultation is an expectorant. The expectorant liquefies the secretions and allows the body's defenses to get rid of the bad material. Cough suppressants should *not* be used without your doctor's advice, because they contain such narcotics as codeine. Over-the-counter cough suppressants may contain dextromethorphan, a close chemical relative.

Glyceryl guaiacolate (Guaifenesin)
If your cat has a dry, hacking cough, a lubricant soothes the inflamed area. If your pet has a cough with mucus, glyceryl guaiacolate liquefies the mucus secretions so that they may be coughed free. It does not suppress the cough reflex, but encourages the natural defense mechanisms of the body.

Read the label: Do *not* use Robitussin® or 2-G® with the additives PE (for the decongestant *phenylephrine*), CF or DM (for the cough suppressant *dextromethorphan*), or AC (for codeine). Use only Robitussin® or 2-G® with only glyceryl guaiacolate (guaifenesin) in 3.5 percent alcohol.

Dosage   ¼ teaspoon every four hours.

Side Effects   No serious side effects, but check with your doctor if the cough persists or the Decision Chart so indicates.

Diarrhea

Kaopectate® is a very safe medication for cats. Do *not* use paregoric—it may be toxic to your cat. See your veterinarian if diarrhea persists or if the Decision Chart so indicates.

Kaopectate®
Kaopectate contains *kaolin* and pectin, which coat the intestinal tract and help to form a solid stool.

Dosage   2 teaspoons per ten pounds of body weight every four hours.

Eye Irritations

For short-term use, apply an ophthalmic ointment such as Neosporin® or Neopolycin® to your cat's eye three or four times daily. These ointments contain three antibiotics: *polymyxin, bacitracin,* and *neomycin.*

Fungus

Tinactin®

If your pet has only one ringworm lesion, you can use this cream. It is available over the counter in drugstores.

Dosage   Apply the cream to the skin lesion with a Q-tip® twice daily. *Note:* Do *not* touch the lesion with your finger.

Side Effects   If the skin becomes more irritated, stop the medication and see your veterinarian. *Note:* Do *not* get the medication in the eye.

Hair Balls

Brushing and combing your cat frequently will help prevent hair balls (swallowed hair from self-grooming). If your cat still vomits hair balls, a lubricant such as white petroleum jelly may help. A commercial hair ball medicine (Kat-a-lax®, Lax-atone®) from your veterinarian or pet store can also be used.

White petroleum jelly
Dosage   ½ teaspoon per ten pounds of body weight. Apply it to the cat's nose and it will be licked off. This can be given once weekly. The jelly melts in the stomach to an oil that lubricates the hair ball for easier passage in your cat's bowels.

Side Effects   Keep in mind that white petroleum jelly has the potential to decrease the absorption of fat soluble vitamins (A, D, E, and K) if given in large doses or for a prolonged time.

Motion Sickness

First, try all the preparations for preventing motion sickness given on page 56.

Bonine®
If you are unsuccessful, an antihistamine called Bonine® (*meclizine hydrochloride*) can be used. It is effective against the apprehension, salivation, and vomiting or diarrhea that some pets experience when traveling. If Bonine® is not successful in eliminating the motion sickness, your veterinarian can provide you with tranquilizers or antihistamines that are effective.

Dosage   12.5 mg. given on an empty stomach one hour before traveling. The dose can be repeated in twenty-four hours.

Side Effects   Your pet may experience drowsiness. *Note:* Do *not* give Bonine® to a pregnant cat—it may cause birth defects.

Pain and Fever

Do *not* give aspirin or Tylenol® to cats without your veterinarian's recommendation. Cats have problems detoxifying and excreting these substances.

Poisoning

To induce vomiting: hydrogen peroxide

If your cat swallows a poison that can be expelled by vomiting, hydrogen peroxide 3 percent works very well. Do *not* induce vomiting if the poison swallowed is a petroleum-based compound or a strong acid or strong alkali (see Swallowed Poisons, page 120). Be sure that the hydrogen peroxide purchased is not a higher strength (such as for bleaching hair).

Dosage 1 teaspoon every ten minutes until your cat vomits. You can repeat this two or three times, if necessary. If this treatment is unsuccessful, 1 or 2 teaspoons of salt or a mustard and warm water solution put on the back of the tongue should induce vomiting.

To absorb poison: activated charcoal

After vomiting, a few teaspoons of activated charcoal mixed in milk or water can be given to absorb the poison if the specific antidote is not known. Activated charcoal can be purchased in drugstores.

To speed passage through the digestive tract: milk of magnesia

Dosage 1 teaspoon per five pounds of body weight once daily.

Skin Irritations

Sterilizing agents and antiseptics

Soap and water is the best way to clean a wound. Hydrogen peroxide (3 percent strength) foams and cleanses wounds very well, and is inexpensive. Betadine®, a nonstinging iodine preparation, kills germs and is a good agent to use on the skin, but it is expensive. To soothe the skin temporarily, calamine lotion can be applied, but it loses its effectiveness when it dries out. It must be washed off and reapplied frequently. *Note:* Do *not* get it in the eyes.

Dosage Cleanse the wounds three times daily. Trim the hair around the wound, if necessary.

Domeboro® solution

This is a soothing wet dressing for relief of skin inflammation. It has antiseptic properties and reduces itching.

Dosage Dissolve one teaspoon or tablet in a pint of warm water. Bathe or apply wet dressings of the solution to the affected skin for fifteen minutes. You can repeat this three or four times daily.

Ointments

A and D ointment soothes irritated skin and can be applied three or four times daily to affected areas. The ointments containing antibiotics (Neosporin®, Neopolycin® and Mycitracin®) can be applied to affected skin three times daily.

Urinary Infections

Acidifiers help control bacterial infections of the lower urinary tract and help prevent a recurrence of crystal or stone formation in the tract.

Vitamin C and juices

Tomato juice and cranberry juice are excellent urinary acidifiers—if your pet will drink them. You can measure their effectiveness by testing urine with litmus paper. If blue litmus paper turns red, the urine is acidic.

Dosage ¼ to 1 cup of cranberry juice or tomato juice per day should be adequate. 100 mg. of vitamin C three times daily.

Vomiting and Stomach Upsets

Kaopectate®, Maalox®, Mylanta®, Pepto Bismol®

All of these products soothe the stomach lining.

Dosage 2 teaspoons of Kaopectate® per ten pounds of body weight every four hours. ½ teaspoon of Maalox® or Mylanta® per ten pounds of body weight every eight hours. ½ teaspoon of Pepto Bismol® per ten pounds of body weight every four hours.

Side Effects Maalox® and Mylanta® may loosen the stools a little. If your pet has a history of heart or kidney disease, consult your veterinarian before using either of these.

THE FIRST AID KIT

This is a *must*. Keep the kit in a convenient location but out of the reach of small children. A fishing tackle box works very well, by the way.

Adhesive tape, 1 inch wide

Gauze bandages, 1-inch rolls

Absorbent cotton

Sterile gauze pads, 3 × 3 inches

Cotton-tipped swabs (Q-tips®)

Rubbing alcohol

Rectal thermometer

Teaspoon

Tweezers

Sharp scissors with rounded ends

Medications (those in bold print on page 70 are the basic requirements)

GIVING PILLS TO YOUR CAT

Caution: Giving pills to cats with neck pain or to vicious cats can be dangerous.

- Place the palm of your hand over your cat's muzzle. With the thumb on one side and your fingers on the other, press hard against and under the upper teeth.
- Tilt the head up slightly. This usually causes the lower jaw to relax and drop a little.
- Using the middle finger of your other hand, push the lower jaw open.
- With your thumb and index finger, place the pill in the center of the tongue near its base.
- Close the mouth quickly and tap your pet's nose with your finger. This will cause the cat to lick and then swallow.
- Fractious cats can be held by the back of the neck. Open the lower jaw with a pencil (always use the eraser end). Toss the pill in the back of the throat and gently tap it down with the pencil.

A plastic pill gun (purchased from your veterinarian or pet shop) is very handy and can save your fingers from getting hung up on your cat's teeth. A flexible tip holds the tablet or capsule within the barrel until deposited in your cat's mouth. A sharp push on the barrel delivers the pill to the back of the throat.

GIVING LIQUIDS TO YOUR CAT

- Hold your cat's head at a 45° angle.
- Make a pouch in the corner of the lip fold by pulling the cheek outward.
- Using a spoon or eye dropper, slowly pour the liquid into the pouch.
- If your cat does not swallow the liquid automatically, jiggle the pouch slightly or tap on the nose with your finger; this will cause it to swallow. Be sure to keep the head at a 45° angle until the liquid is swallowed.

Note: Placing your cat in the bathtub will help avoid mess.

Part **II**

Caring
for Your Cat

HOW TO USE THIS SECTION

This section describes most of the common problems of cats, many of which can be treated at home, without visiting your veterinarian. The system of Decision Charts should help you become confident in diagnosing the problem and using the right treatment for happy results. Prevention is also discussed. Remember the old adage: "An ounce of prevention is worth a pound of cure."

Finding the Right Decision Chart

If you suspect an illness, determine the chief sign—for example, coughing—and look it up in the contents or in the index. Then turn to the correct page. If your cat has more than one problem simultaneously, you may have to use more than one Decision Chart. For instance, if your pet has a cough and runny eyes, check the chart for each problem. If one recommends home treatment and the other advises a visit to your veterinarian, *see your doctor.*

Using the Decision Chart

It is very important to first read all the general information on the particular problem. In many cases, the chart may advise you to see the doctor immediately, but emergency treatment may also be needed before you get to the doctor's office. After reading the information, start at the top of the Decision Chart (do *not* skip around) and answer each question.

If home treatment is indicated, follow all instructions exactly, or the treatment will not be effective. If your cat is not improving, even with good care, *see your veterinarian.*

If the chart indicates veterinary consultation, it does not necessarily mean that the illness is serious. It may mean that more vigorous treatment or further examination and lab tests are needed. "See veterinarian NOW" means *immediate attention is needed.* "See veterinarian within 24 hours" is self-explanatory. "Make appointment with veterinarian" means a visit should be made in the next few days.

The procedures discussed on the next few pages will give you step-by-step guidance on how to handle any emergency. Read the entire section and practice the procedures to become familiar with them *before* you have to use them. Your veterinarian will be happy to help you with any you don't fully understand. I hope you'll never have to use these procedures, but your doctor will be very proud of you for being a prepared and helpful partner if an emergency does occur.

This chapter and Chapter 7, Accidents and Injuries, will help you to recognize an emergency situation. Your job is to preserve your cat's life and to prevent further injury until veterinary care is available. *Note:* There are some other emergencies listed in Chapter 8, Common Problems and Diseases, so scan that chapter as well and become familiar with those situations. In addition, certain problems require emergency treatment from you before going to the doctor's office, so read the descriptive sections carefully *before* an emergency develops.

Chapter **6**

Emergency Procedures

Approaching an Injured Cat

The friendliest animal, if injured, may try to bite because of fear and pain, so approach the cat slowly, talking in a quiet and reassuring voice. Call the cat by name, if it is known. Stop your approach when you are about a foot from the animal. Bend down slowly to the pet's level, still talking calmly. Gradually extend your closed hand, knuckles upward, toward the cat. If no aggression is seen, pet it first with your closed hand. If the animal displays aggression, try reassuring talk for a minute longer. If this is not successful, use restraint (next page).

Next, you should check for vital signs. Be sure the airway is clear and the cat is breathing. If not, give artificial respiration (page 84). Check the heartbeat and pulse (page 20), control any bleeding (page 94), look for signs of poisoning (page 120), treat for shock (page 87), and check for fractures (page 102).

Restraining
an Injured Cat

Remember: The least restraint is the best restraint. Cats fight leashes and may choke to death. A blanket or coat placed over the cat is very safe as long as the animal's breathing is not labored; this works well also with unfriendly cats. Holding the cat by the back of the neck for control is also effective.

Note: Do *not* muzzle a cat. It can be very difficult to do, and it can be dangerous to you and to the cat. Besides, it usually is not necessary.

Giving Artificial Respiration

If there are signs of a breathing problem, such as blue gums, labored breathing, or a staring expression, or if the cat has collapsed, you will need to administer artificial respiration. Before beginning, however, check the pulse (page 20). If you cannot feel it, apply cardiopulmonary resuscitation (next page).

Place the cat on its belly or side. If there is no back or neck injury, extend the head and open the pet's mouth to look for obstructions. Clean the mouth of any blood or mucus with your fingers, then close it. Recheck the pulse.

Now: Inhale; put your mouth over the cat's muzzle, forming an airtight seal; exhale. Remove your mouth and allow the cat's chest to deflate. Repeat this process ten to fifteen times per minute, and continue it until you arrive at the veterinarian's office or veterinary hospital. Be sure to recheck the pulse often while performing artificial respiration. Treat also for shock (page 87).

Giving Cardiopulmonary Resuscitation

If your cat is not breathing and has no heartbeat and pulse, you have an immediate life-threatening situation. If brain tissue is deprived of oxygen for more than four or five minutes, permanent damage or death will occur. Administering cardiopulmonary resuscitation (CPR) may keep the brain tissue from dying. A combination of heart massage and artificial respiration, CPR forces blood out of the heart by simulating the heart's pumping action. To be effective, it must be done rhythmically and in combination with artificial respiration. Veterinary aid is needed quickly as well, so send someone for help while you begin the treatment.

In human medicine, heart attacks (*myocardial infarctions,*) choking, and strokes are common CPR emergencies. These are rare in veterinary medicine, however, so there are only a few instances where CPR is needed. Electrocution, near-drowning, and collapse from congestive heart failure may require CPR. If your cat is unconscious, has no pulse or heartbeat, or is gasping for breath, or if its pupils are dilating, you need to administer CPR. *Note:* If there is massive external or internal bleeding, CPR will *not* be effective because there is not enough fluid in the blood vessels to carry the oxygen.

Respiration

Place your pet on its side. Clean the mouth of blood and mucus. Inhale air, put your mouth over the cat's muzzle, forming an airtight seal, and exhale. Give your pet a new breath every three seconds (twenty per minute), while massaging the heart.

Massage

Place the heel of one hand over the cat's chest, just in back of its elbow, and your other palm on top of that hand. Pump firmly and quickly, doing it once every second (sixty per minute). Hold each thrust for a count of two and release for a count of one. Be careful not be break any ribs or to further injure any rib fractures. Have someone else feel for a femoral pulse (see page 20) as you massage. Discontinue the massage when the heartbeat is restored, but continue the artificial respiration until your cat breathes on its own.

Applying a Tourniquet

Seek veterinary aid immediately. A tourniquet should be used only if direct pressure is unsuccessful in stopping the bleeding. *Never* place a tourniquet over a fracture or a joint.

You can use a handkerchief, a cloth belt, or a piece of cloth as a tourniquet. Adjust it about one inch above the wound by tying a loose loop around the limb. Place a short, strong stick in the loop and twist the tourniquet until the blood stops flowing.

Loosen the tourniquet every ten minutes to allow some circulation. *Note:* Do *not* loosen it in the case of a snakebite (see page 126). Treat the animal for shock (next page) as well.

Treating Shock

Shock is caused by severe insult to your cat's body—heavy bleeding, trauma, fluid loss (from vomiting, diarrhea, or burns), infection, heart failure, or breathing problems. It is a syndrome in which the heart and blood vessels are unable to deliver the nutrients and oxygen to the cells and are equally unable to remove the cells' toxic waste products. If not treated promptly, the shock process may be impossible to reverse and your cat can die.

The major signs of shock are:

1. Pale or muddy gums
2. A weak and rapid pulse (see page 20)
3. Capillary refilling takes longer than two seconds (see page 20)
5. Rapid breathing (over forty breaths per minute)
6. A low rectal temperature (below 100°F), with skin and legs cool to the touch

Shock requires prompt veterinary attention. For immediate aid you should be sure the cat's airway is clear so it can breathe. If not, administer artificial respiration (page 84), check the heartbeat and pulse (page 20), and control any bleeding (page 94). If necessary, apply CPR (page 85).

Maintain body heat (with a blanket or coat) and very gently transport the cat to the veterinary hospital. If your pet is unconscious, keep its head lower than the rest of the body. If possible, phone the hospital so that the staff can prepare for your animal.

Large quantities of intravenous fluids, *corticosteroids**, and oxygen given in time can save your pet's life. In shock, the capillaries are like a dry riverbed. The intravenous fluids flood the capillaries and renew the vigorous blood flow that nourishes the dried-out cells.

Do *not* change the injured pet's position rapidly. A fast lift or rotation can cause shock to move into the irreversible stage.

If the cat is in electrical shock from chewing on wires, there is an added precaution: Do *not* touch the cat if it is still in contact with the current! Unplug the electrical cord from the outlet and then check the cat's pulse and heartbeat and continue treating as for shock. You may also need to treat for burns in the mouth (page 114).

---

*Corticosteroids are hormones produced by the adrenal gland that have many functions, including the ability to help cells fight destructive agents. They are also produced synthetically by pharmaceutical companies, for use in human as well as veterinary medicine.

Water Rescue

Most cats are excellent swimmers, but even the strongest swimmer can drown if it becomes exhausted or falls through thin ice. If your cat begins to drown in a lake or pool, the first thing you should do is send for help. Then try to reach your cat from land with your hand. If you must swim out, try to take a float with you. Grab your cat by the tail or the back of the neck, or let it grab the float with its front legs. Hold on to the cat and swim to shore.

Once you are both safely ashore, hold your cat upside down by the hind legs (hold at the hocks) and give a few sharp shakes to drain excess water from the lungs. Remove any weeds or other hindrances from the mouth. Lay the cat on its side and give artificial respiration (page 84). Check for a pulse (page 20). If there is no pulse or heartbeat, apply CPR (page 85).

You can help to revive the cat by holding spirits of ammonia under its nose. When the cat becomes conscious, wrap it in a blanket or coat to keep warm. If you rescued your cat from ice water, treat it for frostbite and hypothermia (page 112).

Applying a Splint

If you suspect that your cat has fractured its leg, a temporary splint is needed to prevent jagged bone edges from injuring the neighboring blood vessels, tissues, and nerves. *Note:* For stability, a splint should include the joints immediately above and below the fracture. An improperly applied splint is worse than no splint at all.

Place a clean cloth around the limb for padding. Fasten a rolled (U-shaped) magazine, newspaper, or cardboard to the leg with tape.

Many times, the shape of the leg and the cat's resistance to handling when injured will make it impossible to apply a temporary splint. In this case, gently support the limb with a towel, blanket, or board on the trip to your veterinarian's office.

Bandaging

Bandages are used to stop bleeding, to keep dirt and bacteria out of the wound, to keep the edges of the cut together, to support the injured area, and to keep your cat from scratching or excessively licking the wound. Bandages should not be so tight that circulation or breathing is compromised. *Caution:* If the wound isn't clean when you cover it with a bandage, you may hide a developing infection from early discovery, so get the cut clean and keep it clean.

A pressure bandage is any bandage applied with pressure. You can hold the bandage firmly with your hand or tie it in place. A Band-Aid® is another pressure bandage, but it is limited to fairly small cuts and wounds.

Some cat owners leave bandages on too long. They should be changed frequently, every day or two and also if they become wet. The skin has to "breathe," and you have to be sure that the wound is not getting infected—don't wait until you can smell it. For painless removal, apply nail polish remover liberally to the back of the adhesive tape for five minutes. This will dissolve the adhesive and release both skin and hair.

Note: Do *not* let your bandaged cat outside.

You should have the following supplies in your first aid kit:

gauze bandages, 1″ wide

padding, either a cotton roll or a clean cloth

adhesive tape, 1″ wide

Bandaging a Paw, Limb, or Tail

To make a bandage for a paw, limb, or tail, wrap the wound firmly with gauze pads, a gauze roll, or a clean cloth or handkerchief, using a spiral pattern. Place a few strips of tape crosswise at the end of the bandage.

Bandaging

Starting at the toes (or tip of tail), wrap the adhesive tape in overlapping bands securely over the first layer. Be sure to include hair on both sides so the bandage will not slip. To avoid having the lower leg, paw, or tail tip swell, the bandage must include all of the extremity.

Bandaging the Chest or Abdomen

Place a gauze pad or clean cloth over the wound. A *many-tailed bandage* is made by tearing both narrow ends of a large, rectangular piece of clean cloth lengthwise into 1-inch wide strips—but only one-third of the way down. It will fit amply around the chest or abdomen. The strips are tied over your cat's back.

Transporting an Injured Cat

The easiest and gentlest way to carry a cat is in a cat carrier, which is such a good investment! First of all, it will prevent your cat from jumping through the steering wheel or on top of your head while you're driving, and sending *you* to the hospital! Your cat will also be calmer in the veterinarian's reception and exam room—a definite plus for the veterinarian-owner relationship.

If a cat carrier is not available, the one-hand carry is comfortable for your cat and affords secure restraint. The cat's back legs and body rest between your inner forearm and your body. The front legs are held between the fingers of the same arm. Your cat's head can be cradled in your other hand.

If you pinch your cat's front or hind paw and the animal does not react in pain, it may have a spinal injury—paralysis of both hind legs and possibly stiffness or paralysis of the front legs are possible. In this case, very gently slide your cat onto a blanket or board. Even a slight movement of the spine could cause irreversible damage. Check the pulse (page 20) and stanch any bleeding (page 94).

If your cat is seriously ill or injured, it is very important not to make the situation worse. If your pet is in shock (page 87), a fast lift or rotation can cause irreversible harm. Injuries to the spinal cord, chest, abdomen, or limbs can be made worse by inconsiderate handling. A cat carrier, blanket, coat, air mattress, or even a window screen can be used to transport the seriously injured or ill cat.

Chapter **7**

Accidents and Injuries

Cuts and Wounds

Bleeding—even small amounts—frightens many pet owners, but the blood's remarkable clotting mechanism stops most bleeding in five minutes. When a small blood vessel is injured, it *constricts* (narrows) to allow less blood to escape. *Platelets,* which are blood cells, arrive at the scene to plug the hole, and chemicals released by the platelets combine with factors in the blood to produce fiber-like strands called *fibrin,* which complete the blood clot and stop the bleeding.

Skin wound (bleeding from blood vessel)   Constriction (narrowing) of blood vessel   Mobilization of platelets in blood vessel   Fibrin combines with platelets to complete the blood clot

Sometimes the injury to the blood vessel is too large for the clotting mechanism to be effective. Apply direct pressure to the wound for five or ten minutes and allow the clotting mechanism to work; that's usually all that is needed. Use the cleanest material available—gauze pads, sheets, towels, or clothing. A pressure bandage (page 90) can be applied for sustained pressure. If these measures are unsuccessful, a tourniquet (page 86) is needed.

Cut Footpad

The footpad has a lot of blood vessels and can therefore bleed profusely when cut. Since your pet walks barefoot, carelessly discarded beer can pop-tops, jagged broken bottles, and other disposable conveniences are constant hazards. Generally, cats are very good about sidestepping such things, so this should be a rare injury. However, it's good to be prepared.

Home Treatment

Clean the wound with soap and water after the bleeding stops. Hydrogen peroxide (3 percent) can also be used. Do *not* rub the wound hard or the clot may loosen and the bleeding will recur. Gently remove any hair, dirt, or other foreign material from the area.

Wound

Serum and blood cells fill in and bring "building blocks"

Wound contraction

Wounds heal by skin contraction and by the presence of serum and blood cells at the site. Even gaping wounds will heal in time by this process if kept clean. There probably is some truth to the statement that cats lick their wounds to keep them clean and to enhance healing.

Direct pressure with a gauze pad or clean cloth should stop the bleeding of a cut footpad. If you cannot get to a veterinarian, check the wound for dirt or other debris and then bandage firmly. If it starts bleeding again, flush it gently with 3 percent hydrogen peroxide and rebandage.

Shallow footpad wounds do not have to be sutured. Your pet may have a sore paw and a limp for a few weeks, but nightly flushings with clean water and hydrogen peroxide will help heal the wound. If the wound becomes infected, go see your doctor.

What to Expect at the Veterinarian's Office

You should see your doctor if the wound is very deep, very large (longer than one-half inch), very dirty, or has become infected. In these cases, your veterinarian will probably recommend surgery. A narcotic or tranquilizer and a local anesthetic (or general anesthesia) will be used so that your pet will not feel any pain. The

Cuts and Wounds

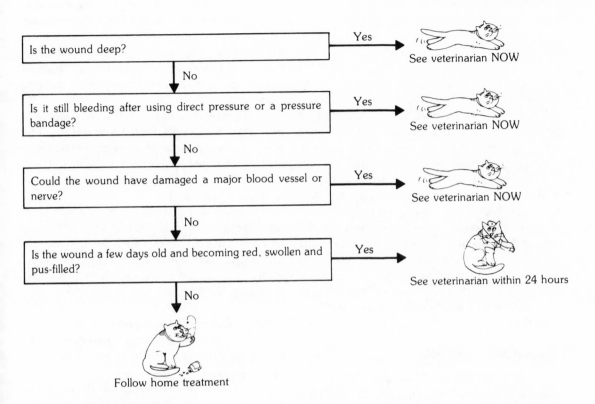

Is the wound deep? — **Yes** → See veterinarian NOW

No ↓

Is it still bleeding after using direct pressure or a pressure bandage? — **Yes** → See veterinarian NOW

No ↓

Could the wound have damaged a major blood vessel or nerve? — **Yes** → See veterinarian NOW

No ↓

Is the wound a few days old and becoming red, swollen and pus-filled? — **Yes** → See veterinarian within 24 hours

No ↓

Follow home treatment

wound will be explored for hair, dirt, and other foreign particles and flushed with sterile water mixed with antibiotics to prevent or eliminate infection. It will be sutured to decrease the healing time and to prevent dirt from reentering. If your cat chews its wounds, or if it is overactive, tranquilizers and/or a special protective collar may be prescribed during the healing period. Your veterinarian will also determine whether antibiotics are necessary.

Deep footpad wounds need to be sutured. Your doctor may also suggest antibiotics if the wound was extremely dirty. Cats are quite resistant to tetanus, but if the wound occurred around stables, your veterinarian may recommend a tetanus shot.

Removing Stitches. Your veterinarian will tell you when the stitches are to be removed. Unless your doctor wants to recheck your pet, you can do the job yourself. Gently grasp a loose end of the knot with tweezers. Using a pair of small, sharp scissors, cut the stitch as close to the skin as possible and pull it out. Cutting close to the skin reduces the chance of contamination and infection.

Cut here

Skin (healed)

Punctures and Animal Bites

One of the saddest things to see is a helpless cat admitted to our hospital after being shot or knifed. Puncture wounds can cause severe bleeding and injury to the internal organs. Veterinary aid is needed immediately.

If your pet was bitten by another animal, that animal should be quarantined for ten days to be sure it does not have rabies (page 138). If you know the owner and can ascertain that the animal has a current rabies vaccination, the quarantine can be done at home. If the owner is not known or if the animal is wild, such as a bat, fox, raccoon, or skunk, quarantine is maintained at a veterinary hospital, a public health facility, or a local pound.

Embedded Fishhook

Cats really are curious, even about things that may hurt them, such as fishhooks. All too often, a cat sniffing around a fishing camp or a cluttered garage can well get a fishhook caught in its lip or nose. Restraining the cat (page 83) is necessary if you are going to remove the hook at home. Remember, just as a fish cannot escape a fishhook once it is embedded, neither can a cat. Therefore, the barb must be pushed through the skin and cut with pliers. The rest of the fishhook can then be removed.

Amputated Tail

If your cat's tail is caught in a slammed car or house door or run over by a car, arrange to see the veterinarian immediately after you apply emergency measures (see Home Treatment).

Home Treatment

EMERGENCY Check the entry and exit areas of puncture wounds. If necessary, give artificial respiration (page 84). Check the heartbeat and pulse (page 20) and control any bleeding (page 94). An amputated tail may require a tourniquet (page 86). Treat also for shock (page 87). Bullet and knife wounds can fracture bones, so a temporary splint (page 89) may be necessary.

The most common result of animal bites is not rabies but simple bacterial infections. The skin is normally a strong barrier against bacteria, but if penetrated, bacteria, hair, and dirt can enter and cause a serious infection or an abscess (page 174) days later.

Clip the hair around the wound with scissors; then clean the wound with soap and water and alcohol and remove any debris. Cover it with a gauze bandage or clean cloth. If the origin of the bite is unknown, quarantine may be necessary. Check with your doctor.

What to Expect at the Veterinarian's Office

Your veterinarian will be concerned about three things: (1) controlling the bleeding (if this hasn't been done); (2) cleaning the wound and possibly suturing it to avoid infection; and, in the case of an animal bite, (3) identifying and confining the other animal.

Your pet may have to be given a tranquilizer and a local or general anesthetic in order to be cleaned and sutured. Antibiotics may be given to avoid infection, especially for dirty fishhook punctures. A rabies vaccination will be given if it is overdue.

If there is dislocation of a tail bone but your cat can move its tail, your veterinarian will probably suggest that no treatment is necessary. However, large gaping wounds with no dislocation will require suturing. Sometimes the nerves, tissue, and bones are damaged beyond repair. Complete amputation of the tail will be recommended in this case.

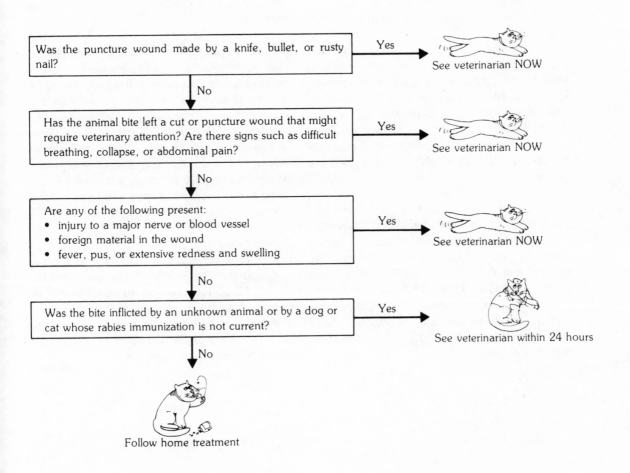

Was the puncture wound made by a knife, bullet, or rusty nail?

Yes → See veterinarian NOW

No ↓

Has the animal bite left a cut or puncture wound that might require veterinary attention? Are there signs such as difficult breathing, collapse, or abdominal pain?

Yes → See veterinarian NOW

No ↓

Are any of the following present:
• injury to a major nerve or blood vessel
• foreign material in the wound
• fever, pus, or extensive redness and swelling

Yes → See veterinarian NOW

No ↓

Was the bite inflicted by an unknown animal or by a dog or cat whose rabies immunization is not current?

Yes → See veterinarian within 24 hours

No ↓

Follow home treatment

Insect Bites and Stings

Some insect bites will cause a local reaction, but a serious systemic reaction occurs only rarely. Bites from poisonous spiders are also rare, but they are life-threatening and need immediate attention.

Since their paws are always on the ground—and often their noses, too—cats can easily be stung by an angry wasp, hornet, or yellow jacket. Swelling and pain of the muzzle or paw may occur; *hives* (bumps that appear suddenly all over the body) may also be seen. A cat will usually cry out when bitten, and if bitten on the muzzle, will continuously rub its face on the ground.

Home Treatment

For bee stings, remove the stinger with tweezers, if you can see it, and apply a paste of baking soda and water to the swollen area to stop the burning and itching. The swelling will subside within twenty-four hours. Most cats do not go into shock from bee stings, but if your pet collapses, administer artificial respiration (page 84) and treat for shock (page 87). See your veterinarian immediately.

If your pet is bitten by a black widow spider or a brown recluse (a brown spider with a white violin-shaped pattern on its back), apply ice packs immediately to the bitten area. The cold constricts the blood vessels there and decreases the local reaction. A tourniquet (page 86) will stop the poison from traveling throughout the body. After applying emergency measures, see your veterinarian.

What to Expect at the Veterinarian's Office

Your veterinarian will need to know what sort of insect or spider bit your cat. If a severe local or systemic reaction has occurred, your doctor will give injections of steroids and antihistamines to counteract the swelling and inflammation. Pain relievers may also be given. Your veterinarian may want to hospitalize and observe your pet for twenty-four hours. If breathing is impaired (this is rarely seen), oxygen will have to be given at the hospital.

Prevention

Watch your cat carefully around wood piles, where spiders like to hide. If your pet generally has severe allergic reactions to insect bites, ask your veterinarian to give you or to prescribe an emergency kit of injectable steroids and antihistamines to keep on hand at home, along with instructions on its proper use.

Insect Bites
and Stings

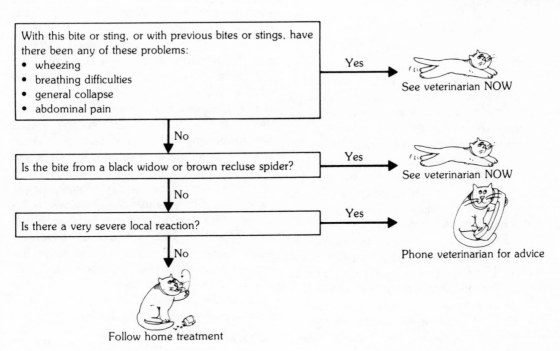

With this bite or sting, or with previous bites or stings, have there been any of these problems:
- wheezing
- breathing difficulties
- general collapse
- abdominal pain

Yes → See veterinarian NOW

No ↓

Is the bite from a black widow or brown recluse spider?

Yes → See veterinarian NOW

No ↓

Is there a very severe local reaction?

Yes → Phone veterinarian for advice

No ↓

Follow home treatment

Convulsions and Seizures

Convulsions are temporary disturbances of electrical activity in the brain that lead to a loss of control of all the cat's skeletal muscles. A severe or lengthy convulsion does not necessarily indicate a serious underlying disease.

The aura, or preseizure period, may last from a few seconds to hours. Common signs are staring, lip licking, twitching, getting restless or nervous, salivating, hiding, wandering, or displaying more affection toward you.

The signs of a generalized seizure are an inability to stand, a loss of consciousness, a loss of bowel and/or urine control, and violent muscle spasms. The cat's body may stiffen and twitch, a frothy saliva may appear, and the eyes may jerk back and forth. After a seizure, the cat will be confused and appear blind and unresponsive, while at the same time salivating heavily and pacing back and forth.

Home Treatment

EMERGENCY Try to hold the cat down gently with a blanket. If you can't do so, clear the area of objects that may injure your pet. Stay calm —watching a seizure can be a frightening experience, but most seizures are not life-threatening. Your pet may have a few seizures in a row. If there is a high fever—greater than 106°F—an ice water bath will help lower the fever. Ice packs placed in the inner thighs and under the front legs are also helpful. See Fever, page 134, for other suggestions.

After the convulsion, calmly and quietly pet your cat and reassure it with your presence. Keep lights and noise to a minimum, since the brain is very sensitive. Seek veterinary aid as soon as you can.

What to Expect at the Veterinarian's Office

Intravenous injections of anticonvulsants and thiamine will be given if the seizures have not stopped. The veterinarian will perform a complete physical examination and will probably suggest hospitalization.

In veterinary medicine, a good history is very important for diagnosis—especially if your pet has had a seizure, since several serious diseases could be indicated: feline infectious peritonitis, toxoplasmosis, lymphosarcoma (leukemia), thiamine deficiency, and epilepsy (which has no known cause) can all bring on convulsions. Another cause of seizures in cats is low blood calcium, which can be seen in a pregnant or nursing mother cat (see Nursing Problems, page 224). Many household chemicals, if ingested, will cause seizures (see Swallowed Poisons, page 120). Finally, if your cat had a head injury followed by unconsciousness within the last two years, this could also be a factor.

Tests may be necessary to diagnose the cause of the seizures. Your veterinarian may recommend several of the following:

1. Blood count (infection, lead poisoning)
2. BUN (kidney disease)
3. Urinalysis (kidney, liver disease)
4. Blood sugar test (low blood sugar, *hypoglycemia*)
5. Blood calcium test
6. Liver function blood tests (liver disease)
7. FIP, FLV, and toxoplasmosis tests

If spinal taps, specialized X rays, and electroencephalograms are required, they are usually done at referral hospitals or universities.

Medication can control convulsions, but it may be necessary to try various doses and even combinations of drugs, so you must be patient. No medication is needed if your cat has only one seizure and the cause is not determined. Occasionally, your veterinarian may not be able to regulate the animal. You should then be referred to a veterinary neurologist (see page 60).

Convulsions and Seizures

Is the seizure still in progress? — Yes → See veterinarian NOW

No ↓

Does your pet have a high fever? — Yes → See veterinarian NOW

No ↓

Phone veterinarian for advice

Bone Fractures

If your cat (1) is not bearing weight on a limb, (2) has a crooked limb, or (3) has limb pain and swelling, you should suspect a break. *Crepitus,* the sound or feel of bone rubbing on bone, is even stronger evidence of a fracture. If a piece of bone is protruding through the skin, there is no doubt.

In a *compound fracture,* a bone fragment penetrates the surface, and severe damage to the skin, muscle, nerves, and blood vessels can result. Delayed healing and infections can be serious problems in compound fractures. Since bone is not very resistant to infection, cover a compound fracture immediately with gauze or a clean cloth and get veterinary assistance.

Limb fractures are not life-threatening, but they should be temporarily splinted so that the jagged bone edges do not injure any neighboring tissues and nerves. Remember: A splint should include the joints immediately above and below the fracture.

Fractures of the spine from trauma are extreme emergencies, especially if your cat is hit by a car. You may see a paralysis of the hind legs and a stiffness (outstretching) of the front legs after trauma.

Home Treatment
EMERGENCY Gently restrain your cat (page 83). Apply ice packs to decrease the swelling and inflammation. Splint the limb (page 89), but do *not* try to reset it. If the break is in the tail, immobilize it with a slender piece of wood or a tongue depresser. If the break is in the cat's pelvis or hindlegs, you will need to transport it by stretcher. See also Lameness, page 156.

What to Expect at the Veterinarian's Office
Your veterinarian will check all other systems to be sure that they were not injured. A radiograph (X ray) is needed to verify the fracture and to determine the best method of repair. Some fractures will heal with external stabilization (splints or casts) alone, while others need internal fixation (metal pins, plates, or wires). Discuss the chances of healing and the cost of each technique with your veterinarian. Today, no cat has to be put to sleep because it has a fracture—a three-legged cat is still more agile than a two-legged person!

Bone Fractures

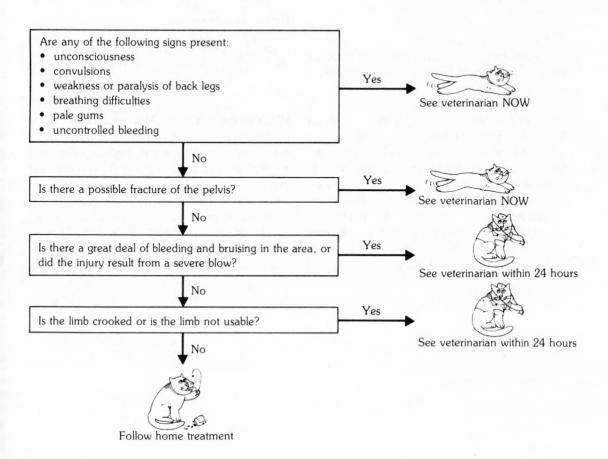

Are any of the following signs present:
- unconsciousness
- convulsions
- weakness or paralysis of back legs
- breathing difficulties
- pale gums
- uncontrolled bleeding

Yes → See veterinarian NOW

No ↓

Is there a possible fracture of the pelvis?

Yes → See veterinarian NOW

No ↓

Is there a great deal of bleeding and bruising in the area, or did the injury result from a severe blow?

Yes → See veterinarian within 24 hours

No ↓

Is the limb crooked or is the limb not usable?

Yes → See veterinarian within 24 hours

No ↓

Follow home treatment

Chest Injuries

If, for any reason, your cat has labored breathing, a blue tongue and gums, or abnormal chest sounds, you should suspect injury to organs in the chest.

Chest injury can occur in any part of the respiratory system (page 21). If bleeding occurs in the chest (hemothorax), if the lung tissue ruptures and air escapes into the chest (pneumothorax), or if the diaphragm ruptures and abdominal contents move into the chest (diaphragmatic hernia), the lungs will not be able to expand to receive fresh oxygen. If the lung tissue is bruised (*traumatic lung syndrome*), oxygen cannot be received. If the heart is bruised (*myocardial irritability*), the blood may not be pumped efficiently. Thus you can see that a chest injury is a potentially life-threatening situation.

Home Treatment
EMERGENCY   Artificial respiration (page 84) and CPR (page 85) may be needed to keep your pet alive. Treat for shock (page 87). Transport gently on a stretcher.

What to Expect at the Veterinarian's Office
Getting oxygen into its system and stabilizing its condition from shock are the highest priorities. If air or blood has to be removed to help your pet expand its lungs and breathe more comfortably, a tube will be inserted in the chest. A local anesthesia in the chest wall will ease its placement.

Once your cat is stable and breathing better, a radiograph of the chest will be taken to see the extent of the injuries.

Chest Injuries

Are any of the following signs present:
- labored breathing
- blue tongue and gums
- abnormal chest sounds

Yes →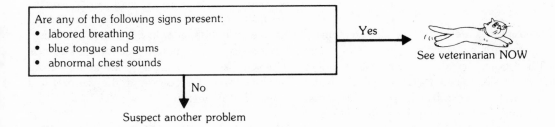

See veterinarian NOW

No

Suspect another problem

Head Injuries

All head injuries are potentially life-threatening, even if there is no outward sign of injury. The skull is a bony casing, and the brain bounces against the skull when there is a blow on the head. This can cause bleeding to occur within and around the brain, and the accumulation of blood can compress the brain.

If your pet is or becomes unconscious, immediate veterinary attention is necessary. Other signs that the brain has been affected are:

1. uneven pupil size (caused by pressure on the brain from bleeding)
2. pale gums
3. a slow pulse (less than 60)
4. limb paralysis or stiffness
5. convulsions

If your cat is unconscious, extend its head and neck and pull the tongue forward. Clean the blood and fluids from the mouth, and transport the animal on a flat, hard surface to the veterinarian or veterinary hospital.

The most frequent cause of serious head injury is being hit by a car. Kittens will also occasionally sustain head injury from being hit by falling objects. Adult cats are fortunate in having large muscles that cover their skulls and cushion some blows to the head. In serious accidents, do *not* overlook possible chest, abdomen, or limb injury, as well.

Home Treatment
EMERGENCY   Observe your cat carefully: Check the pupils, pulse, and gums frequently, and treat for shock. Control any bleeding with direct pressure, using a clean cloth. Remove all blood, mucus, and debris from the mouth and give artificial respiration (page 84), if necessary. If the skull is fractured (see Bone Fractures, page 102), transport your cat on a flat, hard surface to the doctor's office.

If your pet appears normal but has convulsions in four to six months after the injury, check with your doctor. This condition is occasionally seen and requires no medication; the convulsions usually disappear in a few months. This is thought to be a temporary abnormal electrical brain discharge, provoked by the injury, which resolves itself. Of course, if the seizures get worse, further tests will be needed.

What to Expect at the Veterinarian's Office
Your veterinarian will need a good history of the accident that happened. Your pet's head, eyes, ears, nose, throat, and neck will be examined. The back of the eyes will be examined with an ophthalmoscope to check for pressure on the brain and for evidence of hemorrhage. A complete neurological exam, including checking the reflexes, will be done. The chest and abdomen will be examined for injury or internal bleeding. The limbs and pelvis will be checked for fractures or dislocations.

Since bleeding within the skull can be suspected from a thorough physical examination and not by X rays in general practice, skull X rays are helpful only if a fracture is present.

Oxygen and medication (steroids) may be used to reduce brain swelling, but your veterinarian will not give tranquilizers or other medication that may obscure the observation of your pet's improving or deteriorating brain injury. If your cat was unconscious at any time, ask your veterinarian to make sure someone competent will be monitoring your pet through the night; an increasing number of hospitals are equipped for *intensive* twenty-four hour care. (If not, ask if you could monitor the cat at home.) Registration in a university veterinary hospital or an emergency hospital may be requested if one is nearby and if your doctor feels that it would be helpful.

Prevention
Of course, house cats are unlikely to be hit by cars.

Head Injuries

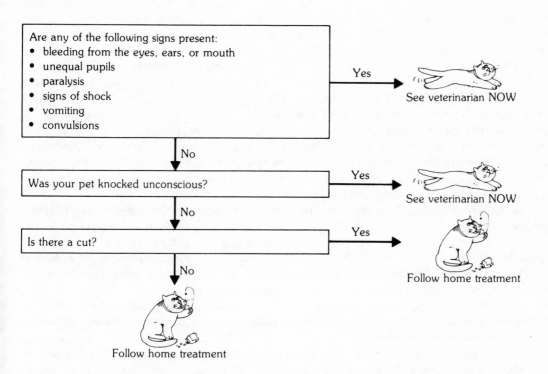

Are any of the following signs present:
* bleeding from the eyes, ears, or mouth
* unequal pupils
* paralysis
* signs of shock
* vomiting
* convulsions

Yes → See veterinarian NOW

No

Was your pet knocked unconscious?

Yes → See veterinarian NOW

No

Is there a cut?

Yes → Follow home treatment

No

Follow home treatment

Eye Injuries

All eye injuries are potentially serious. Whenever an eye or eyelid is injured, an examination by your veterinarian is necessary. Minor injuries to the eye, if not treated properly, can result in vision loss.

The most common causes of eye injuries are auto accidents and fights. These usually result in eyelid lacerations, lacerations of the cornea (the clear membrane in the front of the eye), or internal injury to the eyeball itself. Sometimes the injury is so severe that the eyeball is forced out of the socket, a condition called *proptosis*. The presence of chemicals, such as acids or lye, or foreign objects also requires immediate attention.

Home Treatment

EMERGENCY Chemicals splashed in the eye need to be *immediately* flushed out, using lots of clean water. This must be done as soon as possible to avoid permanent damage to the cornea. Flush five to ten minutes; afterward, apply a clean cloth or gauze bandage to protect the eye from further injury. See your doctor immediately.

Eyelid lacerations can bleed profusely. Applying direct pressure with a gauze or clean cloth to the lid for five minutes should control the bleeding. If the laceration is on the eyeball, cover it with gauze or clean cloth, but do *not* apply pressure.

If a foreign object is under one of the eyelids, your pet will paw at the eye and squint. Of course, these signs are also seen in other conditions, but take a look under the lid—you may see a piece of sand or a loose eyelash. Use a bright light when looking for a foreign body in the eye. Pull the lower lid down with your thumb and inspect the pink conjunctiva that lines the eye and the inner surface of the eyelids; do the same to the upper lid. A cotton-tipped applicator moistened with water and *gently* moved across the conjunctiva can remove the object. You can also flush the inner lid surfaces with clean water while holding the lid open. *Note:* Do *not* try to inspect or swab behind the third eyelid; you may scratch the cornea. If your pet continues to paw at the eye and squint for a few hours, check with your doctor. There may be an injury to the cornea.

Proptosis is an obvious surgical emergency. Since the cause is a severe head injury, check the breathing, heartbeat, and pulse and treat for shock (page 87). Protect the eyeball with a cold, moist gauze sponge or clean cloth so that it will not dry out or be further injured. Control any bleeding with direct pressure. Immediate veterinary help is needed.

What to Expect at the Veterinarian's Office

Your doctor will perform a complete physical if generalized injury from an auto accident has occurred. An ophthalmoscope will be used to inspect all the structures within the eyeball, including under the lids.

A local anesthetic will make it easier to check behind the third eyelid if a foreign body is suspected. If a foreign body is found, a moistened cotton swab or eyewash solution will remove it. An antibiotic ointment is sometimes applied.

A harmless fluorescent dye will be administered and the eye then examined with an ultraviolet light. Whenever the cornea is injured, the dye will confirm the extent of the damage. This procedure is painless. If there is damage to the cornea, antibiotic drops or ointment will be used to protect this delicate membrane from infection. If an *iritis* (an irritation of the colored part of the eye) is present, drops to dilate the pupil are needed. Steroids are used to decrease the inflammation in minor injuries to the cornea (*corneal abrasions*).

In a case of proptosis, your doctor will recommend replacement of the eyeball in the socket *if* the accident just occurred and the globe is not severely damaged. If the vessels and nerves were not injured, vision may be saved.

Eye Injuries

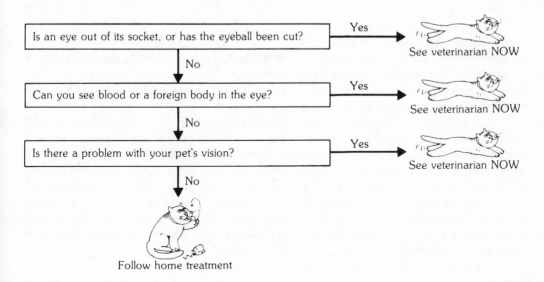

Is an eye out of its socket, or has the eyeball been cut? — **Yes** → See veterinarian NOW

No ↓

Can you see blood or a foreign body in the eye? — **Yes** → See veterinarian NOW

No ↓

Is there a problem with your pet's vision? — **Yes** → See veterinarian NOW

No ↓

Follow home treatment

Severe injury to the eyeball may necessitate removing the eye, or *enucleation*. Cats with one eye or no vision get around remarkably well and are very happy. So do not suggest "putting my cat to sleep" if an eye has to be removed.

Prevention

Keep your cat away when you are working with corrosive materials. Of course, keeping your cat indoors will also avoid fights and auto accidents.

Internal Bleeding

Massive internal bleeding reduces the amount of fluid carrying oxygen and nutrients through the body. If the organs do not get enough oxygen, they die. Immediate veterinary help is needed if profuse bleeding is noted from any body orifice or if your cat shows the following signs: weakness, pale gums, abdominal pain, breathing difficulty, weak pulse. If your cat was injured by an automobile, assume that there is some internal bleeding. Internal bleeding of the stomach is usually indicated by a bright or dark red color to the cat's vomit. If its excrement is dark and tarry or bright red, the intestines may be bleeding. If a red foamy material is coughed up, the lungs may be affected. Some poisons can also cause internal bleeding.

Home Treatment
EMERGENCY   Lay the cat down and cover it lightly. *Note:* Do *not* struggle with it. Transport the animal gently, since its body's ability to carry oxygen is decreased.

What to Expect at the Veterinarian's Office
If possible, call your veterinarian so he or she can prepare for your arrival. The first, most important steps are to provide oxygen and to replace the lost fluids with intravenous fluids and/or blood. Antibiotics to prevent infection and corticosteroids to maintain cellular health will also be given. Your pet will be kept warm with a heating pad or blankets. Its urine output and blood will be monitored to measure progress or deterioration of the condition. If these measures are not sufficient, surgical intervention may be necessary to stop the bleeding.

Internal Bleeding

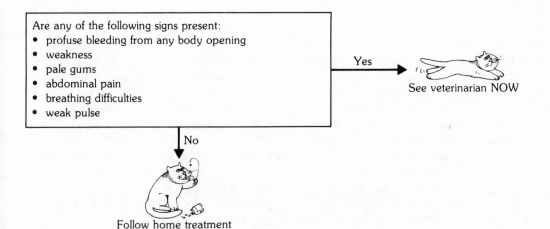

Are any of the following signs present:
- profuse bleeding from any body opening
- weakness
- pale gums
- abdominal pain
- breathing difficulties
- weak pulse

Yes → See veterinarian NOW

No ↓

Follow home treatment

Hypothermia and Frostbite

A cat's fur is generally enough protection against extreme cold, but any long exposure to low temperatures and wind (for example, if the cat is injured and unable to reach shelter) can produce a severe lowering of your cat's body temperature (*hypothermia*). Shivering, stumbling, exhaustion, drowsiness, and a low body temperature (80° to 90°F) may be present.

Frostbite is also rare in cats; however your cat's ear tips and tail may be frozen on very cold days. Their position on your pet predispose them to the full fury of chilly winds and icy temperatures. Frostbitten ear tips may appear leathery and stiff, and the hair on the tips may turn white.

Home Treatment

EMERGENCY   For hypothermia, place the cat in a warm room. Warm water baths, hot water bottles, and an electric heating blanket (carefully used) will increase the body temperature. (Be patient; it increases slowly.) You can measure progress by rectal temperature (page 32) and by the cat's response (it will be more alert). Give warm liquids if your cat is conscious.

If your cat is frostbitten, warm the frozen areas with your hands or with moist, warm (*not* hot) towels. *Note:* Do *not* rub or squeeze. Ointments or pressure dressings should *not* be used because this may further injure the tissue. If your pet has discomfort or pain, or if the skin seems to be becoming infected, see your doctor.

What to Expect at the Veterinarian's Office

If home treatment is unsuccessful, your veterinarian will treat for shock, continue the rewarming methods, and monitor the cat's heart and kidney function.

If any tissue is severely damaged by frostbite, antibiotics will be needed to avoid infection. Pain relievers may be suggested as well. Hasty surgery to repair or amputate the damaged tissue is usually not necessary. If the tissue is kept clean and antibiotics are given, healing usually is seen in a week.

Hypothermia and Frostbite

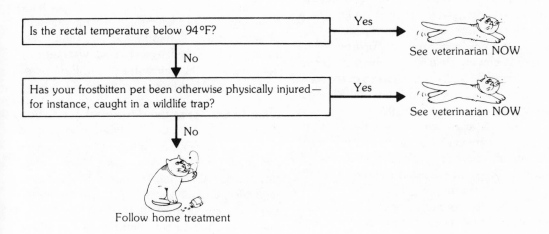

Is the rectal temperature below 94°F? — **Yes** → See veterinarian NOW

No

Has your frostbitten pet been otherwise physically injured—for instance, caught in a wildlife trap? — **Yes** → See veterinarian NOW

No

Follow home treatment

Burns

Most burns in cats occur from coming in contact with hot water, grease, or tar, from stepping on a heated burner, from chewing on electrical wires, from licking hot barbecue grills, or from being trapped in burning buildings. If less than 15 percent of the body is affected, chances of recovery are good. If more than 50 percent of the body is burned, recovery is not anticipated.

Burns are classified by their depth. First-degree burns are very superficial. The skin is red and painful. The hair may be singed but is still attached. Veterinary assistance is not needed, and healing is rapid.

Second-degree burns are more extensive: Severe swelling is present; the skin is red and painful and will slough; healing is slower. In addition, there may be a significant fluid loss from the burn. See your veterinarian.

Third-degree burns are very serious and need emergency veterinary care. The hair falls out, and the skin may be either black or pearly white. Since the entire skin layer has been destroyed, infection and fluid loss are great dangers. The burn is painless, however, because the nerves in the area have been destroyed. Healing is very slow unless a skin graft is performed.

Home Treatment

EMERGENCY Clip hair away from a first-degree burn with scissors, then flush the area with cold water. Gently dry it with clean or sterile gauze. You can also apply cold compresses. *Note:* Do *not* use ointments. Deeper second- or third-degree burns should be seen by your veterinarian immediately. Simply cover the affected area with a clean cloth (*not* cotton), treat for shock (page 87), and go to your doctor. *Note:* Do *not* apply water, antiseptics, or ointments.

Cats that are burned by chewing on electric cords should be seen by your veterinarian, also. There will be burns on the lips, tongue, and gums but the threat to life is that the heart may stop or that fluid may get in the lungs (*pulmonary edema*). Feel the chest for the heartbeat and feel for the femoral pulse. If there is no heartbeat, and your pet is not breathing, begin CPR (page 85).

For chemical burns, run a shower or hose down your cat and keep the water running until all traces of the chemical are gone. Then cover the affected area with a clean, cold, wet gauze or cloth and treat the animal for shock. For electrical burns, see Treating Shock, page 87.

What to Expect at the Veterinarian's Office

Your veterinarian will determine the severity of the burns. Clipping, cleaning, and giving antibiotics may be all that is needed. More serious burns may require intravenous fluids, steroids, antibiotics, and pain relievers. Hospitalization is also necessary for these cases since close nursing care is required to save your pet's life. If the burns are extensive and your cat survives, skin grafts may be necessary.

A kitten that has bitten through an electric cord may have burns just in the mouth that require antibiotics to prevent infection and anti-inflammatory drugs to reduce swelling. If the current has injured the heart or lungs, intensive treatment for shock, including oxygen, may be needed to save its life.

Prevention

Don't allow your cat to lie below the stove when cooking, since a pot of boiling water or oil can easily be tipped over. If your pet insists on lying near the stove because it can't resist the wonderful smells, use the back burners whenever possible. Do *not* let your cat lie on the stove when the burners are hot. Many cats are heat-seekers and can burn themselves severely on the stove. At the dinner table, never pass hot food over your pet's head. Many hot foods have been spilled on a pet waiting for a free handout.

Whenever a kitten in the teething stage (three to eight months) is left in a room unobserved for a long period of time, unplug the electric appliances that are not being used.

114

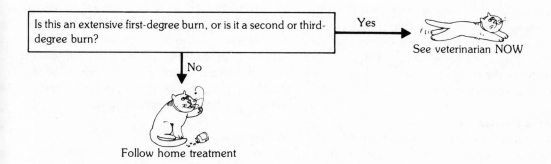

Is this an extensive first-degree burn, or is it a second or third-degree burn?

Yes → See veterinarian NOW

No ↓

Follow home treatment

Smoke Inhalation

Fire does not injure by burning alone: Smoke contains very little oxygen and a lot of carbon monoxide. Other poisonous gases may be present as well, from burned plastic, textiles, and rubber. These add more trouble. Thus a fire not only burns the breathing tubes and lungs, but it also poisons your cat.

Home Treatment
EMERGENCY Remove your cat to fresh air. Check its breathing and use artificial respiration (page 84). Treat your cat for shock (page 87), then seek veterinary aid.

What to Expect at the Veterinarian's Office
If your cat is conscious, and there is no blood-tinged sputum being coughed up and no fluid in the lungs, humidified oxygen and steroids may be given to try to prevent such problems as severe pneumonia from developing during the critical period—the next forty-eight hours. Pain-relieving medication may be given to ease some of the breathing distress. X rays will be taken during your cat's hospitalization to monitor the lung damage. If everything goes well, follow-up X rays will probably be taken two to four weeks after the injury. If your cat is unconscious, is coughing up blood-tinged sputum, or has pneumonia, the outlook is more serious.

Prevention
Smoke alarms should be installed, and any other fire prevention measures should be taken. Your local humane shelter or fire department can provide you with a decal for your door that will notify the fire department of the number of pets to look for and their usual location in your home in case of fire.

Smoke Inhalation

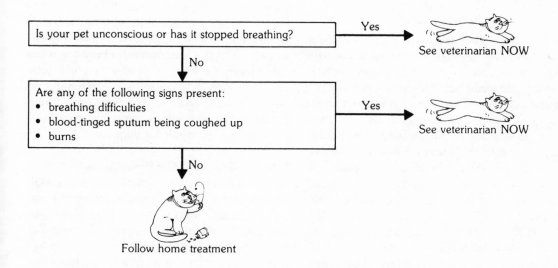

Is your pet unconscious or has it stopped breathing? **Yes** → See veterinarian NOW

No

Are any of the following signs present:
- breathing difficulties
- blood-tinged sputum being coughed up
- burns

Yes → See veterinarian NOW

No

Follow home treatment

Heatstroke

In heatstroke, the body is completely unable to lower its fever. All the mechanisms normally used to regulate body temperature, such as panting, are ineffectual. Heatstroke occurs often in cats that are kept on hot days in areas where shade and water are lacking. It also occurs in pets that are left in unventilated, hot, parked cars. Cats with short noses (Himalayan or Persian cats), old, or fat pets are especially prone to heatstroke, since they are less able to regulate their body temperature in warm or hot environments.

The signs of heatstroke are dramatic and include a rectal temperature of over 106°F, extreme panting, a fast-pounding pulse, weakness, a staring expression, and collapse.

Home Treatment

EMERGENCY   A high body temperature must be lowered rapidly to avoid brain damage or death. As in the treatment for fever, a cold water bath or shower must be given immediately. Ice applied to the head and between the thighs is beneficial. Being in an air-conditioned room also helps bring down the fever. If the body temperature has not dropped to 103°F in ten minutes, a cold water enema may be necessary. See the section on Fever, page 134, for instructions on giving a cold water enema. *Note:* After a cold water enema, improvement *cannot* be measured by rectal temperature.

If your cat stops panting, seems more relaxed, and responds normally to your voice, you are doing well. Give your pet ice cubes or a small amount of water. Great fluid loss occurs during heatstroke, and this must be replaced. Once your pet seems improved, a doctor should examine it. If this is impossible, check the rectal temperature for the next twelve hours. If your cat's condition gets worse, seek veterinary aid quickly. Be sure your car is well ventilated during the trip to the doctor. Keep applying ice cubes to the head and between the thighs.

What to Expect at the Veterinarian's Office

If your emergency treatment was successful, your veterinarian will examine your pet to make sure that there is no permanent brain or organ damage. If emergency treatment at home was not successful, it will be necessary to replace lost water and treat for shock (intravenous fluids and steroids). Cold water baths and enemas will be continued. Oxygen will be given if needed, and your cat will be hospitalized so that it can be observed closely for twenty-four hours.

Prevention

Adequate ventilation, shade, and free access to water are necessary. If you have to leave your cat in the car on a warm day, be sure that you park in the shade and keep the window cracked for ventilation. Carry water in the car for your pet. Check car-bound cats frequently: Remember, the sun changes direction. *Note:* If your pet is short-nosed, old, or fat, these precautions may not be enough. Try keeping them in a cool room with an adequate water supply.

Heatstroke

Is your pet's rectal temperature over 103° even after emergency procedures? Does it still pant and seem tense and unresponsive?

Yes → See veterinarian NOW

No ↓

Follow home treatment

Swallowed Poisons

Cats, when curious, can get into a lot of trouble by swallowing products that are around the house or in the garbage.

Home Treatment

EMERGENCY   If your cat swallows a poison (see the Decision Chart), call your poison control center immediately and get veterinary aid. Take the poison container and a sample of the vomit to the veterinarian. If your cat stops breathing, give artificial respiration (page 84). If you cannot reach your veterinarian or poison control center, check for the poison on the following lists and give the prescribed treatment. If the poison cannot be identified, force your cat to swallow egg whites, milk of magnesia, and/or milk (see Giving Liquids to Your Cat, page 77).

List A: Petroleum Products, Acids, and Alkalies

Dishwasher granules	Oven cleaner
Drain cleaner	Paint remover
Floor polish	Paint thinner
Furniture polish	Shoe polish
Gasoline	Toilet bowl cleaner
Kerosene	Wax (floor or furniture)
Lye	Wood preservative

Signs of poisoning by these products are bloody vomit, diarrhea, shock, depression, coma, convulsions (sometimes), coughing, abdominal pain, and redness around the mouth. *Note:* Do *not* induce vomiting! Make your cat swallow milk, egg whites, or olive oil to decrease absorption of the poison. Treat also for shock (page 87).

Acids and alkalies can also burn the mouth and skin, so flush these areas with large amounts of water. Apply a sodium bicarbonate paste to acid burns. Apply vinegar to neutralize alkali burns.

List B: Other Known Poisons

Acetone	Insecticides
Alcohol	Linoleum (lead salts)
Algae toxins	Matches
Amphetamines	(*Note:* Safety
Aspirin	matches are non-
Antifreeze	toxic)
Arsenic	Medicines
Bleach	Moth balls
Carbon tetrachloride	Mushrooms, wild
Chlordane	Paint, lead-based
Cosmetics	Perfume
Crayons	Pine oil
DDT	Rat or mouse poison
Deodorants	Red squill
Detergents	Roach poison
Fabric softener	Shellac
Fireworks	Sleeping pills
Fluoroacetates	Snail bait
Garbage toxins	Strychnine
Hair dye	Suntan lotions
Hexachlorophene	Thallium
(in certain soaps)	Warfarin
Indelible markers	Weed killer

Signs of poisoning by these products include severe vomiting, diarrhea, delirium, collapse, coma, and convulsions. If your cat is conscious, induce vomiting: Mix equal amounts of hydrogen peroxide (3 percent strength) and water and administer one tablespoon of this fluid. A mustard and water solution also works well. Another way to induce vomiting is to put a few tablespoons of salt on the back of the cat's tongue; repeat this until vomiting occurs. Then treat for shock (page 87).

What to Expect at the Veterinarian's Office

If your cat is unconscious, oxygen and intravenous fluids will be given. Other life-preserving procedures, such as stomach pumping, may be necessary. Hospitalization will be required.

If your cat is conscious, treatment will depend upon the particular poison swallowed and whether an antidote is known.

Swallowed Poisons

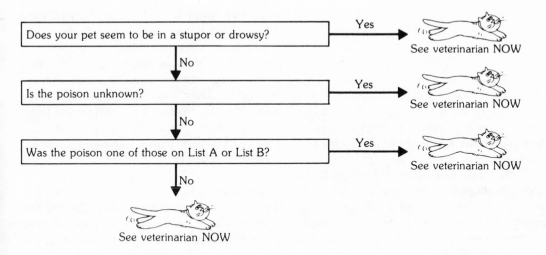

Does your pet seem to be in a stupor or drowsy? — Yes → See veterinarian NOW

No ↓

Is the poison unknown? — Yes → See veterinarian NOW

No ↓

Was the poison one of those on List A or List B? — Yes → See veterinarian NOW

No ↓

See veterinarian NOW

Carbon Monoxide Poisoning

Exhaust fumes contain carbon monoxide. If your cat is put in the trunk of the car with the motor running or in a car with a poor exhaust system, carbon monoxide poisoning can occur. See also Smoke Inhalation, page 116.

Carbon monoxide blocks the transportation of life-giving oxygen to the body cells. If oxygen cannot get to the cells, death will occur. The signs of carbon monoxide poisoning are weakness, cherry-red gums, twitching muscles, and an elevated temperature.

Home Treatment
EMERGENCY Get your cat into fresh air. If breathing has stopped, give artificial respiration (page 84). Seek veterinary assistance at once.

What to Expect at the Veterinarian's Office
If you provided immediate aid, no further treatment may be necessary, and you can probably take your cat home. If not, oxygen (to counteract the carbon monoxide) and intravenous fluids (to treat for shock) may be needed, especially if your pet hasn't recovered by the time you reach the veterinarian's office. Observation for a few days in the hospital may be suggested if your cat is recovering slowly.

Prevention
Never put your cat in a car trunk. Be sure that your car's exhaust system is in good working order. If camping, do *not* use propane gas stoves or heaters in an unventilated tent.

Carbon Monoxide Poisoning

Has your pet stopped breathing? ——Yes——→ See veterinarian NOW

No ↓

Follow home treatment

Poisonous Plants

Cats may be curious and chew up your house plants. Following are some common houseplants that are dangerous to your cat:

Christmas cherry: The berry is poisonous.
Dieffenbachia, also called Dumb cane: The leaves can cause vomiting, diarrhea, swelling of the tongue, and even suffocation.
Dried arrangements: The seed pods and beans of tropical plants may be highly toxic.
Ivy: The leaves can cause breathing and stomach illness.
Mistletoe: The berries are highly toxic and can cause vomiting, diarrhea, and convulsions.

The following outdoor plants can also be hazardous if chewed and/or swallowed:

Castor bean	Lobelia
Daphne	Mistletoe
Foxglove	Monkshood
Horse chestnut	Nightshade
Jimson weed	Poison hemlock
Larkspur	Water hemlock
Laurels	Yew
Lily-of-the-valley	

Home Treatment
EMERGENCY If you discover that your cat has dined on a houseplant, call your poison control center immediately and get veterinary aid. If you don't know the name of the plant, take it along to the veterinarian's office. Give artificial respiration (page 84), if necessary. If you cannot reach a poison control center or your veterinarian, see Swallowed Poisons, page 120, and follow the treatment.

What to Expect at the Veterinarian's Office
If your cat is unconscious, oxygen and intravenous fluids will be given. The stomach may be pumped, as well. Hospitalization will probably be required, since other life support procedures may be necessary.

If your cat is conscious, vomiting will be induced. Treatment will depend on the particular poison and whether the attempts to make your cat vomit have been successful.

Prevention
There is one step that you can take to prevent poisoning from houseplants: Do *not* keep known poisonous plants in the house! If you just can't do without that beautiful plant that is potentially hazardous, the following may prevent its ingestion:

1. If your cat is kept strictly indoors, daily walks outside (on a harness) and being allowed to chew the grass may cure the houseplant gourmand. *Note:* Be sure that your lawn has not been sprayed with weed killers.

2. If your cat cannot be walked, grow indoors some grasses that your cat may eat, such as wheat or oats. A bellyful of either of these may satisfy the "chewing-of-the-green" urge.

3. Most cats love catnip—they eat both fresh leaves and dried. You can grow your own. It is a perennial and comes up year after year. Sit back and watch your cat's antics after a catnip snack. You'll see a lot of rolling and acts of bravado.

4. If you catch your cat nibbling plants, spray the cat with your plant mister at the time of the "crime" to convince your cat to stay away.

5. Moth balls or cayenne pepper in the soil may irritate your cat's "smeller." Cats don't

| Has your pet stopped breathing? | Yes → See veterinarian NOW |

No ↓

Follow home treatment

like to be irritated and, therefore, may stop chewing the plants. *Note:* Some mothballs contain *naphthalene,* which causes a hemolytic anemia if ingested by the pet.

6. Of course, keeping the hazardous plants out of reach is a very smart step and will usually work, unless your pet is determined to be "Supercat."

Snakebites

Cats are not bitten by snakes very often because they are "street smart" and usually stay away from poisonous snakes. Snake venom attacks the blood cells and/or nervous system and can cause immediate pain, severe swelling, weakness, vomiting, diarrhea, bleeding from the nose and anus, paralysis, convulsions, and coma.

Home Treatment
EMERGENCY   Identify the snake by checking the fang marks. A poisonous snake usually leaves just two marks (fangs) in the skin. A non-poisonous snake usually leaves U-shaped teeth marks, and the bite is not very painful.

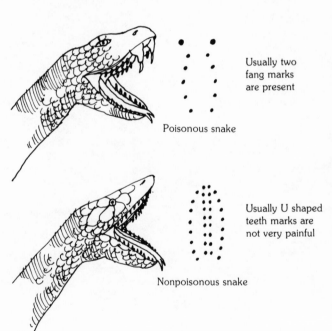

Usually two fang marks are present

Poisonous snake

Usually U shaped teeth marks are not very painful

Nonpoisonous snake

If the snake was poisonous, apply a tourniquet (page 86) between the bite and the heart. You should be able to get one finger under the tourniquet, so that the wound can ooze slightly. Leave the tourniquet on for one to two hours maximum. Keep your cat quiet and lying down. Clip the hair over the wound with scissors. Apply alcohol to the wound and make a shallow linear (not X-shaped) cut over the fang marks using a flame-sterilized knife or razor. Use a suction cup to suck out the venom. You can use your mouth also—but only if there are no open sores. Spit out the venom—do *not* swallow it. Repeat for fifteen minutes. Leaving the tourniquet on, wash the wound with soap and water and apply cold compresses. Clean the wound with alcohol.

If your cat is struggling too much, just apply a tourniquet and see the veterinarian as quickly as possible.

If the snake was nonpoisonous, apply cold compresses and clean the wound with soap, water, and alcohol.

What to Expect at the Veterinarian's Office
Hospitalization will be necessary. Additional suction of the wound will be done. Ice packs will be applied to decrease pain and tissue damage. *Antivenin*, if available, will be given to neutralize the venom. Shock treatment, antibiotics, fluids, steroids, and possibly oxygen may be needed.

Prevention
Keep your pet away from known snake-infested areas. Keep an antivenin kit handy.

Snakebites

Are the fang marks those of a poisonous snake?

Yes → See veterinarian NOW

No ↓

Follow home treatment

Toad Poisoning

When I took my Florida veterinary license boards ten years ago, a slide of a toad was one of the "name it and the problem it causes" questions. Since I had come from a northern veterinary school, I assumed that this was either so unimportant that it was never taught me or I had considered it so irrelevant that I never stored it in my memory. After passing the boards, I practiced in Florida and found out quickly that there the Bufo toad is as common as oranges. It is found in other areas, too, but the Florida variety seems to be much more deadly.

Bufo toads are slow-moving creatures, and a cat may pick one up in its mouth. The wartlike salivary glands on the back of the toad's neck release a poison that, after being rapidly absorbed through the cat's mouth and stomach lining, causes heart irregularities. Within minutes, the cat will shake its head, salivate profusely, and become uncoordinated. The breathing and heart rates become rapid. Collapse, convulsions, and death can occur within fifteen minutes.

Home Treatment

EMERGENCY   Wash out your cat's mouth with a hose immediately if you see that contact has been made with a Bufo toad. Be sure not to tilt the head all the way in the air as you do so, or water may go down the cat's breathing tubes. See your veterinarian immediately.

What to Expect at the Veterinarian's Office

Intravenous drugs will be administered to correct the heart irregularities. If you have already rinsed out the cat's mouth yourself and have managed to get the cat to the veterinarian quickly, your cat has the best chance for survival.

128

Toad Poisoning

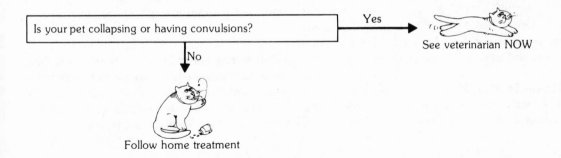

Is your pet collapsing or having convulsions? —— Yes —→ See veterinarian NOW

No

Follow home treatment

Porcupine Quills

Curiosity will not only kill a cat; it can sometimes transform it into a furry pin cushion. Porcupine quills are usually found embedded in the head, nose, and mouth.

Home Treatment
The quills can be softened with vinegar and removed more easily using pliers, by slowly twisting out each quill. This is *extremely* painful, and it may be difficult to restrain your cat without sedation. If you get the quills out, be sure to cleanse the puncture wounds with an antiseptic, since quill wounds can get infected very easily.

What to Expect at the Veterinarian's Office
Your veterinarian will remove the quills after administering a tranquilizer or general anesthesia. The wounds will be thoroughly cleansed, and your cat will be given antibiotics.

Porcupine Quills

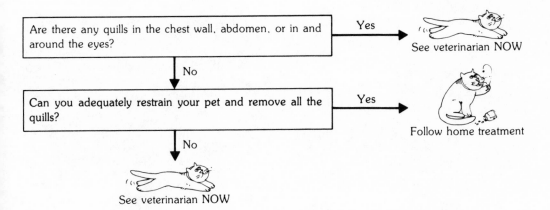

Are there any quills in the chest wall, abdomen, or in and around the eyes? → **Yes** → See veterinarian NOW

No ↓

Can you adequately restrain your pet and remove all the quills? → **Yes** → Follow home treatment

No ↓

See veterinarian NOW

Chapter 8

Common Problems and Diseases

Fever

In cats, a body temperature above 103°F is a fever, but an elevated temperature is not necessarily a sign of illness. Many healthy pets will have a variation in temperature of one or two degrees depending on the time of day, its emotional state and amount of activity, or the environment, such as riding in a hot automobile. Muscle activity and food digestion are the most important ways cats produce heat to maintain body temperature. Some healthy animals that are nervous will shake so much (i.e., increase their muscle activity) at the doctor's office that a 104°F temperature may be recorded.

The most common causes for persistent fevers in cats are viral and bacterial infections. Examples are panleukopenia (viral), skin abscesses (bacterial), respiratory infections (viral and/or bacterial) and feline infectious peritonitis. Other causes are heat stroke (environmental), *eclampsia* (low blood calcium), and cancer (lymphosarcoma or leukemia).

The hair coat of most cats insulates against heat loss or heat gain. If it is a hot day, the only way they can lower their body temperature is by panting, since they do not have sweat glands (except on the foot pads). If they are in a closed, unventilated car on a hot day, the panting mechanism will not be able to lower the body temperature enough, and heat stroke will result.

Bacteria, viruses, and probably cancer cells cause fever by stimulating certain white blood cells to produce chemical substances called *pyrogens*. Pyrogens can be helpful in combating unwanted invaders. Therefore, fever is not always a bad sign—it may mean that your pet's body is responding to the challenge and fighting the infection.

There are a number of signs that will tell you when your cat has a true fever. Depression, a sad expression, and lack of appetite are common signs. Some cats seem cold and shiver; others feel hot and pant or seek cool places. You may also notice an increase in both the heart and and respiratory rates.

Feline Infectious Peritonitis (FIP)

Feline infectious peritonitis (FIP) is a contagious viral disease of wild and domestic cats that does not infect humans. The disease has an insidious onset: The cat is lethargic, has progressive weight loss, a loss of appetite, and a fever that does not respond to antibiotic therapy. Fluid may accumulate in the abdomen and/or chest. The eyes, central nervous system, and abdominal organs may be ravaged by the inflammatory reaction. At this writing there is no cure, and supportive therapy will prolong life for only a short time. Euthanasia is the most merciful solution, should your cat develop FIP.

The FIP virus may cause no signs, only mild signs (sneezing, watery eyes, and a nose discharge), or the full-blown disease as described above. Researchers are currently trying to determine why all infected cats do not get the full-blown disease. These fortunate cats unfortunately become carriers and pass the virus to others. Your veterinarian can diagnose FIP by a thorough physical exam, analysis of abdominal or chest fluid, a positive FIP antibody test, and other laboratory data.

The FIP virus is suspected to cause the "kitten mortality complex," which includes the deaths of unborn fetuses, newborn kittens, and very young kittens. The Cornell Feline Research Laboratory (New York State College of Veterinary Medicine, Cornell University, Ithaca, New York 14853) is studying FIP in the hope of developing effective treatment and a vaccination. The support of cat lovers is needed. Please write to the laboratory for further information.

Home Treatment

Take your cat's temperature as you did during the home physical, using a rectal thermometer, which has a rounded, stubby tip. Shake down the thermometer and apply vaseline or mineral

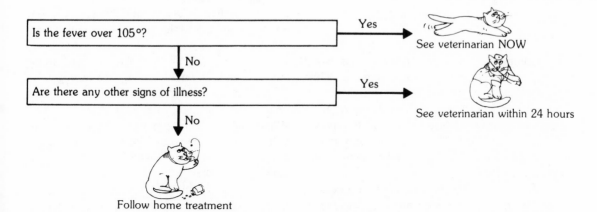

Is the fever over 105°? — **Yes** → See veterinarian NOW

No

Are there any other signs of illness? — **Yes** → See veterinarian within 24 hours

No

Follow home treatment

oil to the bulb. Restrain your cat (page 83), lift its tail, and gently slide the thermometer into the anus. Leave it in for three minutes. It is helpful to wrap your cat in a blanket or sheet, leaving its tail end exposed, and hold it between your arm and body. This leaves at least one hand free to hold in the thermometer, which might break if the cat moves a lot. But remember that cats dislike restraint. Remove the thermometer and read the mercury level as you normally do. *Note:* Do *not* administer aspirin, which can cause a toxic reaction. And do *not* "starve" a fever, since the body needs more fuel (calories) than usual in this weakened state.

If the fever is over 105°F, see Heatstroke on page 118. A cold water bath or shower must be given immediately to lower the body temperature before brain damage or death results. Ice applied to the head and inner thighs is also beneficial. If the body temperature has not dropped to 103°F in ten minutes, a cold water enema may be necessary. Fill an enema bag with cold water and ice cubes. Lubricate the tip and insert it gently into the anus. Hold the bag high until your cat shows signs of discomfort, then let the water drain out. *Note:* After a cold water enema, improvement *cannot* be measured by rectal temperature.

If your pet has a fever and is not vomiting, be sure that it eats and drinks. The caloric (energy) requirements increase when heat increases because energy is used faster and must be replaced. There is also an increased need for fluids in the feverish body. If your pet will not drink voluntarily, see Giving Liquids to Your Cat, page 77. *Note:* Water should *not* be given if your pet is vomiting. In this case, let it lick ice cubes.

Cats that will not eat or drink and cannot be nursed by you should be seen by your doctor as soon as possible, especially if your pet's condition deteriorates.

What to Expect at the Veterinarian's Office
Again, a fever may be a *sign* of illness. If your pet has a fever along with other signs and is getting worse, do not hesitate to see your veterinarian. Your doctor will do a complete physical examination. Blood tests, urinalysis, and X rays may be necessary to find the cause of the fever.

If an infection is suspected, antibiotics will be given. Intravenous or subcutaneous fluids may be administered if your pet has not been able to take in enough fluids to meet the body's daily needs. Fluid therapy is very important for pets that will not eat or drink.

Panleukopenia (Distemper)

Panleukopenia (pan = all, leuko = white blood cells, penia = lessening—destruction of white blood cells) is a highly contagious viral disease. It is seen in all members of the cat family, from house cats to lions. It is not infectious to humans and it does not cause "bad temper" (distemper). The death rate in infected, *unvaccinated* young cats is very high.

The virus damages body cells, suppressing the immune response and allowing bacteria to do further damage. The antibiotics kill the bacteria, thus giving the body time to overwhelm the virus and repair the damage. If your cat can be kept alive for a week, the chance for recovery is good.

The virus has a predilection for intestinal cells and bone marrow. Its general signs are a high fever (104° to 105°F), loss of appetite, weakness, vomiting, and diarrhea (sometimes bloody). Since these signs are so similar to those of other serious problems, such as leukemia, toxoplasmosis, some poisonings, and intestinal obstructions, a visit to your veterinarian is essential and should be done immediately.

The virus is spread by direct contact with the saliva, vomit, urine, or feces of an ill cat. The virus is very hardy and most disinfectants are ineffective in destroying it. There is no drug that specifically kills the virus.

Home Treatment
Your doctor may ask you to be an active partner in helping your cat get well, because good nursing care is as important to recovery as the antibiotics and fluids that your veterinarian will administer. The important things are to provide adequate nutrition, to maintain body condition and to help fight infection, and fluids, to prevent dehydration, primarily from the vomiting and diarrhea.

Your cat may not feel like eating or drinking, but small, frequent feedings of raw egg yolks or cooked eggs, milk, strained baby foods, and boiled chicken will help with the nutrition. Water, milk, and chicken broth will help with the fluids. See the Decision Charts and Your Cat's Home Pharmacy for remedies for vomiting and diarrhea.

Most cats with panleukopenia should be treated since the majority will survive. Good nursing care, good veterinary care, patience, and love and understanding can be very rewarding.

What to Expect at the Veterinarian's Office
Since the signs of panleukopenia are similar to those of other diseases, blood tests and X rays may be necessary for diagnosis and for determining the proper treatment regimen. Of course, a complete physical examination will be done. Your doctor may suggest home care and possibly frequent veterinary visits as the best treatment plan. Antibiotics, fluids, antivomitins, antidiarrheals, vitamins, and sometimes blood transfusions are needed to help your cat recover.

Prevention
The kitten series of vaccinations should begin at seven to nine weeks of age, with the last one given at twelve to sixteen weeks of age. Yearly boosters are needed to keep up the antibody level and to keep the body's "memory system" on guard.

Panleukopenia
(Distemper)

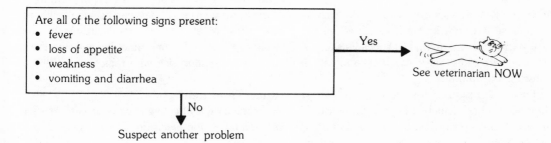

Are all of the following signs present:
• fever
• loss of appetite
• weakness
• vomiting and diarrhea

Yes → See veterinarian NOW

No

Suspect another problem

Rabies

The word rabies evokes fear, and rightfully so. A viral disease that attacks the brain, it is seen in many warm-blooded animals, especially skunks, raccoons, foxes, bats, coyotes, dogs, and cats. It *is* infectious to humans.

One of the signs of the disease is a change of behavior: There may be restlessness, extreme shyness, or aggressiveness. In fact, wild animals may seem tame. Their pupils are dilated, as well.

In the *furious stage,* the animal will bite at anything in its way. Loud noises or bright lights can stimulate the biting attacks. The animal also becomes uncoordinated. In this stage, the animal may die during convulsions or it may go on to the *dumb stage.*

In the dumb stage, the paralysis of the throat causes voice changes, salivating, and an inability to eat or drink. The lower jaw will be paralyzed and unable to close, and the tongue and lower jaw will hang loose. Generalized paralysis, coma, and death follow.

The virus is spread by the bite of a rabid animal—the virus-laden saliva enters the wound. Airborne transmission in caves inhabited by bats has been reported. (Just a word here about bats—they are shy and helpful creatures. At dusk, many types of bats can be seen catching mosquitos. Most bats are good citizens of our spaceship earth—leading quiet lives, doing their job and not getting sick with rabies).

Home Treatment

No home care is effective. See your veterinarian *immediately* if the Decision Chart applies.

What to Expect at the Veterinarian's Office

An animal suspected of being rabid will be quarantined and public health officials will be notified.

Prevention

Keep your cat's rabies vaccination up to date. The first vaccination is given between three and six months of age. A booster is given at one year and then annually thereafter.

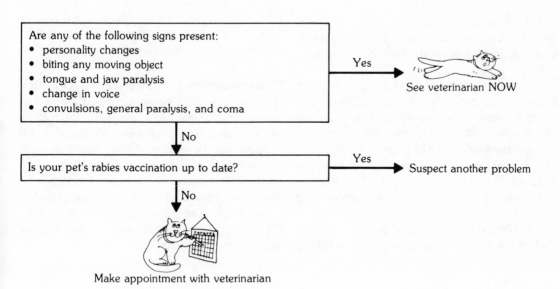

Are any of the following signs present:
- personality changes
- biting any moving object
- tongue and jaw paralysis
- change in voice
- convulsions, general paralysis, and coma

Yes → See veterinarian NOW

No ↓

Is your pet's rabies vaccination up to date?

Yes → Suspect another problem

No ↓

Make appointment with veterinarian

Increased Water Intake

Water is essential for life and your pet obtains it from foods as well as liquids, since the metabolism of food (especially fats) also produces water.

Cats need about 30 ml. (1 oz.) per pound of body weight daily, but lactation, fever, hot weather, exercise, and water loss from vomiting and diarrhea will increase your pet's need. Dry foods that contain only 10 percent moisture will also increase water consumption. In addition, certain medications, such as antibiotics and corticosteroids, may cause your cat to become very thirsty.

However, excessive thirst is seen as well in such serious illnesses as diabetes and kidney disease. Therefore, veterinary attention may be necessary.

Home Treatment
An increased water intake in an alert and active pet is of no concern. Keep your cat's water bowl filled. If there are any signs of illness or if you are concerned about the amount of water consumed, see your veterinarian.

What to Expect at the Veterinarian's Office
If your cat is drinking an increased amount of water, bring a fresh urine sample to the doctor's office. The urinary system and the possibility of diabetes can be evaluated from this sample. A complete history and physical examination will be done. If vomiting or diarrhea is thought to be the cause of the fluid loss and increased thirst, a stool sample and bowel X rays will be taken. Blood tests may be needed to check the status of all the internal organs.

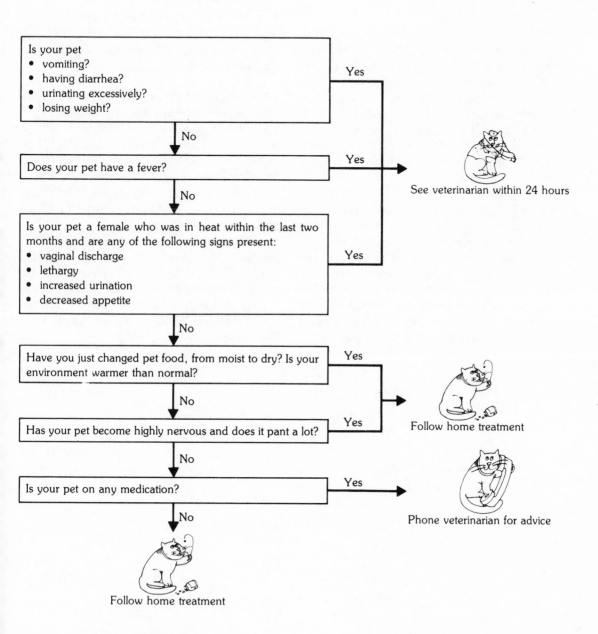

Is your pet
- vomiting?
- having diarrhea?
- urinating excessively?
- losing weight?

Yes →

No ↓

Does your pet have a fever?

Yes → See veterinarian within 24 hours

No ↓

Is your pet a female who was in heat within the last two months and are any of the following signs present:
- vaginal discharge
- lethargy
- increased urination
- decreased appetite

Yes

No ↓

Have you just changed pet food, from moist to dry? Is your environment warmer than normal?

Yes →

No ↓

Has your pet become highly nervous and does it pant a lot?

Yes → Follow home treatment

No ↓

Is your pet on any medication?

Yes → Phone veterinarian for advice

No ↓

Follow home treatment

Increased Appetite

More exercise, a cold environment, pregnancy, and nursing will increase the need for food, especially for calories and good quality protein. However, an increased appetite could mean something more. For example, the early signs of diabetes, which is seen frequently in cats, are an increased water consumption, increased urination, weight loss despite a voracious appetite, and possibly depression and vomiting (these last two are late signs).

Worms may also cause an increased appetite, although they could equally decrease the appetite or cause no change at all. Still, you should not rule out worms (see page 44).

If your pet has a voracious appetite, but the food just passes out as unformed stools and dramatic weight loss occurs, pancreatic, liver, and intestinal problems (in which the food is not absorbed or used properly) may be indicated. These require veterinary attention, also.

Home Treatment

If you suspect that more exercise, a cold environment, pregnancy, or nursing may have increased your cat's caloric and protein requirements, no professional treatment will be necessary, in all probability. You should, however, read the section on nutrition (page 33). Any other dramatic appetite changes require veterinary consultation.

What to Expect at the Veterinarian's Office

Since an increased appetite can be caused by so many things, your doctor will take the time to get a good history and to perform a complete physical exam. Blood tests, a fecal exam, and a urinalysis may be needed. Prepare for the visit by not feeding your cat in the morning and by taking urine and stool samples to test for diabetes and worms, respectively.

A word about diabetes: Most owners of diabetic pets do a remarkable job in giving the daily insulin injections and checking the urine. Although the disease can not be cured (as of this writing, at least), a controlled diabetic can still live a happy life. If your cat is diagnosed as a diabetic, please treat it.

Increased Appetite

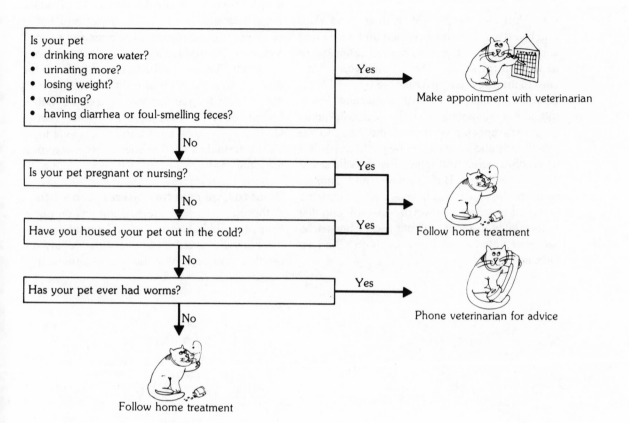

Is your pet
- drinking more water?
- urinating more?
- losing weight?
- vomiting?
- having diarrhea or foul-smelling feces?

Yes → Make appointment with veterinarian

No

Is your pet pregnant or nursing?

Yes

No

Have you housed your pet out in the cold?

Yes → Follow home treatment

No

Has your pet ever had worms?

Yes → Phone veterinarian for advice

No

Follow home treatment

Decreased Appetite

Cats—just like people—have their good days and bad days. If your pet is alert and active and shows no signs of illness but has not eaten any or all its food for a day or two, don't worry. Cats who roam free are sometimes fed by neighbors, or else they feed on rodents or garbage. While this is not advisable, it could obviously affect your cat's appetite at home, and begging on your hands and knees won't help if your pet has eaten elsewhere. And remember the effect that environment has. Both humans and animals consume less food and have less of an appetite in warm weather. However, loss of appetite (*anorexia*) is also seen with many cat illnesses, so see your veterinarian if the Decision Chart so indicates.

Home Treatment

If your cat is not eating and you cannot see your veterinarian, force feeding may be necessary to provide the calories, nutrients, and water necessary for survival. Strained baby foods, soft boiled eggs, raw egg yolks, whole milk, and boiled chicken are good sources of calories and protein. You can also try feeding your pet's regular food by hand: Place a small amount of food on the roof of your cat's mouth with your finger, a spoon, or a tongue depressor. See also Giving Liquids to Your Cat, page 77. *Note:* Forced feeding is *not* to be used instead of a veterinary visit. It should be used in coordination with professional care.

What to Expect at the Veterinarian's Office

A thorough physical examination will be done. Sometimes blood tests, X rays, a urinalysis, and stool samples will be necessary to identify the problem and determine the best treatment.

Decreased Appetite

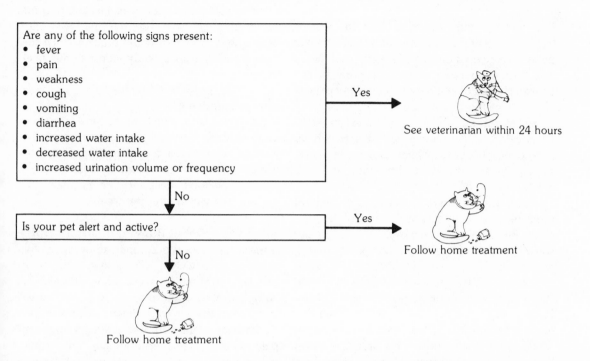

Are any of the following signs present:
- fever
- pain
- weakness
- cough
- vomiting
- diarrhea
- increased water intake
- decreased water intake
- increased urination volume or frequency

Yes → See veterinarian within 24 hours

No ↓

Is your pet alert and active?

Yes → Follow home treatment

No ↓

Follow home treatment

Underweight

Cats that are underweight or have lost weight usually are not receiving enough calories. If your pet is burning up more calories than usual (living in a hot environment, exercising more, or becoming excited over a nearby female in heat will all do it), eating a new food that may not be as digestible, or eating less food (and therefore fewer calories), weight can be lost. If you have moved recently, brought another new pet home, or had a baby, your cat may be upset and may not eat well.

But, weight loss can occur from medical problems as well. In certain diseases of the pancreas, liver, and intestines the food is not absorbed properly (diarrhea and/or vomiting will be present also). A weight loss accompanied by increased urination and water intake may indicate the presence of diabetes or kidney disease. Heart disease (such as heart valve disease) can cause a weight loss called *cardiac cachexia*, in which the body does not get the proper nutrition because of poor circulation. Worms can steal the nutrition needed by your cat's body. The list of medical problems that can cause weight loss is endless, so an examination by your veterinarian is essential.

There is nothing really wrong with being just a little underweight, however. Healthy pets that are on the lean side seem to have fewer joint, heart, lung, and pancreatic problems. To find out your cat's proper weight, consult your veterinarian.

Home Treatment

If your cat is alert, active, and does not seem ill, you could try increasing the caloric intake (see Feeding Your Adult Cat, page 38). Check the weight desired, the caloric needs, and the amount of food necessary to maintain that weight, and weigh your pet weekly.

What to Expect at the Veterinarian's Office

If the weight loss is accompanied by signs of illness, or if no weight gain is seen with the increased food intake, see your veterinarian. A complete history and physical examination will be done and your cat's dietary and bowel patterns will be scrutinized. Blood tests, a stool sample, urinalysis, electrocardiogram, and X rays may be necessary to find the underlying cause for the weight loss.

Underweight

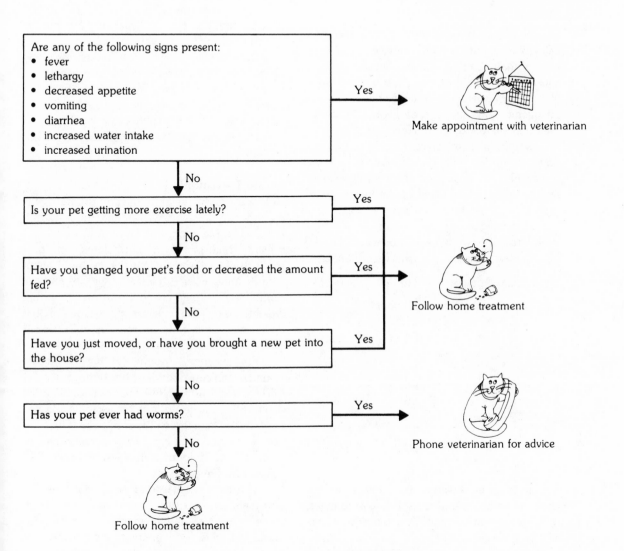

Are any of the following signs present:
- fever
- lethargy
- decreased appetite
- vomiting
- diarrhea
- increased water intake
- increased urination

Yes → Make appointment with veterinarian

No ↓

Is your pet getting more exercise lately? **Yes**

No ↓

Have you changed your pet's food or decreased the amount fed? **Yes** → Follow home treatment

No ↓

Have you just moved, or have you brought a new pet into the house? **Yes**

No ↓

Has your pet ever had worms? **Yes** → Phone veterinarian for advice

No ↓

Follow home treatment

Overweight

Obesity in cats, in most cases, is from too many calories and not enough exercise. Fat people seem to have fat pets. I'm convinced that this is caused by an eating pattern ("just a little bit more won't hurt") shared between owner and pet. If fat people don't exercise enough, why should their pets have a different life-style?

Weight gain can be very insidious until one day you say "What happened!" As a pet matures or gets old, its metabolism and activity changes, and its caloric intake should be reduced accordingly. People have the same problem keeping off that extra weight after the "middle years" arrive. What are the "middle years" for a cat? The following chart explains a cat's age in human terms:

Cat Age	Human Equivalent
6 months	10 years
1 year	15
2 years	24
4	32
6	40
8	48
10	55
12	65
14	70
16	80
20	100

If there is an increase in caloric intake, a slow-down in metabolism (due to body-age changes), or a decrease in exercise (due to action on your part or to a lazy or aging pet), a weight gain will be seen. *Hypothyroidism* (a lack of thyroid hormones) is rare in cats, and an *ovariohysterectomy* (removal of the ovaries, tubes, and uterus in a female) does not seem to cause a weight gain.

But sometimes owners misinterpret a weight gain or "large belly" as a fat problem when in reality a heart, liver, or kidney problem (with fluid accumulation in the abdomen) or a hormone imbalance is the cause. Overweight cats can have more pancreatic (diabetes and inflammation of the pancreas), heart, lung, and joint problems because these parts are continually being overstressed by the excess fat and weight. Surgery and healing can also be extremely difficult in an overweight cat.

Your veterinarian is *also* overstressed by obese pets. It makes the physical examination more difficult because it's harder to hear the heartbeat and lung sounds and to feel the internal organs. Trying to find a vein for blood tests or intravenous fluids in a fat pet can be a major undertaking.

Home Treatment

Before starting a weight reduction program, it is a good idea to have your veterinarian perform a physical and, if necessary, blood tests to rule out related health or hormone problems. The program itself involves finding the desired weight (see Feeding Your Adult Cat, page 38) and the number of calories needed to maintain that weight. Feed your cat just 60 percent of that daily total until the cat reaches the desired weight.

For instance, if your cat weighs twelve pounds, and ten pounds is the desired weight, 400 calories × 60% = 240 calories should be fed daily until your cat weighs ten pounds. Be patient, it may take three or four months. Once the goal is reached, you can slowly increase the calories to the calorie maintenance level (400 calories for ten pounds).

The cat's normal food or special prescription diets can be used for the weight reduction program, but all family members must cooperate. No table food or treats are allowed because these add considerable calories. Keep a weekly record of your cat's weight. If there is not a steady weight loss, contact your veterinarian. *Note:* If your pet roams free and is fed by neighbors, gets into trash, or hunts for rodents, forget about weight reduction.

Take a "before" and an "after" picture of your cat. Your veterinarian will be proud of you and your pet's accomplishment. A sincere owner who practices good preventive medicine for his

148

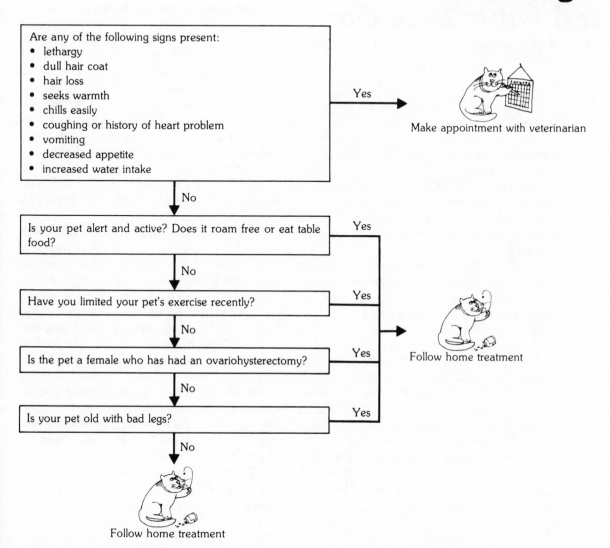

Are any of the following signs present:
- lethargy
- dull hair coat
- hair loss
- seeks warmth
- chills easily
- coughing or history of heart problem
- vomiting
- decreased appetite
- increased water intake

Yes → Make appointment with veterinarian

No ↓

Is your pet alert and active? Does it roam free or eat table food? — **Yes**

No ↓

Have you limited your pet's exercise recently? — **Yes**

No ↓

Is the pet a female who has had an ovariohysterectomy? — **Yes**

No ↓

Is your pet old with bad legs? — **Yes**

→ Follow home treatment

No ↓

Follow home treatment

---

pet is deeply respected by veterinarians. I want to share with you a postcard I received this summer from my patient Smokey Meisner, on vacation in the Poconos:

Dear Doctor Sheldon,
I am feeling fine, eating well, running, and feeling full of pep. My sugar color chart is staying between blue negative and +1. My owners are happy and enjoying their vaca-

tion because of how you help me. They appreciate you, and I love you!
    Lick, lick, lick!
    Smokey Meisner

Smokey had been terribly overweight but went on a diet and lost it all. The Meisners brought me "before" and "after" pictures, and the difference is truly amazing. Smokey, I am sad to say, became a diabetic (a high risk with obesity) but is otherwise happy.

Spraying, Scratching, and Other Behavior Problems

Cats have been a favorite companion of human-kind for about five thousand years. Their grace, beauty, and regal bearing have charmed kings and common folk alike. During this time, the cat was quite independent. It did not live in close quarters, did not share the social pressures common to modern times, and was not bred selectively. These factors singly or in combination are thought to contribute to an increase in behavior problems.

Both intact and neutered male cats (and to a lesser extent, females) may back up to vertical objects, such as furniture and drapes, raise and quiver the tail, and squirt a small amount of urine on the object. This is called *spraying*. *Note:* This is *not* to be confused with *urolithiasis* or *cystitis* (page 208). Spraying is thought to make the surroundings more familiar and comfortable to the cat because they have the cat's own smell, and to let others know that Morris, Jaws, or Ralph "was here." If the cat perceives a threat to its environment, such as a new addition to the household (another pet, a new baby), a furniture change, or a new cat in the neighborhood, spraying may be seen. In these cases, however, it will probably be temporary.

Home Treatment

Castrating the male cat before sexual maturity solves the spraying problem before it begins, but castration after maturity is still highly effective (see page 227). If castration doesn't appeal to you, try placing mothballs or the cat's food bowl in the "spray zone." Cat's don't go to the bathroom where they eat and they detest the smell of mothballs, so this may eliminate the problem, especially if it is a temporary aberration. *Note:* Do *not* use mothballs if small children are in the household. Some mothballs contain naphthalene, which causes a hemolytic anemia if the cat licks or chews the mothball. Hormones or a new home for the cat may be needed if the behavior persists.

Cats are very proper about their toilet habits: They cover their bowel movements in their territory (if their mothers taught them correctly, this is the litter box). A change of litter type, infrequent cleaning of the litter box, or any perceived environmental threats can disrupt this habit. First of all, try to correct the environmental change. Clean the area and place the feeding bowl or mothballs nearby. If flowerpot soil has become the new bathroom, a few mothballs placed in the soil or some cayenne pepper sprinkled on top should send your cat back to its litter box. If your cat is having loose bowel movements outside of the litter box, see Diarrhea, page 200.

Thumb sucking or sucking on pacifiers or other objects is a favorite pasttime of small chil-(cont.)

Spraying, Scratching, and Other Behavior Problems

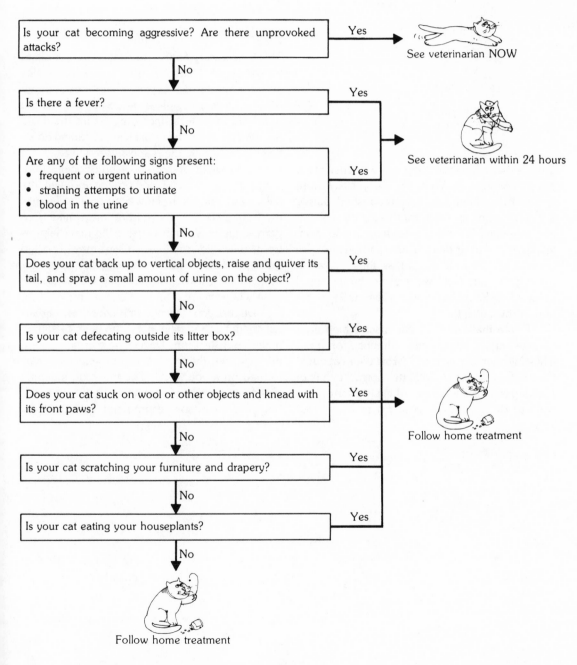

Is your cat becoming aggressive? Are there unprovoked attacks? — **Yes** → See veterinarian NOW

↓ **No**

Is there a fever? — **Yes**

↓ **No**

Are any of the following signs present:
- frequent or urgent urination
- straining attempts to urinate
- blood in the urine

— **Yes** → See veterinarian within 24 hours

↓ **No**

Does your cat back up to vertical objects, raise and quiver its tail, and spray a small amount of urine on the object? — **Yes**

↓ **No**

Is your cat defecating outside its litter box? — **Yes**

↓ **No**

Does your cat suck on wool or other objects and knead with its front paws? — **Yes** → Follow home treatment

↓ **No**

Is your cat scratching your furniture and drapery? — **Yes**

↓ **No**

Is your cat eating your houseplants? — **Yes**

↓ **No**

Follow home treatment

Spraying, Scratching, and Other Behavior Problems

(cont.)

dren, especially when they are anxious, tired, hungry, or stressed. Well, cats—especially those that were orphaned or undernourished during the nursing period—may try to suck your blankets, sweaters, pants, or anything made from wool, your skin or hair, or its own body. At the same time, they will knead as they do when nursing. A firm "No!" and a shake by the scruff of the neck should be helpful in eliminating or reducing this behavior.

Confrontation: Your cat is scratching your favorite chair, your new drapes, or your Ishfahan oriental rug! Don't throw your cat out to the dogs. First try to modify this normal behavior (clawing trees is a way of marking territory). You can't sit down and ask your cat to leave your "trees" alone, but you can place a scratching post near the object being damaged. When you see your cat scratching other things, place it near the post and move its front legs and claws on the scratching post. If this fails, declawing may have to be considered.

Declawing

This is necessary only if your cat is using its claws on people or destroying your home furnishings by refusing to use a scratching post. Some owners, if their cat plays outdoors, tolerate the damage to furniture since they realize there is a greater chance of the cat's falling or sliding down from a tree if only the rear claws are used. A cat is not damaged physically or emotionally from the declawing, and it *could* protect itself with the back claws and teeth. However, a cat still *thinks* the front claws are present and may make dangerous mistakes, such as using the now-helpless front paws for defense. Cats may also go through their usual scratching motions (it's thought to be a way of removing worn nails, as well) when they get up in the morning.

Discuss your feelings with your veterinarian; talk to friends and neighbors who have cats; then make your decision. Declawing can be done at any age, but there is less stress when it is performed on a young cat. The times of neutering (five to six months of age) and spaying are good. Many veterinarians recommend that only the front claws be removed, since the back claws rarely damage furniture.

Most cats recover remarkably well from this surgery. A few cats are tender for a week or two after surgery; they may touch the paw lightly to the ground or occasionally hold it up. When the bandages are removed, I advise using shredded newspaper with just a few granules of kitty litter in the litter box for one week after surgery. This will reduce the chances of irritation or infection while the paws are healing.

A general anesthesia is used for the operation, because the claws and the area from which they grow (*basal germinal cells*) are removed. Some doctors suture the digits afterward. The paws should be kept bandaged for two or three days after surgery.

What to Expect at the Veterinarian's Office
If any of the behavior problems have not been modified by the Home Treatment, please consult your veterinarian. Each cat, just like each human, is a unique personality, and a discussion of your cat and your home situation with your veterinarian may be very helpful.

Recently, the University of Pennsylvania veterinary hospital established a referral clinic (sponsored by the National Institutes of Health) to handle problems that owners have with their animals. The staff includes a veterinary neurologist, an animal behavior specialist, a social worker, and a human psychiatrist.

Spraying, Scratching, and Other Behavior Problems

(cont.)

Note: An aggressive cat can be dangerous! This situation requires an immediate discussion with your veterinarian. To avoid future injury, it is very important that kittens be socialized to humans and any other household members (dogs, birds, etc.) during the critical socialization period —five to sixteen weeks of age. (Please read Training Your Cat, which begins on page 51.) Improper socialization is a major cause of future aggressive behavior, although there may also be an inherited basis. Kittens may go through a phase when they "hunt" your feet or ankles; this can be stopped by a sharp "No!" or by diverting the kittens' attention to other playthings. A cat that is well socialized to humans is a very great pleasure.

Skunk Encounters

You will become a truly seasoned pet owner the day your cat comes home looking like a cat but smelling like a skunk. And you may not have to wait long: Kittens are more curious about skunks than are adult cats.

Home Treatment
Before you begin to make your cat "de-scent," put on a pair of rubber gloves. Wash your cat's eyes with warm water, and bathe its entire body with soap and water. Towel dry and soak your cat with tomato juice (you can add a little diluted lemon juice). This whole process may have to be repeated a few times.

Throw away your cat's collar—you'll never get the smell out of it.

What to Expect at the Veterinarian's Office
If the eyes are extremely irritated, your doctor will flush them with sterile water. The cornea will be examined for damage. An eye antibiotic (with or without steroids) will be dispensed.

Are the eyes seriously inflamed? → **Yes** → See veterinarian NOW

↓ **No**

Follow home treatment

Lameness

Neither an owner nor a veterinarian can always tell by eye or feel whether a bone is broken. If your cat is limping badly and you suspect a fracture, have an X ray taken (see Bone Fractures, page 102).

Two not-uncommon problems can cause a weakness of your cat's hindlegs. The first is a *pelvic fracture,* which is generally seen in cats that have been hit by cars. The second is called *arterial thromboembolism.* This sudden blockage of the artery that supplies blood to both hindlegs is being recognized more often in cats of all ages. The syndrome usually occurs suddenly: The cat exhibits severe pain and a weakness or paralysis of both hindlegs, which are cool to the touch because no warm blood is reaching them. No femoral pulse (see page 20) can be felt. Clots can develop in the lung, brain, or other organs, and shock and death can occur suddenly. The cause is not known but is thought to be an underlying heart condition called *cardiomyopathy* that causes clots to be carried from the heart to distant blood vessels in the body.

Besides these two major causes, there are other reasons for lameness. Tar, paint, and thorns can stick to your cat's footpad and between the digits. When your cat trys to chew off these substances, its paws can get irritated. The irritation, in turn, makes your pet tender on the paw and then lame. This is a frequent occurrence. Many cats are brought to the doctor with a "broken leg" which is actually a lameness caused by an abscess (page 174).

Tissues that connect the bones of a joint and give it stability during movement are called *ligaments.* Sometimes these are stretched (*strained*), slightly torn (*sprained*), or completely torn. The most common ligament sprain or complete tear is seen in the knee of the cat. The *anterior cruciate ligament* prevents the knee bones from rubbing together, so a partial or complete tear will cause severe pain. Your doctor will be able to determine the degree of tearing.

Something else that should be mentioned here is *paper bone disease (osteoporosis),* which can be seen in growing kittens that are fed a diet with the wrong balance of calcium and phosphorus (an all-meat diet) and not enough vitamin D-3. In this case calcium is lost from the bones. The kitten is reluctant to walk, has pain in the legs, and may stand with its paws turned inward. Its bones are fragile and fracture easily.

Osteoarthritis (bony changes in the joint) is the end result of joint instabilities that were not or cannot be corrected satisfactorily, of joint injuries, or of the aging process (one old fellow called it "older-itis"). After sleeping or lying down, your pet is stiff and feels pain that seems to disappear as your cat moves around.

Dislocation

Dislocations of the hip joint are occasionally seen in cats that have been hit by cars. The hip joint is a snug "ball and socket" arrangement. Trauma can tear the muscles and tendons over the hip and pop the ball out of the socket, causing a dislocation, or a *luxation,* of the hip joint. If the hip is dislocated, the cat may not be able to place the leg on the ground. Fractures of the pelvis may accompany traumatic injury to the hips.

Home Treatment

Time and activity restriction (home confinement) can be tried for a few days, if the chart so indicates. *Remember:* Cats *cannot* be given aspirin to decrease the pain and inflammation.

If tar or paint is the problem, soak the paw in mineral or vegetable oil for twelve to twenty-four hours and then bandage it for another twelve to twenty-four hours. Wash the paw with soap and water after removing the bandage. Thorns or other foreign objects can be removed from the paw with your fingers or tweezers.

Any lameness that gets worse or lasts longer than three days should be checked by your veterinarian.
(cont.)

Lameness

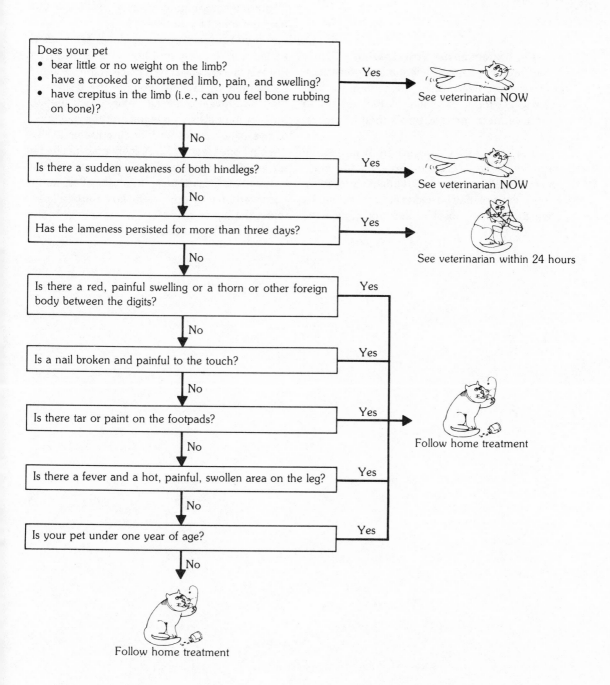

Does your pet
- bear little or no weight on the limb?
- have a crooked or shortened limb, pain, and swelling?
- have crepitus in the limb (i.e., can you feel bone rubbing on bone)?

Yes → See veterinarian NOW

No ↓

Is there a sudden weakness of both hindlegs?

Yes → See veterinarian NOW

No ↓

Has the lameness persisted for more than three days?

Yes → See veterinarian within 24 hours

No ↓

Is there a red, painful swelling or a thorn or other foreign body between the digits?

Yes →

No ↓

Is a nail broken and painful to the touch?

Yes →

No ↓

Is there tar or paint on the footpads?

Yes → Follow home treatment

No ↓

Is there a fever and a hot, painful, swollen area on the leg?

Yes →

No ↓

Is your pet under one year of age?

Yes →

No ↓

Follow home treatment

Lameness

(cont.)

What to Expect at the Veterinarian's Office
If the fragments are in adequate alignment, a pelvic fracture needs only confinement for four to six weeks for good healing. If they are not in good alignment, pins or plates may be necessary.

The chances for recovery from an arterial thromboembolism are not good, and recurrences (usually severe) are frequent. Surgery to remove the clot may be necessary and should be done as soon as possible after you notice the signs. Drugs to decrease clot formation will also be tried. X rays of the chest are usually taken to see the health of the heart and lungs, since heart failure may accompany the clots. An electrocardiogram may be needed.

If you suspect a dislocated hip, see a veterinarian within twenty-four hours, since recent hip dislocations are easier to replace in the socket. A radiograph (X ray) will confirm the dislocation and may reveal other hip injury, such as fractures of the pelvis. A general anesthesia is given to relax the muscles and, by firm manipulation, the hip bone is replaced. A splint may be needed for ten days to prevent unnecessary movement in the joint. Occasionally, the dislocation can be corrected only by *open reduction* (surgically entering the hip area).

SKIN PROBLEM CHART

Problem	Itching	Color	Skin Appearance	Major Location	Age Seen	Duration	Other Signs
Allergic inhalant dermatitis	Severe	Red to yellow, with pus	Crusty areas if infected	Generalized	Begins at one to three years of age	Usually seasonal, unless house is dusty	Bites paw, rubs face, sometimes sneezes
Flea bite dermatitis	Moderate to severe	Red to yellow, with pus; moist	Some hair loss; crusty areas if infected	Base of tail, lower back, inner thighs, neck	Over six months	Warm weather, unless fleas are in house	
Contact dermatitis	Sudden and severe	Red or yellow, with pus; flat	Raised if infected	Neck (around flea collar), armpits, abdomen, between digits	Any age	Until controlled, unless plants are abundant (seasonal)	
Ticks	Moderate	Yellow to red	Scabs; yellow to red moist areas if infected	Ear flaps, between digits, head, neck, shoulders	Any age	Until controlled	
Rodent ulcer	None	Red	Thickened, ulcerated areas	Upper lip; less commonly, inside mouth, between digits, belly, and rear legs	Any age	Until controlled	
Feline acne	None	Gray to yellow, with pus	Pimples, blackheads, crusty areas	Chin	Any age	Until controlled	
Ringworm*	Occasional	Red	Hair loss; round, scaly, inflamed areas	Face, front legs, paws	Usually young	Until controlled	
Abscess	None	Red	Swollen, soft, hot areas; scabs	Anywhere—face, legs, tail base	Any age	Until controlled	Fever, appetite loss, lethargy, lameness if on leg

*Infectious to humans and other animals

Allergies

Your cat's body has a remarkable immune system of antibodies, which are protein substances produced by cells called lymphocytes, that destroy antigens that invade the body, such as viruses and bacteria. This system can become supersensitive to such foreign particles as flea saliva, pollen, house dust, and wool, however, and this supersensitivity can produce chemicals that cause an *allergy,* a severe inflammatory reaction.

Allergic inhalant dermatitis has not been as well documented in cats as it has in dogs. It is caused by a supersensitivity to certain particles in the air such as pollen from trees, ragweed, grass and other plants, house dust, feathers, and wool. The allergy follows a predictable history:

1. It is inherited, so if the parents had it, the offspring probably will, too.
2. It is seasonal—the signs appear about the same time every year.
3. The signs begin between six months and three years of age.
4. The signs include severe biting and scratching, licking the paws, sneezing, rubbing the face, and generalized redness.

Home Treatment

Home treatment is directed toward symptomatic relief and avoiding the foreign particle, or *allergen.* If the offending allergen is thought to be house dust, vacuuming daily and using Dust-seal (L. S. Green Associates, 162 W. 56th Street, New York City 10019) in the environment may help. If wool or feathers are thought to be the culprits, eliminating as many things composed of wool or feathers as possible is recommended.

Bathing your cat with a mild shampoo (such as baby shampoo) will soothe any skin inflammation and remove any allergens on the hair coat. Calamine lotion or Domeboro® solution can be applied to the irritated skin. Hydrogen peroxide (3 percent) and antibiotic ointments are also helpful.

If the signs persist, see your veterinarian. Other skin diseases that may cause similar signs are flea bite dermatitis (page 162) and contact dermatitis (page 164).

What to Expect at the Veterinarian's Office

Your veterinarian will take time to get a good history. He or she may be able to identify the allergen in your pet's environment.

If allergic inhalant dermatitis is the problem, two avenues of treatment are possible—steroids or hyposensitization. Most veterinarians, at this time, use a low dose of steroids to relieve the itching. *Note:* Steroids should *not* be given for long-term treatment because they have some very serious side effects.

The other type of treatment involves testing for the allergy. It can be a long and frustrating treatment since the cats seem to keep developing allergies to new and different foreign particles. Allergy testing and hyposensitization is not used much in cat medicine at this time.

Allergies

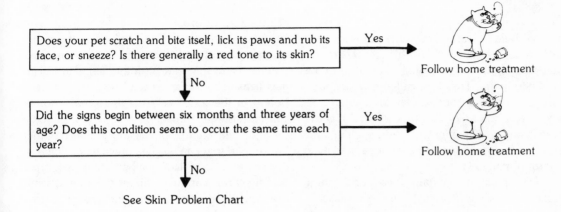

Does your pet scratch and bite itself, lick its paws and rub its face, or sneeze? Is there generally a red tone to its skin? **Yes** → Follow home treatment

No ↓

Did the signs begin between six months and three years of age? Does this condition seem to occur the same time each year? **Yes** → Follow home treatment

No ↓

See Skin Problem Chart

Flea Bite Dermatitis

Internal parasites aren't the only parasites your cat has to contend with in this life: There are numerous insects that would like to call your pet's skin home. These are called *external parasites* and include such dastardly creatures as ticks, fleas, mites, lice and flies. They can cause severe itching, skin infections, and even internal problems such as tapeworms, anemia, and even a form of paralysis.

Preventing or treating these unwelcome creatures is accomplished by using insecticidal preparations. Understanding their life cycles will give you an edge in this battle, and the following discussion should be beneficial. Ticks and mites are discussed separately, on pages 166 and 167.

Any cat older than six months of age can develop an allergy to flea saliva. Fleas are thin, wingless, brown insects that are extraordinary jumpers and move through the hair coat rapidly. The flea injects its saliva under the cat's skin as an aid in retrieving its meal (the cat's blood). The saliva acts as foreign material that can cause your pet to itch and bite itself profusely. Even people may be bitten by hungry fleas; their favorite human areas are ankles and waists, and the bites are very itchy.

Hair loss and skin infection are characteristic, especially on the lower back, neck, and inner thighs, favored flea feeding sites. The hair loss usually has a pattern: a triangular patch on the lower back and patches at the tail base, on the neck, and on the inner thighs. You may even see fleas jumping or moving in these areas, although often you won't see fleas on your cat. Flea droppings are the black specks (digested blood) found primarily on the hairs of the lower back. To test, place the droppings on white paper and moisten them with water. If they turn red, they are flea droppings; if not, they are dirt.

Before treating for fleas, check to see if your cat might have allergic inhalant dermatitis (page 160) or contact dermatitis (page 164).

Home Treatment

You must control fleas on all animals in the household and in the environment. A natural control agent that can be tried *before* your cat gets fleas is brewer's yeast. Mixing 0.1 gm. per pound in the food daily seems to make some cats "distasteful" to fleas.

For flea control on all the animals in the household, you can use flea powders or dips, or flea collars or medallions. When using dips, read the directions carefully. Sponge your pet with the dip, avoiding the eyes, and repeat as the directions indicate. *Note:* Do *not* apply dips to open sores.

If you use a flea collar, use the recommended size for your cat. The flea collar must be aired for a few days before you place it around your pet's neck. If the skin underneath the flea collar becomes red and hair is lost, *remove* the collar. Some animals are sensitive to the chemical. *Note:* Do *not* combine flea collars or medallions with other insectides. For example, don't dip your cat and then put a flea collar on it.

There has recently been some discussion about the wisdom of animals or their owners inhaling the vapors in the collars. If your pet sleeps on your bed, it might be prudent to remove the flea collar until the morning.

Since fleas spend most of their life cycle *off* your cat, controlling or treating the environment is most important to avoid that frustrating "Where are the fleas coming from? I sprayed my cat a month ago!" routine. Vacuum weekly for a few months, especially rugs, upholstery, cracks and crevices, and closets. Throw the vacuum bags away after vacuuming; otherwise, the fleas will hatch in your vacuum, closets, etc. Wash or throw away the cat's bedding. Finally, a commercial insecticide should be sprayed around your house periodically for a few months. If you

Flea Bite Dermatitis

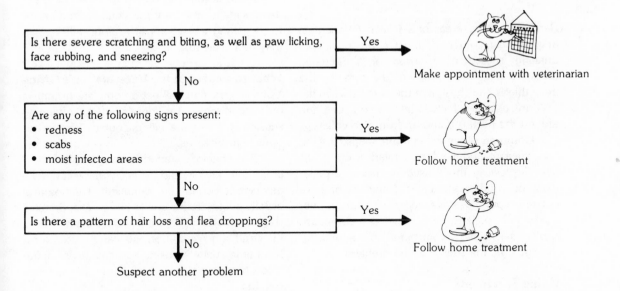

Is there severe scratching and biting, as well as paw licking, face rubbing, and sneezing? — **Yes** → Make appointment with veterinarian

No ↓

Are any of the following signs present:
- redness
- scabs
- moist infected areas

— **Yes** → Follow home treatment

No ↓

Is there a pattern of hair loss and flea droppings? — **Yes** → Follow home treatment

No ↓

Suspect another problem

think it might stain something, test by spraying only a small area first.

Your cat should be treated from the end of the winter through the first frost if you live in a varied climate.

What to Expect at the Veterinarian's Office
If you have tried everything and your cat is still scratching, see your veterinarian. He or she will make sure that none of the "rule-outs" are present. If a flea bite allergy is suspected, corticosteroids, which can reduce or stop the itching, will be prescribed. If there are open sores, your doctor may give you antibiotics, a medicated shampoo and topical ointment to use. Be sure to discuss flea control for the pet *and* the house to avoid a recurrence of the problem.

Contact Dermatitis

Reddened, itchy areas of skin can be seen on any cat that comes in direct contact with an irritating substance. Hairless or thin-coated areas, such as the abdomen, the armpits, the inner thighs, the chest, and the area between the toes are usually affected. In addition, irritation around the neck is common from flea collars.

Common other irritants are soaps, insecticides, flea collars, wool (particularly wool rugs), dyes (especially those used in nylon carpets), paint, or wood preservatives. Have any of these entered your cat's life recently? Poison ivy, poison oak, pollens, and grasses can also cause contact dermatitis. If your pet is on a new drug, this could be the source of the problem.

Home Treatment
First, try to identify the offending substance. If you think you have found the culprit, try to eliminate it from your cat's environment.

To relieve the itching, apply calamine lotion to the red areas three times daily. Cool compresses of Burrow's solution (Domeboro®),

applied for fifteen minutes every six hours, is an alternative. *Note:* Cats should *not* be given antihistamines without your veterinarian's OK.

If the lesions are extensive, if home treatment is ineffective, or if the skin infection seems to be getting worse, a visit to your veterinarian may be necessary.

What to Expect at the Veterinarian's Office
Your veterinarian will get a complete history in order to discover the identity of the offending substance. He or she will, of course, first rule out other skin diseases.

An antibiotic-steriod cream applied four times daily and steroid tablets work well, even if the culprit cannot be identified. Treatment is usually necessary for one to two weeks. Steroids should not be used for long periods of time, but if the condition recurs, steroids can be used for a short time again. Your doctor may advise medicated baths and cold applications of Burrow's solution.

Prevention
Air out a new flea collar for three days before using it, and buy the recommended size for your cat. If a neck irritation is seen, do not use a flea collar.

Contact Dermatitis

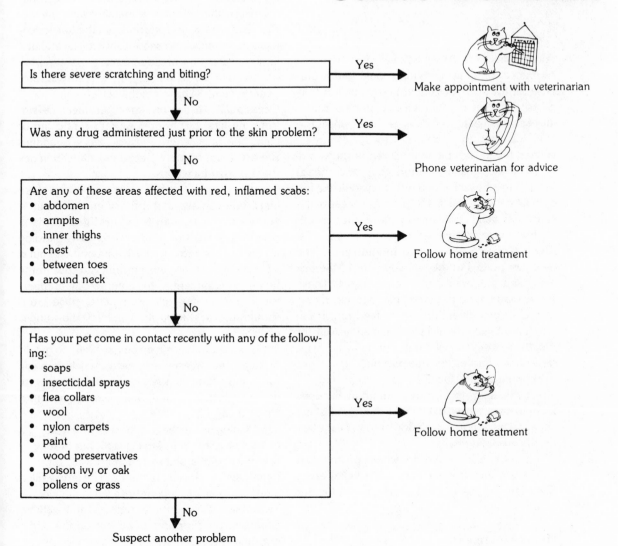

Is there severe scratching and biting? — **Yes** → Make appointment with veterinarian

No ↓

Was any drug administered just prior to the skin problem? — **Yes** → Phone veterinarian for advice

No ↓

Are any of these areas affected with red, inflamed scabs:
* abdomen
* armpits
* inner thighs
* chest
* between toes
* around neck

— **Yes** → Follow home treatment

No ↓

Has your pet come in contact recently with any of the following:
* soaps
* insecticidal sprays
* flea collars
* wool
* nylon carpets
* paint
* wood preservatives
* poison ivy or oak
* pollens or grass

— **Yes** → Follow home treatment

No ↓

Suspect another problem

Ticks

I don't think even Albert Schweitzer, who had a reverence for all living things, could find a purpose for the tick's existence. In my opinion, any parasite that sucks your own or your pet's blood, lays approximately 5,000 eggs, and transmits a fatal disease to humans (Rocky Mountain spotted fever) is not a good citizen of the world!

These disgusting creatures bury their heads in the skin and suck blood until they look like fat, brown beans. At this point, probably because it is so fat that it can't hold on any more, the tick falls off the host and lays the 5,000 or more eggs. The eggs hatch one or two months later. The next two phases in the development of the tick are called the larval and nymph stages. These stages may last quite a long time, because different ticks need different hosts to feed on. In the dormant stages, the ticks can patiently wait for months—or even hibernate during the winter—under bushes, in the ground, or in your own home until a suitable host comes along.

Ticks seem to be more common on dogs than on cats. This may be due either to a distinct chemical attraction for the dog or to the cat's fastidious grooming habits.

Ticks can be found anywhere on the skin but they prefer the ear flaps, interdigital areas (between the toes), head, neck, and shoulder areas.

Home Treatment

Tick removal is surrounded by many myths and old wives' tales. Some of the popular methods—using a match to burn off the tick or using gasoline or kerosene—are overkill: They will get rid of the tick, but they may also injure your cat! Instead, just grasp the tick close to where it is embedded with your fingers or tweezers (by the way, a tick does *not* get its whole body under the skin!) and firmly pull it out. Soaking the tick with alcohol or nail polish remover (*acetone*) will plug up its breathing holes and make removal easier.

Burn the tick with a match *after* removal. Please do not flush one tick down the toilet; ecologically, it makes no sense to waste several gallons of water on one tiny insect.

After a tick is pulled out, a scab will form over the area. (This is not the tick growing back!) Occasionally, a tick bite may get infected—not from the bite, but from your cat's scratching or biting the area where the tick was embedded. Read the appropriate Decision Chart for treatment of skin infections.

Since female ticks can lay 5,000 or more eggs, you can see that if those eggs are laid in your home or kennel, a serious infestation will occur. (The sight of thousands of ticks crawling up the walls is enough to tick anybody off!) Your veterinarian can dispense products to use in the home environment. The commercial products found under flea bite dermatitis, page 162, should also help keep the tick infestation under control.

An exterminator may be necessary to get rid of heavy tick infestations, because ticks can live for a long time in the cracks and crevices of floors, woodwork, and walls without having a blood meal.

"Chiggers" is the popular name for the red or harvest mite. In its larval stage, it is orange or red, the size of a pinhead, and parasitic on most mammals (dogs, cats, humans). The larvae hitch a ride on your leg or your pet's leg in the woods. Their bite causes severe redness and itching. Chiggers can be found anywhere on the body, but their favorite hangouts are the head, neck, ear canals and flaps, and abdomen. After getting a good blood meal, the larvae drop off and become nymphs. Later they develop into adult chiggers, which feed on plants. The adult chigger lays eggs that develop into larvae, which are the only parasitic form.

If only the ears are affected, use the same treatment for ear discharges (page 182). Your veterinarian will dispense a safe insecticidal prep-

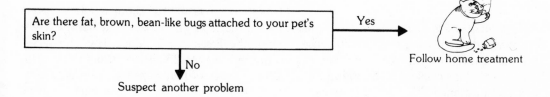

Are there fat, brown, bean-like bugs attached to your pet's skin? **Yes** → Follow home treatment

↓ **No**

Suspect another problem

aration if a generalized infestation is present. An antibiotic-steroid cream will control the itching.

You can prevent chigger problems on your cat by using an insecticidal preparation during warm weather (the same as for fleas, page 162).

The white mite known as "walking dandruff" is large enough to see. This mite causes itching and can affect cats, humans, and dogs. The same insecticides administered for fleas, used for about three weeks, are effective.

The adult fly and its larvae (*maggots*) occasionally cause skin problems. Maggots develop from eggs that are laid by flies. If they are in wounds, remove them with tweezers. Clean the area with Phisohex® and apply an antibiotic ointment to the wound.

Lice look like very small white oval specks that are seen best with a magnifying glass. They are spread by direct contact and cause severe itching. They spend their whole life cycle on the pet. Fortunately, lice are not seen very often on cats. A bath is effective. After drying, an insecticide can be used.

Rodent Ulcer

It seems to me unfair that rodents have their names attached to a disease they do not cause. In fact, the cause of rodent ulcer is not known, although researchers conjecture that the cause is either a derangement in the immune system or a virus.

Rodent ulcer is a thickened, red, and ulcerated sore most commonly found on the upper lip. Other areas that may be affected are the inside of the mouth, the spaces between the digits, the skin of the belly, and the back of the rear legs.

Home Treatment
See your veterinarian as soon as possible, because early treatment is extremely important.

What to Expect at the Veterinarian's Office
Most diagnoses of rodent ulcer are made easily, by inspection. But sometimes the veterinarian needs to perform a blood test or a biopsy (see page 68) to confirm the diagnosis.

If the infection is not too extensive, your veterinarian will inject corticosteroids directly into the sore and/or prescribe corticosteroid tablets to be taken for about a month. Most rodent ulcers will disappear if treated early—at least, the first time. Unfortunately, the recurrence rate is 10 to 25 percent within six months. Other modes of treatment for recurring rodent ulcers are *megestrol acetate* (Ovaban®), agents that stimulate the immune system, radiation therapy, and surgery. *Note:* Megestrol acetate (Ovaban®) should *not* be used in intact females. Although it works well, it can have some side effects, such as increased appetite, water intake, urination, and weight gain. One cat treated with Ovaban® developed hypothyroidism.

This disease requires patience from the veterinarian, the owner, and the cat because treatment is sometimes lengthy (in fact, a cat should be treated for at least a month with one agent before another drug is tried) and recurrences are not uncommon. But it is so satisfying to see the rodent ulcer respond to treatment and *never* come back.

Rodent Ulcer

Is there a red, ulcerated sore on the lips or elsewhere?

Yes ───────►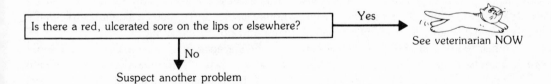

See veterinarian NOW

No ↓

Suspect another problem

Feline Acne

Some cats have a tendency to get bacterial infections (*acne*) on the chin. There are numerous oil glands in this area, and oil and dirt may accumulate, causing blackheads and inflammation around the hair follicles and oil glands. This can progress, if not treated, to a deep skin infection.

The cause of feline acne is not known. Cleanliness may be a factor, since lazy chin cleaners seem to have more infections. A genetic predisposition is probably involved as well, since the condition is seen frequently in littermates and their parents.

Home Treatment
Wash daily with Phisohex® or Phisoderm® and rinse thoroughly. A human acne medication containing benzoyl peroxide, such as Oxy-5®, seems to work well, too, but avoid contact with the eyes or mouth. Apply once daily for three days only. If undue skin irritation, flaking, or dryness develops discontinue using the ointment and consult your veterinarian. These products remove the excess oil, cleanse the skin surface, and decrease the bacteria on the skin. If they are not available, apply rubbing alcohol gently to the chin and don't rinse it off.

Feline acne, if treated early, can heal in a week or two. Unfortunately, the condition recurs, but cleaning the chin daily might prevent recurrences. If the chin infection is severe or does not respond to home treatment, see your veterinarian. Occasionally, a ringworm lesion may be found on the chin.

What to Expect at the Veterinarian's Office
Your veterinarian will prescribe antibiotics (for two or three weeks in some cases) and will probably be proud of you for starting the above cleansing program and will encourage you to continue.

Feline Acne

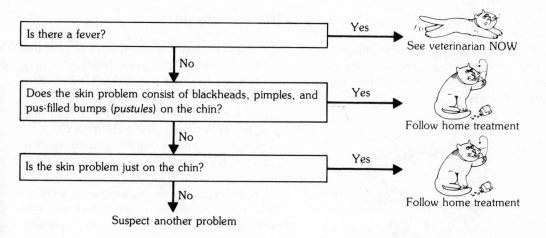

Is there a fever?	**Yes** → See veterinarian NOW
↓ No	
Does the skin problem consist of blackheads, pimples, and pus-filled bumps (*pustules*) on the chin?	**Yes** → Follow home treatment
↓ No	
Is the skin problem just on the chin?	**Yes** → Follow home treatment
↓ No	
Suspect another problem	

Ringworm

Ringworm is a fungus infection of the skin that can be transmitted to your cat by other infected animals, by humans, or by contact with the soil. Pets under one year old and children are more susceptible than adults.

Ringworm lesion

The classic ringworm lesion is a rapidly spreading, circular, hairless, scaly area surrounded by an outer edge that is red. However, ringworm lesions do not always take on the classic form. Your doctor has further tests to verify this diagnosis.

Home Treatment

A single fungus lesion can be treated with *tolnaftate* (Tinactin®), which you can purchase in the drugstore. The pet's bedding, combs, brushes, leashes, and collars should be sterilized or discarded, since reinfection from fungus spores is a constant danger. Clean and vacuum your house and throw the vacuum bag away. If there is more than one small lesion on your cat, see your doctor.

What to Expect at the Veterinarian's Office

Your doctor will use an ultraviolet light (one type of fungus will fluoresce green), a skin scraping, and/or a fungal culture to diagnose ringworm. The treatment of choice for ringworm is topical Tinactin® or Conofite® combined with *griseofulvin*, an oral medication, for at least one month.

Ringworm

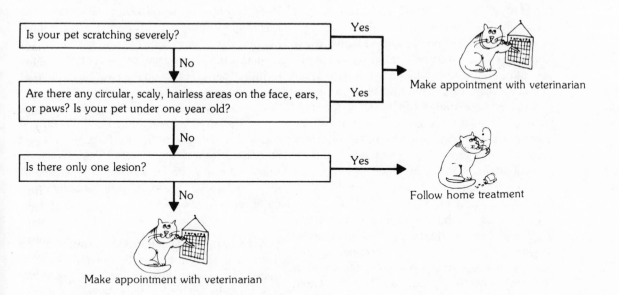

Is your pet scratching severely? — **Yes** → Make appointment with veterinarian

No ↓

Are there any circular, scaly, hairless areas on the face, ears, or paws? Is your pet under one year old? — **Yes** → Make appointment with veterinarian

No ↓

Is there only one lesion? — **Yes** → Follow home treatment

No ↓

Make appointment with veterinarian

Abscesses

An abscess is a walled-off collection of pus caused by a bacterial infection. (Pus is a collection of live and dead bacteria, dead tissue, white blood cells, and other cells called on to defend your pet's body.) Any damage to the skin, especially lacerations or puncture wounds, can admit bacteria into the underlying tissue. If the cat's body cannot fight the bacteria, tissue will be damaged and an abscess will form. An abscess is potentially dangerous: If prompt medical and/or surgical attention is not provided, the infection can spread to the chest, brain, heart, kidneys, or liver via the blood stream.

An abscess is characterized by a warm swelling that is painful to the touch. Your cat may also be lethargic and have a fever. A common occurrence is having a cat brought to the office with a lameness and lethargy that have become worse over a few days. Pressing on each area of the limb, hip, or shoulder may elicit pain. The owner thinks the cat's leg is broken, but a swelling and a scab over a healed bite wound can be felt. The cat's rectal temperature can be 104° to 105°F.

Home Treatment

EMERGENCY A cat that has an abscess should be seen by your doctor, since the potential for tissue damage or death from bacterial toxins is high unless proper wound cleaning and/or surgery and antibiotic treatment are done.

If it is impossible for you to see a veterinarian, you will have to treat the abscess at home. If the abscess is open and draining, probe and clean the wound with a cotton-tipped applicator. Remove any hair, wood slivers, or other matter that may be in the wound. Pour a small amount of hydrogen peroxide (3 percent) into the wound, three times daily, or use an eye dropper or turkey baster. Press on the swelling to help the hydrogen peroxide flush the wound.

If the abscess has not burst, apply hot towels to the area to help bring it to a head. When you can feel a soft spot in the swelling, use a clean razor blade to nick the swelling. The pus should drain out easily. Probe and flush the wound as explained above. Try to get your cat on antibiotics as soon as possible.

What to Expect at the Veterinarian's Office

Your doctor will probe the wound for dirt, debris, and foreign material and may flush the abscess with antibiotic, sterile saline, or hydrogen peroxide solutions or surgically *debride* (remove dead and infected tissue) the area. A drain may be left in the wound to allow flushing of the wound for a few days. Antibiotics will be given for one week.

Prevention

Cleaning wounds promptly with soap and water or hydrogen peroxide and gently probing for hair, dirt, or foreign material will prevent many infections (see Cuts and Wounds, page 94).

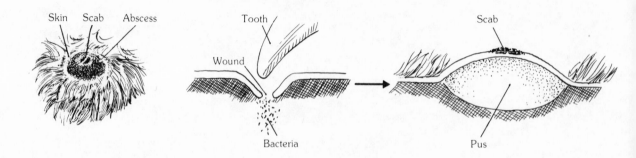

Skin Scab Abscess

Tooth

Wound

Bacteria

Scab

Pus

174

Abscesses

Are any of the following signs present:
- a swelling that is warm and painful to the touch
- lethargy
- fever

Yes →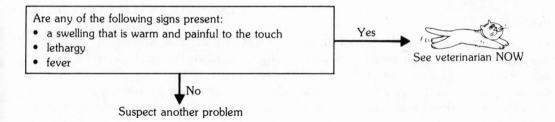

See veterinarian NOW

No

Suspect another problem

Lumps and Swellings in the Breasts

Breast tumors are seen in female cats older than seven years of age. The incidence may be greater in cats who have not been spayed (also called an ovariohysterectomy) before their first heat (see Preventing Pregnancy, page 226). See your veterinarian.

A nursing female can develop an infection in one or more breasts (*mastitis*) in which the breast becomes red, hot, hard, and painful. This may be accompanied by fever and loss of appetite. The cat may lose interest in the kittens, who in turn become restless and weak because of the infected milk.

A mother cat can have engorged breasts after weaning, but they will not be red, hot, hard, or painful. In addition, the cat will remain alert and active and will still eat well.

The breasts may enlarge about two months after the heat period. If the cat is not pregnant, this is due to normal hormone changes. Milk can be produced and other signs of false pregnancy (page 219) can occur.

Home Treatment

If the mother cat has mastitis, your doctor will prescribe antibiotics. *Note:* Do *not* let the kittens nurse, since the antibiotics in the milk could be toxic. This means hand-feeding very young kittens (under two or three weeks old). See page 223 for directions.

Also keep the kittens away if the mother has engorged breasts after weaning, since nursing will stimulate the milk production. Apply cold compresses to the breasts. Improvement should be seen in one to three days; if not, contact your doctor. No treatment is necessary for the slight breast swelling seen in females during the heat cycle.

What to Expect at the Veterinarian's Office

Breast tumors can range in size from smaller than a pea to masses involving the whole gland. They can also be benign (not cancerous) or malignant (cancerous), so see your doctor *early*—do *not* wait for the nodules to get larger. Your doctor will palpate the breast and the adjacent lymph nodes for evidence of malignancy. If the nodule is thought *not* to be a cyst, a radiograph of the chest will be taken to check for the possible spread (*metastasis*) of a malignant tumor. If the X ray is normal, your doctor may recommend surgical removal of the nodule and a biopsy (microscopic examination of a tissue sample) of both it and the adjacent lymph nodes. If the nodule is malignant, further therapy will be considered (see Cancer, page 233).

Mastitis is usually treated successfully with antibiotics.

Lumps and Swellings in the Breasts

Are hard lumps felt in any gland? —— Yes ——▶ Make appointment with veterinarian

No ↓

Is the nursing female's breast red, hot, hard, and painful? —— Yes ——▶ Phone veterinarian for advice

No ↓

Follow home treatment

Lumps and Bumps on the Skin

If the face suddenly becomes swollen, or if bumps appear all over the skin, this is probably an allergic reaction to insect bites (page 98). If a warm, painful, reddish swelling appears anywhere on the skin (common areas are the lower legs, head, or tail base) and your cat is feverish and lethargic, an abscess is probably present (page 174). If the bump moves freely—i.e., it is not attached to the skin underneath—and is not painful or enlarging, follow the Home Treatment.

Home Treatment
If none of the above signs are seen, watch the lump. If its appearance changes or your cat seems uncomfortable, contact your doctor. If no change is seen, ask about the lump on your next visit.

What to Expect at the Veterinarian's Office
If the tumor is benign, such as a *lipoma* ("fatty tumor") or a *sebaceous adenoma* (a cauliflower-gray, hairless growth), your doctor will probably advise no treatment unless it becomes irritated. Any suspicious skin growths should be removed and biopsied. Skin tumors, if malignant, are the most curable cancers.

Lumps and Bumps
on the Skin

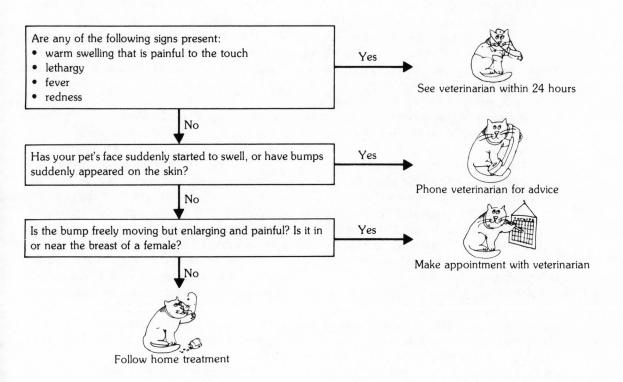

Are any of the following signs present:
- warm swelling that is painful to the touch
- lethargy
- fever
- redness

Yes → See veterinarian within 24 hours

No ↓

Has your pet's face suddenly started to swell, or have bumps suddenly appeared on the skin?

Yes → Phone veterinarian for advice

No ↓

Is the bump freely moving but enlarging and painful? Is it in or near the breast of a female?

Yes → Make appointment with veterinarian

No ↓

Follow home treatment

Eye Discharges

Your cat has only two eyes. Therefore, a seemingly minor eye problem could rapidly turn into a major catastrophe. See your veterinarian *immediately* if the chart so indicates.

If your cat is closing its eye in pain, has irregular pupils, or is bumping into objects, first see Eye Injuries, page 108. A discharge of thick yellowish or green pus indicates conjunctivitis, an inflammation of the membrane that lines the eyelid and part of the eyeball. If fever, cough, or weakness accompanies the conjunctivitis, a systemic disease may be present (see Rhinotracheitis, page 43).

Kittens less than two weeks old whose eyes have not opened yet may get an acute bacterial conjunctivitis. A large reddened swelling will appear under the closed lids. Veterinary attention is needed to flush the eye and to provide the proper medication. If you have to treat it yourself, gently pull the lids apart and flush the eye with clean water three times daily.

If your cat has a watery eye discharge, licks its paws, sneezes, and rubs its face on the floor, see Allergies, page 160. A constant watery discharge that does not seem to bother your pet is probably an abnormal overflowing of tears, called *epiphora*. It is hereditary in certain breeds—Persian cats, for one. The hair in the inner corner of the eye is always moist and stains a dark brown. It can be caused by misplaced eyelashes, blocked tear ducts, nasal fold hairs irritating the eye, or an eyelid defect.

Home Treatment
See your veterinarian today if the chart indicates that this is necessary. Otherwise, mild irritations can be treated with Neosporin® or Neopolycin® *ophthalmics* (for eyes only!). Follow the directions for human use.

If your cat has a "pushed-in" face and the nasal fold hairs seem to be irritating the eyeball, it may help to press down the nasal fold hairs with a little bit of vaseline.

What to Expect at the Veterinarian's Office
Your veterinarian will check the eyelids, vision, reaction of the pupil to light, and the inner eye with a special magnifier that has its own light source, called an *ophthalmoscope*. A green dye called *fluorescein* is used to see if the tear ducts are open and if the cornea is healthy. A complete physical will also be done, since the eye infection may be part of a systemic disease.

Antibiotic eyedrops or ointments are frequently given for eye infections. Cortisone-type eye medicine should be prescribed very infrequently, since certain infections (such as herpes) may get worse with these medicines. If herpes is diagnosed, special eyedrops and other medicines will be needed.

Misplaced eyelashes or eyelid defects may have to be corrected surgically. Blocked tear ducts may need to be flushed out if the medication is not working.

Eye Discharges

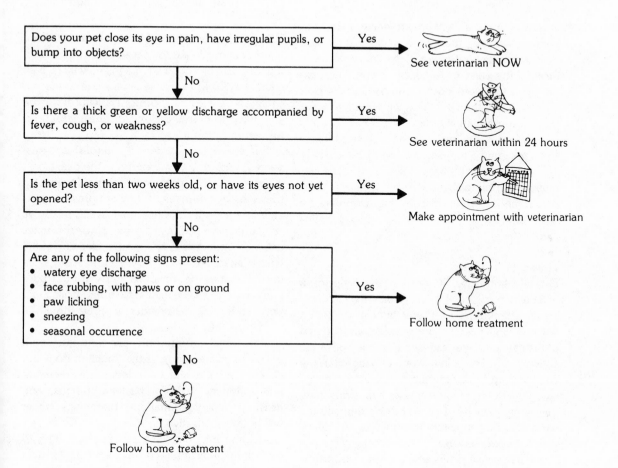

Does your pet close its eye in pain, have irregular pupils, or bump into objects?   **Yes** → See veterinarian NOW

No ↓

Is there a thick green or yellow discharge accompanied by fever, cough, or weakness?   **Yes** → See veterinarian within 24 hours

No ↓

Is the pet less than two weeks old, or have its eyes not yet opened?   **Yes** → Make appointment with veterinarian

No ↓

Are any of the following signs present:
- watery eye discharge
- face rubbing, with paws or on ground
- paw licking
- sneezing
- seasonal occurrence

Yes → Follow home treatment

No ↓

Follow home treatment

Ear Discharges

A small amount of light brown, waxy material in your cat's ears is probably normal. It is produced by glands in the outer part of the ear canal and it protects the ear canal and ear drum. The next time you visit your doctor and the ear exam is normal, smell the ears. You will then know the odor of a normal ear.

Ear infections may exhibit a slight redness, some pus, and a foul-smelling odor. Head shaking and ear scratching are also seen. The ear may be painful to the touch. If this happens, be sure to check the ear flap for bite wounds or a *hematoma* (a tumor or swelling that contains blood).

Home Treatment
Ear infections usually require the help of a veterinarian, since the cat's ear canal is complexly shaped. If you are unable to see a veterinarian, clean the inner ear flap and the part of the canal that you can see with baby oil and a cotton swab. Use a few drops of baby oil in the ear canal and massage the ear to break up the wax and debris. Hold the ear flap straight up over your pet's head so you don't damage the ear drum and gently remove any wax and debris with the cotton swab.

Place a few drops of 70 percent isopropyl alcohol in the ear twice daily. Massage the ear canal to be sure that the alcohol makes its way to the bottom of the L-shaped ear canal. If there is no improvement in two or three days, see your doctor. If there is improvement, continue the treatment for ten days.

Thorns or ticks on the ear flap or at the opening of the ear canal can cause your cat to scratch its ear. Use your fingers or tweezers to remove it. Apply 70 percent isopropyl alcohol to the irritated area so that it won't become infected.

If there are no signs of ear infection and a small amount of light-brown waxy material is present, use baby oil or alcohol and a cotton swab to clean the ear as explained above.

What to Expect at the Veterinarian's Office
Your doctor will find the cause of the ear inflammation. An otoscope (a magnifier with a light source) will be used to examine the entire ear canal and ear drum. Some pets with very sore ears have to be tranquilized or anesthetized for this examination.

If ear mites (*otodectes cyanotis*) are suspected, your doctor will examine the dry, black, waxy material under the microscope, looking for the eight-legged mites. If they are present, your veterinarian will dispense an insecticidal or oil preparation to put in the ears. Since the mites can hide under the debris, proper cleaning of the waxy material is essential for a cure. Also, since the mites may live on other parts of your pet's body and are contagious to other household pets, an insecticidal powder or spray should be used on all the animals.

Bacterial ear infections can be treated with antibiotic preparations. If the infection does not clear up or if it recurs, your doctor will do culture and sensitivity tests for bacteria, fungus, and yeast on the exuded matter so that the treatment will be more effective.

Some ear infections can be frustrating to treat. If the infection is chronic, your doctor may suggest surgery to keep the ear dry and enhance drainage. The success rate of surgery is very high.

Prevention
Keep an eye on the ear! Check your cat's ears weekly for early signs of trouble, such as slight redness. Clean the wax occasionally from the ear canal, but remember that a certain amount of wax is normal and protective. Place cotton in the ears before bathing because soap and excessive moisture may lead to inflammation.

Ear Discharges

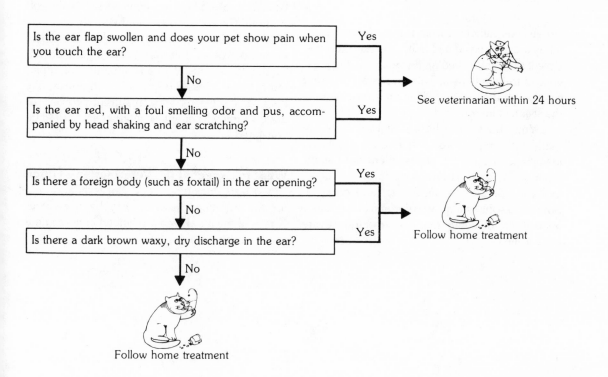

Is the ear flap swollen and does your pet show pain when you touch the ear? — **Yes** →

No ↓

Is the ear red, with a foul smelling odor and pus, accompanied by head shaking and ear scratching? — **Yes** →

See veterinarian within 24 hours

No ↓

Is there a foreign body (such as foxtail) in the ear opening? — **Yes** →

No ↓

Is there a dark brown waxy, dry discharge in the ear? — **Yes** →

Follow home treatment

No ↓

Follow home treatment

Nosebleeds

Nosebleeds can occur from trauma (if your cat is hit by a car or has a bad fall), infection, tumors, violent sneezing, bleeding disorders, or the presence of foreign bodies. The cat has a rich blood supply in the nose, and bleeding can occur with the slightest injury.

You should also be aware that there are many bleeding disorders that are now being identified. In these instances, there are usually other signs, such as red blotches on the gums and ears, pale gums, weakness, and collapse. Some poisons such as Warfarin can cause generalized bleeding that can include severe nose bleeds.

Home Treatment
The cat's nose consists of a bony part and a soft part (the *turbinates*). The area of the nose that is usually involved in nosebleeds lies within the soft portion. Cats are nose breathers, so they will naturally resist any attempt to clear the nose, especially when the air passage is blocked. Squeezing the nostril for a few minutes or applying cold compresses or ice across the nose may help. If nosebleeds are a recurrent problem or are becoming frequent, a veterinarian should be consulted.

What to Expect at the Veterinarian's Office
Blood tests, including blood clot tests and tests for autoimmune diseases, may be necessary. X rays of the nasal area are helpful in finding the cause of the nosebleeds.

Nosebleeds

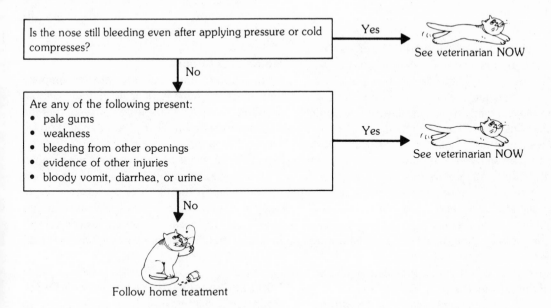

Is the nose still bleeding even after applying pressure or cold compresses? — **Yes** → See veterinarian NOW

No ↓

Are any of the following present:
- pale gums
- weakness
- bleeding from other openings
- evidence of other injuries
- bloody vomit, diarrhea, or urine

Yes → See veterinarian NOW

No ↓

Follow home treatment

Runny Nose

The nose is responsible, in large part, for your cat's perception of the world. A cat's sense of smell is remarkable. All the smells of the world filter through it—but so do viruses, bacteria, pollens, and, sometimes, thorns. These "invaders" can cause a runny nose. Nasal secretions contain antibodies and tissue fluid that fight these unwanted particles and flush them outside the body. The sneeze is a remarkable reflex in your cat's body to attempt to expel the irritant.

If your cat's nose and eyes have a thick yellowish discharge and your pet is lethargic, breathing heavily, coughing, and/or has a fever, a serious respiratory infection, such as rhinotracheitis, may be present.

A discharge from one nostril may be due to a thorn or other object that has lodged in the nose as your cat inspected its environment. Older cats can have sinus infections or tumors involving one side of the nose. An uncommon cause of runny noses in cats is allergies.

Cats with a clear, watery nasal discharge and sneezing will often have other signs simultaneously, such as paw licking, face rubbing, watery eyes, and scratching. This problem lasts longer than a viral infection (often for weeks or months) and occurs most often seasonally, when pollen particles or other allergies are in the air. House dusts and molds may aggravate the allergic runny nose.

Whether your pet's nose is cool and moist or warm and dry is not a good indication of its health or body temperature.

Home Treatment

Since the cat's nasal passages are so complex, any infection there is difficult to treat without your veterinarian's help. If you suspect that the problem may be an allergy, see that section for more information.

You will need to contact your veterinarian to treat respiratory infections properly. Increase the humidity in the air with a vaporizer, especially in a small room, such as the bathroom, to help liquefy the nasal discharge. Humidifiers also help stop irritation when heated air dries out the respiratory passages.

What to Expect at the Veterinarian's Office

Your doctor will make a thorough examination of your cat's nose, mouth, and throat. If a respiratory infection is suspected, antibiotics may be dispensed. Steroids and/or antihistamines will help if the runny nose is an allergic sign. A foreign body in the nose must be removed, with or without anesthesia.

Severe respiratory infections, trauma, or poisoning may demand more intensive treatment, laboratory tests, and radiographs (X rays).

Runny Nose

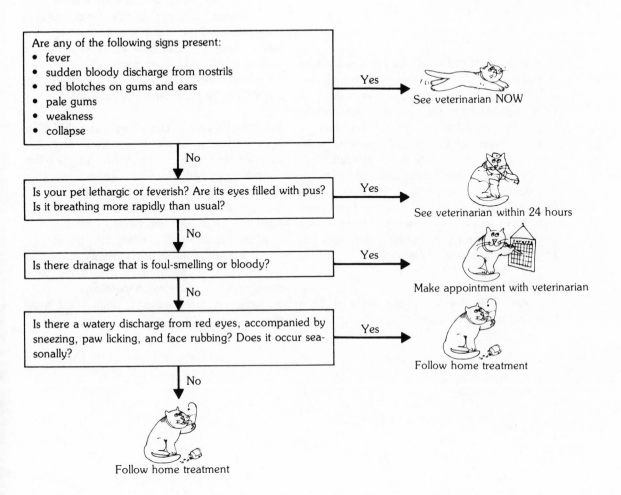

Are any of the following signs present:
- fever
- sudden bloody discharge from nostrils
- red blotches on gums and ears
- pale gums
- weakness
- collapse

Yes → See veterinarian NOW

No ↓

Is your pet lethargic or feverish? Are its eyes filled with pus? Is it breathing more rapidly than usual?

Yes → See veterinarian within 24 hours

No ↓

Is there drainage that is foul-smelling or bloody?

Yes → Make appointment with veterinarian

No ↓

Is there a watery discharge from red eyes, accompanied by sneezing, paw licking, and face rubbing? Does it occur seasonally?

Yes → Follow home treatment

No ↓

Follow home treatment

Coughs

Any irritation of the breathing tubes will trigger one of your cat's best defense mechanisms—the cough reflex. In a cough, a violent rush of air cleans material from the breathing tubes and the lungs. Pollens and pollution can irritate the respiratory system, and even mild irritations to the breathing tubes will initiate the cough reflex.

If your cat's cough is accompanied by fever, difficult breathing, weight loss, low energy, blue gums and tongue, and a history of heart murmur, heart disease, or a malignant tumor, see your doctor. Your pet may have a serious disease needing veterinary assistance.

Home Treatment
To help clear the unwanted material from breathing tubes, use a cool mist vaporizer in the bathroom or take your pet into the bathroom and turn on the hot shower to produce thick clouds of steam. Some relief from the congestion should be seen in fifteen minutes. If there is no improvement, see your doctor. If your pet becomes more distressed in the "steam room" or when using the cool mist vaporizer, stop the treatment and see your doctor. Cough syrup containing just guaifenesin can be used. See Your Cat's Home Pharmacy, page 69.

What to Expect at the Veterinarian's Office
An examination of the throat, neck, and chest will be made. If a pneumonia or lung involvement is suspected, blood tests and a chest X ray will be taken. Antibiotics will be prescribed if a bacterial infection is suspected. Cough depressants may be given if the cough is severe enough to injure the delicate breathing tube lining.

If a heart problem or metastasis (spread) of a malignant tumor is suspected, blood tests, radiographs and an electrocardiogram will be necessary to diagnose and monitor the treatment.

Coughs

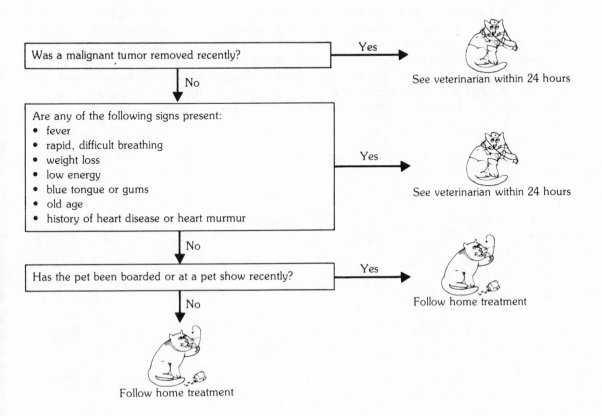

Was a malignant tumor removed recently? — **Yes** → See veterinarian within 24 hours

No ↓

Are any of the following signs present:
- fever
- rapid, difficult breathing
- weight loss
- low energy
- blue tongue or gums
- old age
- history of heart disease or heart murmur

Yes → See veterinarian within 24 hours

No ↓

Has the pet been boarded or at a pet show recently? — **Yes** → Follow home treatment

No ↓

Follow home treatment

Hoarseness

Hoarseness is usually caused by an inflammation of the larynx ("voice box"), a condition called laryngitis. The cat's meow may sound different or may be temporarily lost. Bacterial or viral infections are common causes of laryngitis. So are overworked vocal cords, clearly a factor in the hoarseness of cats that meow constantly when boarded or when on the trail of sexual adventure.

Home Treatment
Time is the best remedy if there is no fever or no other signs of illness. If no improvement is seen in three days, see your veterinarian.

What to Expect at the Veterinarian's Office
If an infection is suspected, blood tests or radiographs of the chest may be needed. For treatment of coughs, see page 188.

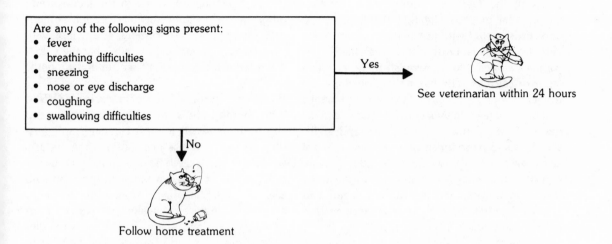

Are any of the following signs present:
- fever
- breathing difficulties
- sneezing
- nose or eye discharge
- coughing
- swallowing difficulties

Yes → See veterinarian within 24 hours

No → Follow home treatment

Mouth Odor

Bad breath in cats is commonly due to problems involving the teeth and gums. Cats develop *plaque* (the mucous film that develops if you don't brush your teeth) just as humans do. Since very few owners brush their pets' teeth, the plaque hardens into a brownish material called *tartar* or *calculus*. The tartar that you *don't see* (under the gum) loosens the delicate membranes that hold the teeth in their sockets, and infections develop around the receding gums and teeth. This is called *periodontal disease,* and it is not easily missed by the owner: The odor is quite powerful, the tartar is prominent on the canine teeth and molars, and the gums are red and swollen. In addition, your cat may drool or have trouble chewing.

Tumors and overgrowth of gum tissue will cause a foul mouth odor. The cat needs veterinary care. A very sweet mouth odor combined with lethargy and increased water intake, urination, and appetite may indicate diabetes. See your doctor and take a urine sample to be checked for sugar.

Cats rarely need to have a cavity filled because they don't get cavities very often.

Home Treatment
Don't worry if your kitten is only a few months old and has "garlic breath"; this is normal. It is caused by certain "good" bacteria that live in the mouth. In a few months this odor will disappear.

Prevention of periodontal disease is important, since chronic mouth infections constantly spread bacteria and toxins to the kidneys and other organs. In time, this takes its toll on your pet. If the tartar is just forming, scrape it off with your fingernail, but keep in mind that the culprit is the tartar that you *don't* see, under the gum.

What to Expect at the Veterinarian's Office
If the mouth odor is caused by dental tartar and gum inflammation, a teeth cleaning (and possibly an extraction) is necessary. Very few cats will tolerate their teeth being scraped by the special instrument called a tartar scraper—and *no* cats will tolerate the ultrasonic teeth cleaners—while they are awake, so sedatives or anesthesia are necessary. If your cat is middle-aged or older, your doctor may perform a blood test to check the health of the kidneys before using a sedative or anesthesia. The heart will be monitored before, during, and after the teeth cleaning.

If teeth need to be extracted or if the teeth and gums are very unhealthy, your doctor will prescribe antibiotics. Since the bacteria can spread through the bloodstream, antibiotics will prevent an infection from developing in the mouth or in some distant organ (the liver or kidney, for instance). They may be started a few days before the teeth cleaning.

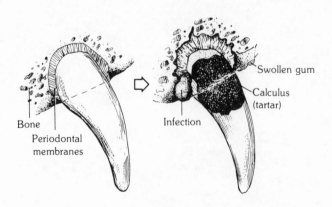

Bone
Periodontal membranes

Infection

Swollen gum
Calculus (tartar)

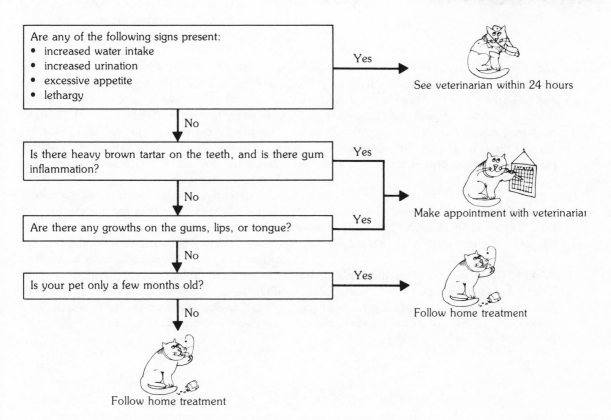

Are any of the following signs present:
- increased water intake
- increased urination
- excessive appetite
- lethargy

Yes → See veterinarian within 24 hours

No ↓

Is there heavy brown tartar on the teeth, and is there gum inflammation?

Yes →

No ↓

Are there any growths on the gums, lips, or tongue?

Yes → Make appointment with veterinarian

No ↓

Is your pet only a few months old?

Yes → Follow home treatment

No ↓

Follow home treatment

Prevention

The time to prevent future dental problems is before tartar forms, or after your doctor cleans the teeth. Cleaning your cat's teeth at least twice weekly with a children's tooth brush or gauze pad is the ideal way of increasing the time interval between professional teeth cleanings. Most cats don't like the foaming and fizzing of human toothpastes, so use a salt-water or bicarbonate of soda solution to clean the outer surface of the gums and teeth. The inner surface collects tartar much more slowly, and since most pets resist the process, don't bother cleaning it. It is best to start this routine when your pet is a kitten. Handle firmly but gently. You can clean the outside of the teeth rapidly, in about thirty seconds.

Set up a regular teeth cleaning schedule with your veterinarian and have him send you a reminder card. Some cats need a teeth cleaning every six months; others can go a year or two between cleanings.

I'm not a big believer in hard bones, hard rubber toys, dry food, or hard biscuits that purport to clean teeth. If these *were* helpful, I'm sure your dentist would suggest that you chew on a soup bone while you're watching television.

Shortness of Breath

Cats pant in hot weather to regulate their body temperature. They also pant when they are frightened or nervous. These are normal body reactions and are *not* shortness of breath. If your cat is truly having trouble breathing in or breathing out and is gasping for breath, there is probably a serious obstruction in the chest or breathing tubes.

Home Treatment
EMERGENCY Give artificial respiration (page 84) and see your veterinarian immediately.

What to Expect at the Veterinarian's Office
Your veterinarian will perform a careful examination of all systems. Your pet may need oxygen at this time. If there has been evidence of trauma (such as an auto accident), X rays will be taken when your cat is stabilized. An outdoor pet that has no fever and sudden breathing problems may have a chest injury from being in a fight or hit by a car.

An old cat with a history of coughing and heart disease who develops sudden shortness of breath may have a failing heart. Cardiomyopathy (a sudden degeneration of the heart muscle of a cat at any age) can also cause the heart to fail. Oxygen and drugs are necessary to strengthen the heart. Electrocardiograms and X rays are indicated.

There are other common diseases that your doctor will consider if your cat has shortness of breath: eclampsia in nursing cats (page 224), anemia, internal hemorrhage from bleeding disorders or trauma (page 110), fever from infection or heat stroke (page 118), tumors (page 237), or feline infectious peritonitis (page 134). Hospitalization is almost always necessary for a pet that has shortness of breath.

Shortness of Breath

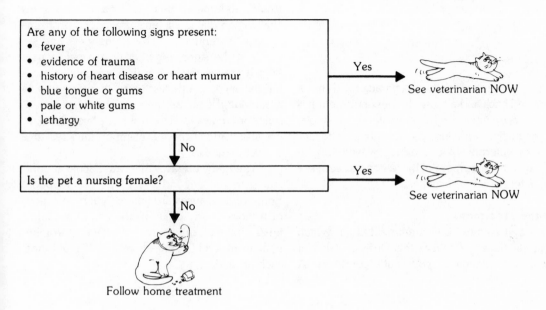

Are any of the following signs present:
- fever
- evidence of trauma
- history of heart disease or heart murmur
- blue tongue or gums
- pale or white gums
- lethargy

Yes → See veterinarian NOW

No ↓

Is the pet a nursing female?

Yes → See veterinarian NOW

No ↓

Follow home treatment

Acute Abdominal Pain

Acute abdominal pain is characterized by a hunched back and a tense, tender abdomen. It is often accompanied by bloody vomit or stools, unproductive vomiting, painful attempts to urinate or defecate, bloody urine, or weakness in the legs. If one or more of these signs is seen, see the veterinarian *immediately*.

Home Treatment

The best treatment is no treatment at all. Watch your cat closely. Recheck this Decision Chart if there is a change in your cat's condition. A phone call or visit to your veterinarian may be necessary.

What to Expect at the Veterinarian's Office

Acute abdominal pain is one of the most challenging diagnostic and procedural problems for your veterinarian. The suddenness and severity of the signs, coupled with a pet in pain (which makes the physical exam difficult) calls for patience, gentleness, and thoroughness to determine if your pet needs to be treated medically or surgically. The history, physical exam, lab tests, and X rays are important keys to a correct diagnosis.

The many diseases that cause acute abdominal pain are beyond the scope of this book. Some of the causes are inflammation, infection, or tumors of any organ in the abdomen; intestinal, urinary, or arterial blockage (thromboembolism); and the ingestion of certain poisions, such as lead.

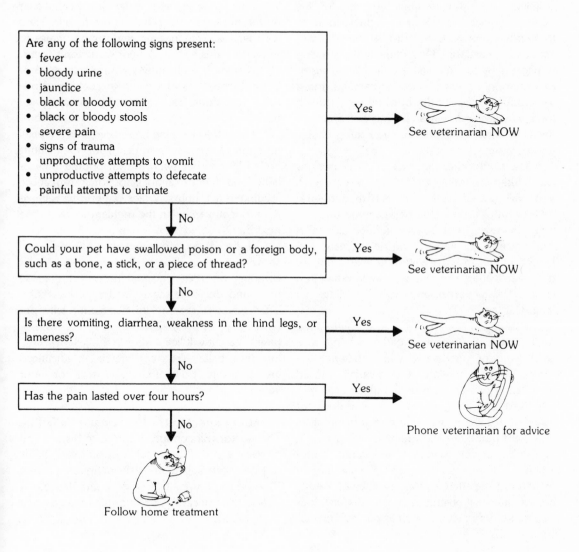

Acute Abdominal Pain

Are any of the following signs present:
- fever
- bloody urine
- jaundice
- black or bloody vomit
- black or bloody stools
- severe pain
- signs of trauma
- unproductive attempts to vomit
- unproductive attempts to defecate
- painful attempts to urinate

Yes → See veterinarian NOW

No ↓

Could your pet have swallowed poison or a foreign body, such as a bone, a stick, or a piece of thread?

Yes → See veterinarian NOW

No ↓

Is there vomiting, diarrhea, weakness in the hind legs, or lameness?

Yes → See veterinarian NOW

No ↓

Has the pain lasted over four hours?

Yes → Phone veterinarian for advice

No ↓

Follow home treatment

Vomiting

Vomiting is a reflex by which your cat forcibly expels stomach or upper intestinal contents through the mouth. Cats have "sensitive" stomachs and vomit easily. Most of the time, vomiting is triggered by a mild irritation called *acute gastritis,* commonly caused by eating garbage, moist cat food that stays in the bowl all day, spoiled food, tin foil, and bones. If your pet does not have any other signs of illness you can probably use the Home Treatment.

There are other fairly common causes, as well. While grooming itself, your cat can catch and swallow a lot of hair with its barbed tongue. These clumps of hair (hair balls) can accumulate in the stomach and be vomited occasionally. Any pet that gobbles its food or overeats may have vomiting episodes a short time after eating. Excess salivation and vomiting while riding in a car is called motion sickness (see Traveling with Your Cat, page 56).

Two misconceptions should be mentioned here. First, cats sometimes gag and bring up a small amount of foamy, white material but remain normal afterward. This is usually caused by irritation in the throat area and is *not* vomiting. Second, if your pet eats grass and does not vomit, it usually means only that your pet likes grass, not that there is something wrong.

See your veterinarian if the Decision Chart advises a visit. Vomiting can indicate inflammation of the pancreas, the presence of foreign bodies, intestinal obstructions, liver disease, kidney failure, or infections such as panleukopenia.

If your cat is on medication and is vomiting, call your doctor, since the medication may be causing it. Vomiting will also interfere with the absorption of the medicine that your pet is taking.

Home Treatment

Take away food *and* water for twenty-four hours, but give your cat ice cubes to lick. They will decrease the nausea and supply water in small amounts so that dehydration won't occur.

Maalox®, Mylanta®, Kaopectate®, or Pepto-Bismol® can be given to coat the stomach. See Your Cat's Home Pharmacy, page 69.

Once the vomiting has stopped, feed small amounts of chicken broth (from boiled chicken), *boiled* hamburger (with the fat poured off), or baby food. If your cat does not vomit, repeat the feeding in two hours. Water can also be reintroduced. You can begin the regular diet again the next day.

If the cat occasionally vomits hair balls and shows no other signs of illness, more regular combing and brushing will remove the loose hairs and decrease the formation of hair balls. Smear ½ teaspoon white petroleum jelly per ten pounds of body weight on the cat's nose or paw. The cat will lick it off and the jelly will coat the hair ball. Also, commercial medications are available from your pet store or your veterinarian.

What to Expect at the Veterinarian's Office

The doctor will conduct a complete history and physical exam. If your cat is dehydrated, fluids will be given subcutaneously or intravenously. Blood tests, a urinalysis, a stool sample, and X rays may be necessary to determine the cause of the vomiting.

198

Vomiting

Are any of the following signs present:
- fever
- black or bloody vomit
- lethargy, weakness
- unproductive retching
- severe abdominal pain
- frequent unsuccessful attempts to urinate
- bloody stools

Yes → See veterinarian NOW

No ↓

Is your pet taking any medication?

Yes → Phone veterinarian for advice

No ↓

Follow home treatment

Diarrhea

One of the most common problems in cats is diarrhea, the elimination of watery, runny, or soft stools. Usually, the condition lasts for only twenty-four to thirty-six hours and home treatment is fine, unless the diarrhea persists and your pet gets severely listless. If your cat has bright red blood in the stools, black, tarry stools, severe abdominal pain, or fever, or if it persistently vomits or attempts to vomit, see your veterinarian promptly.

Sometimes medication such as antibiotics can change the number and kind of bacteria that normally live in your pet's intestines. This can cause diarrhea. If your cat is on medication, call your veterinarian.

Many cats do not have enough of an enzyme called *lactase*, which breaks up a large sugar molecule in milk called *lactose*. Consequently, the lactose "pulls" water into the intestinal tract to soften the stools.

Very often diarrhea is caused by diet—i.e., by eating "exotic" things, such as garbage, tin foil, candy, the family's table food (especially spicy foods), and bones. Excess fat in the diet, or sudden pet food changes, can sometimes cause diarrhea as well.

Worms and other intestinal parasites can irritate the intestine and cause diarrhea that is sometimes bloody.

Kittens with diarrhea may quickly develop severe fluid losses. Be sure to maintain adequate fluid intake. Assessing dehydration is discussed on page 31.

If you suspect a chemical or plant to be the cause, see Swallowed Poisons, page 120. However, neither is a common cause of diarrhea.

Home Treatment

You can manage diarrhea by changing the diet and giving Kaopectate® to coat the intestinal tract and firm the stools.

Except for kittens, who have only a small caloric reserve, no food should be given for twenty-four hours. *Note:* Do *not* take away water.

After the one-day fast, you can give small, frequent feedings (four to five small meals) of *boiled* hamburger or chicken with boiled rice for four or five days. Cooked eggs and cottage cheese can then be added. Be sure to bring the food to room temperature before feeding, since food that is too hot or too cold can cause diarrhea. The small, frequent feedings give the intestine enough time to digest the food. Over the next few days, mix this diet with an increasing amount of your cat's regular food.

If the diarrhea persists beyond forty-eight hours, contact your veterinarian.

What to Expect at the Veterinarian's Office

The doctor will conduct a complete physical exam, paying particular attention to the abdomen. Blood tests, a fecal exam, and a urinalysis may be needed if an infectious (panleukopenia) or systemic (kidney disease, diabetes, pancreatitis) disease is suspected. A plain X ray or a barium series may be necessary to define the area of inflammation or the intestinal obstruction (such as string or a rubber ball). Sometimes, *intussusception* (telescoping a loop of the bowel into the adjacent loop of bowel) is obstructing the digestive tract. Intestinal obstruction is not uncommon in kittens and usually requires surgery. Tumors of the intestinal tract in cats can be seen in leukemia.

If your cat is dehydrated, intravenous or subcutaneous fluids may be required.

Prevention

Do *not* give your cat table food (especially spicy food) or milk, if it causes loose stools. Do *not* feed it bones. They serve no useful purpose but they *do* splinter, and the razor-sharp pieces can cut or perforate the intestines.

Have your veterinarian check your cat's stool samples for worm eggs often—particularly at vaccination time.

Do *not* let your cat play with yarn, string or any toys they can chew up or swallow. These can cause a fatal intestinal blockage.

Diarrhea

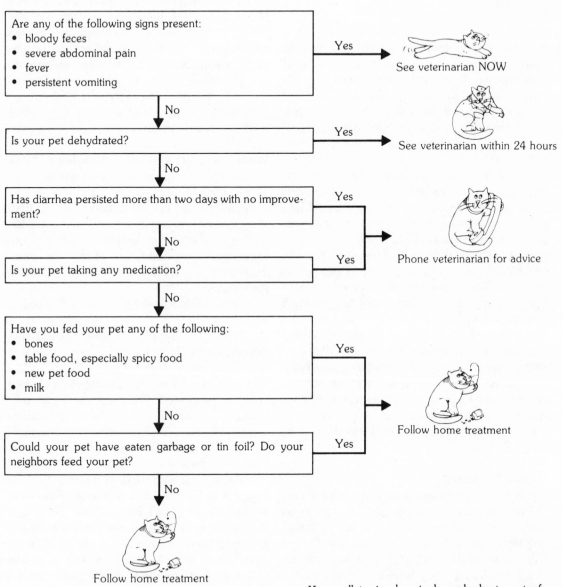

Are any of the following signs present:
- bloody feces
- severe abdominal pain
- fever
- persistent vomiting

Yes → See veterinarian NOW

No ↓

Is your pet dehydrated?

Yes → See veterinarian within 24 hours

No ↓

Has diarrhea persisted more than two days with no improvement?

Yes →

No ↓

Is your pet taking any medication?

Yes → Phone veterinarian for advice

No ↓

Have you fed your pet any of the following:
- bones
- table food, especially spicy food
- new pet food
- milk

Yes →

No ↓

Could your pet have eaten garbage or tin foil? Do your neighbors feed your pet?

Yes → Follow home treatment

No ↓

Follow home treatment

Keep all toxic chemicals and plants out of the way of your cat's curiosity.

Cats that run loose, unsupervised, can get into garbage, poisons, and other disease-causing snacks. You can avoid these situations by confining your pet indoors. House cats have less chance of finding dangerous things to eat.

Constipation

Constipation is characterized by straining to move the bowels or by having infrequent bowel movements. If your cat is not straining and is alert, active, and eating well but has not defecated in two or three days, don't panic. Not even Amtrak is always on time, so why should your cat's bowel movements be on such a strict schedule?

Ingesting bones, wood, or other indigestibles is the leading cause of constipation. Less common causes are the ingestion of hair balls from cleaning themselves and the slower intestinal movements of older animals.

A cat that has impacted feces (hard feces in the colon) makes frequent, straining attempts to defecate. The animal may be listless or *anorectic* (without appetite) and may vomit or pass small amounts of blood-streaked, foul-smelling feces. Some long-haired cats get feces stuck and matted over their anus. Consequently, they cannot defecate. This is called *pseudocoprostasis*.

Note: Male cats strain with a urinary blockage that many owners confuse with constipation. If your male cat squats with no elimination, see Painful, Frequent, or Bloody Urination, page 208.

Home Treatment

Take your cat's temperature (page 32). It may be normal or slightly elevated. You can try to relieve mild constipation by adding over-the-counter laxatives such as Metamucil® or Mucilose® to the food. Adding water to a dry food diet may also be helpful. Also try adding mineral oil, which lubricates and softens the stools, to the food. Add 1 teaspoon per ten pounds of body weight, but don't give mineral oil for more than three days—prolonged use decreases the absorption of vitamins. *Note:* Do *not* administer it directly into the mouth, as it is

very bland and may pass into the respiratory system before your cat can cough. Mineral oil in the lungs will cause a pneumonia.

If your cat is straining to pass small amounts of blood-streaked, foul-smelling feces, you can try a pediatric Fleet® enema if your veterinarian recommends it. Follow the directions on the package and stay in touch with the veterinarian.

Pseudocoprostasis is cured very simply by trimming the hair and matted feces from the anus using scissors. Bathe the area and apply a soothing cream if it is irritated.

What to Expect at the Veterinarian's Office

If your cat has impacted feces trapped in the colon, your doctor will perform a complete physical. He or she will palpate the impacted feces in the colon and do a rectal exam. In addition, your doctor may suggest a radiograph to study the extent and cause of the impaction. Sometimes a piece of bone is found lodged in the rectum.

Repeated warm water enemas will probably be necessary to relieve the blockage.

Keep your cat's water bowl filled. Dehydrated pets can have hard, dry feces.

When cats groom themselves, their barbed tongues can capture large clumps of hair, which are then swallowed. These hair balls can contribute to constipation. An oil-based gel such as Laxatone®, Kat-a-lax®, or white petroleum jelly can prevent problems (see Your Cat's Home Pharmacy, page 69).

As your cat ages, so does the muscle in the intestine. It becomes lazy and moves the feces through the intestines much slower. The longer the feces stay in the intestine, the more water is removed from them, making the stool much drier. Give an oil-based gel and mix stewed or raw fruits and vegetables in the food—prunes live up to their reputation! Be sure that an old cat's water bowl remains filled, because adequate fluid intake is very important.

To help prevent pseudocoprostasis, keep the anal area of your long-haired cat clipped of excess hair.

Constipation

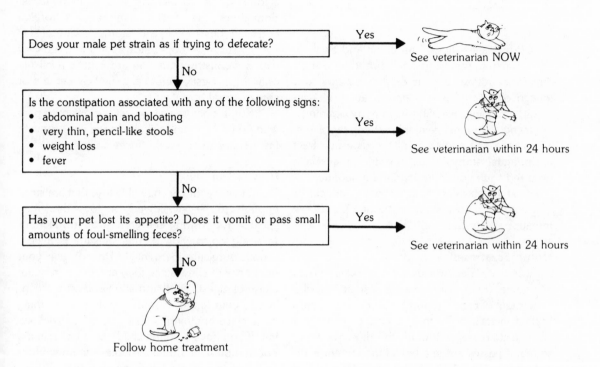

Does your male pet strain as if trying to defecate?

Yes → See veterinarian NOW

No

Is the constipation associated with any of the following signs:
- abdominal pain and bloating
- very thin, pencil-like stools
- weight loss
- fever

Yes → See veterinarian within 24 hours

No

Has your pet lost its appetite? Does it vomit or pass small amounts of foul-smelling feces?

Yes → See veterinarian within 24 hours

No

Follow home treatment

Swallowed Foreign Objects

Cats (especially kittens) can chew and swallow enough paraphernalia to stock a moderate-sized department store. If your cat has swallowed a foreign object and is vomiting or attempting to vomit, coughing, bleeding from body openings, or having abdominal pain or breathing problems, a blockage or perforation of the digestive tract (esophagus, stomach, or intestine) may have occurred. See your veterinarian *immediately*. If your cat has swallowed a known chemical or medicine or a suspected poisonous plant, see the appropriate Decision Charts.

Home Treatment
EMERGENCY You will usually need veterinary assistance. If you cannot reach a doctor, feed a large meal of cat food and bread or cotton balls soaked in milk or broth to coat the object and cushion its passage through the digestive tract, so that it passes out in a bowel movement without causing injury. This is especially important if you suspect that a pin or piece of glass has been swallowed. Check with your doctor as soon as possible and check the feces daily for the object.

What to Expect at the Veterinarian's Office
Your doctor may take plain and barium radiographs to determine the position of the foreign object. Surgery is necessary if the foreign object is too large or too sharp to pass out in the feces. Sometimes the doctor can remove foreign bodies in the esophagus or stomach without surgery, by using a scope. However, these are very expensive instruments and are usually available only at university veterinary medical centers or some central hospitals.

Some doctors will expect the object to pass with no problem and will discharge your cat with instructions to check the feces daily.

Prevention
Do not give your cat chewable toys that are small enough to be swallowed or toys that may splinter. Keep string and yarn away from kittens (a string obstruction of the intestine is a *very* serious surgical emergency). Do not give your pet bones to chew since they are also a frequent cause of digestive inflammation and obstruction. Watch your kittens carefully during the teething stage since anything is "fair game" for swallowing. If you have a young child *and* a kitten in the house, you have double trouble—you need four eyes. After a play period, be sure that all your child's playthings are accounted for and have not been chewed by your pet. After sewing, account for all thread and needles.

Swallowed Foreign Objects

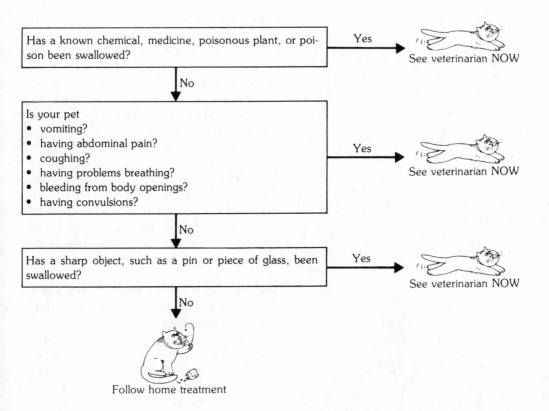

Has a known chemical, medicine, poisonous plant, or poison been swallowed?

Yes → See veterinarian NOW

No ↓

Is your pet
- vomiting?
- having abdominal pain?
- coughing?
- having problems breathing?
- bleeding from body openings?
- having convulsions?

Yes → See veterinarian NOW

No ↓

Has a sharp object, such as a pin or piece of glass, been swallowed?

Yes → See veterinarian NOW

No ↓

Follow home treatment

Anal Problems

Tapeworms (see page 50) can cause itching of the anal area as they pass out the anus. Your cat may lick the anal area, or "sleigh-ride": slide along on its rear-end with the back legs lifted.

Cats have anal sacs located on each side of the anus that are equivalent to the skunk's scent glands and were probably used by your pet's ancestors to spray enemies or to mark a territory. The fluid has a sharp, pungent odor.

Cats seldom have problems with these sacs. The anal sacs are normally expressed when your pet exercises vigorously or moves its bowels. If the secretion in the anal sacs is not emptied by exercise or defecation, impaction and infection can occur. Your pet will lick the anal area and "sleigh-ride" or scoot along the ground. If an infection occurs in one or both sacs, the area adjacent to the anus will become red, swollen,

Holes on anus

Anal sac

and painful. When the abscess ruptures, pus or blood-tinged fluid may drain from it.

An irritation of the anal area can also develop from diarrhea. The fluid is acidic and can scald the anus.

Home Treatment
If the anal sac becomes infected, your veterinarian should treat it.

You may try to treat an impacted anal sac at home. *Note:* Cover the anal area with a tissue or gauze pad when expressing the anal sacs. If the secretions get on your rug or clothes, the smell can be very difficult to remove. Place your thumb and index finger at the 3 o'clock and 9 o'clock positions outside the anal area. Squeeze firmly toward the center. The anal sac contents should exit from holes on the anus.

Anal irritations from diarrhea can be treated by bathing with a medicated soap and applying calamine lotion, white petroleum jelly, or antibiotic ointment.

What to Expect at the Veterinarian's Office
Anal sac infections can be treated by flushing the sac with sterile water and antibiotics. Your doctor may hospitalize your pet for a few days or may treat the animal on an out patient basis. Anal abscesses need more vigorous therapy.

Chronic anal sac infections are best treated by removing the sacs surgically.

Prevention
Since cats express the anal sac while running, regular exercise is very important.

If your pet is prone to impactions, frequent expressing of the sacs by you or your doctor will lessen the chances of anal infections or abscesses.

Flea control and keeping your cat indoors will prevent tapeworms.

Anal Problems

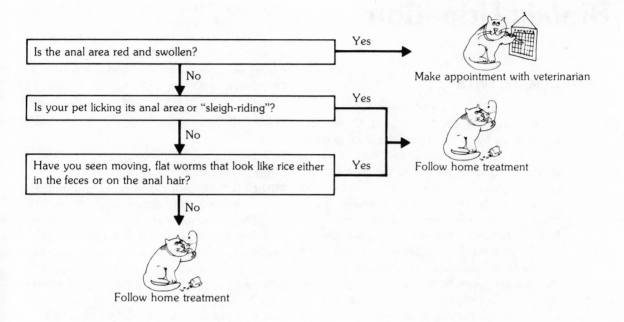

Is the anal area red and swollen? — **Yes** → Make appointment with veterinarian

No ↓

Is your pet licking its anal area or "sleigh-riding"? — **Yes** → Follow home treatment

No ↓

Have you seen moving, flat worms that look like rice either in the feces or on the anal hair? — **Yes** → Follow home treatment

No ↓

Follow home treatment

Painful, Frequent, or Bloody Urination

IN MALE CATS

A common problem in males is an inflammation or infection of the bladder (*cystitis*). Other signs of cystitis are frequent, urgent urination; blood in the urine; frequent licking of the penis; urinating in unusual places—on the carpet, in sinks, on sofas; vomiting; and fever.

Cystitis is frequently complicated by a blockage of the urethra (the tube from the bladder that goes through the penis), usually caused by sand-like crystals (*urolithiasis*). The urethra in the male is very small, and it doesn't take many crystals to cause a blockage. If the blockage is not relieved rapidly, your cat can die of *uremia*, a condition in which the toxic products that are normally eliminated in the urine build up in the blood. Loss of appetite, vomiting, weakness, and dehydration are ominous signs of a very serious situation, such as impending kidney failure or death.

Trauma such as being hit by an auto or being kicked can injure or rupture the bladder. You may see blood in the urine, or perhaps the evidence can be checked only microscopically, by your doctor.

If your pet is urinating more than usual and is drinking excessive amounts of water, diabetes or kidney disease may be the cause.

IN FEMALE CATS

The previous discussion, for males, applies with just a few qualifications. The female's urethra has both an advantage and a disadvantage: The advantage is that the urethra can expand more easily; therefore, the stones and crystals that form can be passed easier and generally without blockage. However, the urethra is also much shorter (the disadvantage); therefore, bacteria from the outside have an easier time invading the bladder and causing troublesome and recurrent bacterial infections.

Female cats in heat will occasionally urinate in unusual places. This is probably caused by sexual excitement or by a mild temporary inflammation of the urinary opening. If your pet seems to be healthy and happy but the strange urination doesn't stop in a few days, see your veterinarian.

Home Treatment

EMERGENCY   If your cat is straining to urinate, seek veterinary aid *immediately*. A cat that hasn't been able to urinate for twenty-four hours may die. If your male cat is urinating a good stream, but there is blood in the urine, you should see your veterinarian. It may be only an inflammation or infection of the lower urogenital tract (bladder, prostate, or urethra), but it could lead to a blockage. Give your pet vitamin C or cranberry or tomato juice to drink to acidify the urine (see Your Cat's Home Pharmacy, page 69). Either will act as a natural antibiotic if bacteria are present. Most cats like tomato juice better than the sweet cranberry juice.

What to Expect at the Veterinarian's Office

Try to collect a urine sample: Place only a few granules of kitty litter in a clean, dry litter box. Transfer the urine thus collected to a clean, dry container. Refrigerate the sample if your appointment is an hour or more away from collection time.

Your veterinarian will perform a complete physical examination. If there is a partial or complete obstruction of the urethra, the bladder may be as large as an orange and painful to the touch. In this case, your cat will have to be *catheterized* (i.e., a tube will be placed into the urethra) and the blockage of crystals will be dispersed by flushings with sterile water. This procedure is usually done under general anesthesia. (cont.)

Painful, Frequent, or Bloody Urination

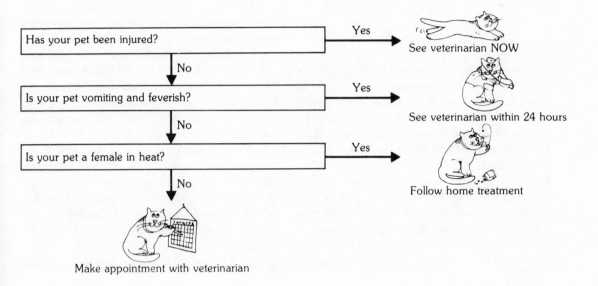

Has your pet been injured?	Yes →	See veterinarian NOW
No ↓		
Is your pet vomiting and feverish?	Yes →	See veterinarian within 24 hours
No ↓		
Is your pet a female in heat?	Yes →	Follow home treatment
No ↓		
Make appointment with veterinarian		

Painful, Frequent, or Bloody Urination

(cont.)

The health of the kidneys may be determined by blood tests before the anesthesia is given. At the time of catheterization, a sterile urine sample may be collected to determine if bacteria are causing or complicating the cystitis and, if so, what antibiotic will be effective. X rays may be taken of the bladder to rule out bladder stones or tumors. Fluids are usually given intravenously or subcutaneously to increase urine flow and to remove the toxic products that were retained during the obstruction. Antibiotics, *antispasmodics* (to relax the muscles of the bladder and relieve pain), and *urinary acidifiers* (if the crystals are found only in neutral or alkaline urine and the kidney tests are normal) will be used. It is necessary to hospitalize and carefully monitor your pet's kidney function and urination.

Urolithiasis is one of the most frustrating conditions that your veterinarian has to treat, and the blockage can recur very easily. Recurrent blockages are best treated with a surgical procedure called a *urethrostomy*, in which a larger opening is made in the urethra. This does not cure the disease but it provides a larger hole for the passage of the crystals and decreases the chance of another blockage. If there are stones in the bladder, they can be removed by *cystotomy* (bladder surgery).

If a bacterial infection is present (this is uncommon), an antibiotic should be prescribed. Months of treatment may be necessary to clear up the infection. Bacteria can move up into the kidney or *seed* (multiply) in the bladder wall and can be difficult to eradicate. Culture, sensitivity, and urine tests—not just the outward appearance of a cure—are important follow-ups. Many times, infections can move up the urinary tract and remain "silent," while slowly deteriorating your cat's kidneys.

If your cat has been injured and there is visible or microscopic blood in the urine, your doctor will want to monitor the damage and repair to the urinary system with blood tests and urinalyses.

Prevention

Since the cause of the male cat's urinary problem is not known, methods for preventing a recurrence are controversial. A few suggestions that seem to help are adding just a pinch of salt to the food to increase water intake and thus increase urination, thereby flushing out the bladder and decreasing crystal formation. Feeding cat foods low in ash (magnesium and other minerals) may help. Both dry and moist cat foods that contain more than 3.5 percent ash (wet weight) should be avoided. Long-term urinary acidifiers may be recommended. Two acidifiers that can be purchased in drug stores or your pet store are DL-

Methionine® (250 mg. three times daily) or ascorbic acid (vitamin C) tablets. One vitamin C tablet (100 mg.) three times daily should acidify the urine. Any long-term medicine should only be given with your doctor's consultation. Litmus paper can be used to check the effectiveness of the acidifiers.

Recurrence of bacterial infections and/or bladder stones may be prevented by antibiotics, acidifiers, or alkalinizers, depending on the type of bacteria isolated and the type of stone formed. Unfortunately, recurrence of these problems is high.

Vaginal Discharge

A serious infection of the uterus in an intact female cat is called *pyometra*. It can occur any time, but it is more common one to two months after a heat period, when the uterus seems to have a better environment for bacterial growth. Your cat may lose its energy and appetite, increase its water intake and urination, and vomit fairly often. You may also notice a fever and a swollen abdomen. If the cervix is open, there will be a yellowish or greenish foul-smelling vaginal discharge. If the cervix is closed and there is no vaginal drainage, rapid deterioration or death can occur. See your doctor immediately. Uterine infections can also be seen a few weeks after the birth of kittens. A red or brownish discharge is present, along with some of the signs seen in pyometra. Again, see your doctor as soon as you can.

An infection of the vagina is not very common in cats.

Home Treatment

No treatment is necessary for the slight mucous discharge of the female just entering or in heat. For other discharges, professional care is necessary.

What to Expect at the Veterinarian's Office

An ovariohysterectomy is the treatment of choice for uterine infections, since in most cases medication is unsuccessful. Pyometra is life-threatening, so immediate surgery is required. Antibiotics and intravenous fluids are usually administered during surgery to prevent systemic infection, shock, and kidney failure that can complicate the problem. Hospitalization is important for monitoring your cat's vital signs afterward.

Prevention

Be sure that your cat gives birth in clean surroundings. If your cat did not have a trouble-free delivery, have your doctor check for retained fetuses or placentas within twenty-four hours, and ask him to give an injection of hormones to involute the uterus.

Watch your cat carefully for one to two months after a heat period. If any signs of pyometra are present, see your doctor immediately.

If you do not intend to breed your cat, schedule an ovariohysterectomy *before* the first heat. Besides eliminating the chance of contracting pyometra, having the procedure done this early may prevent breast cancer (see Lumps and Swellings in the Breast, page 176).

Vaginal Discharge

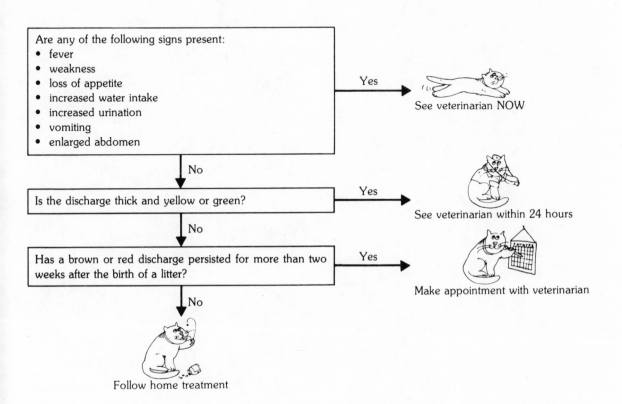

Are any of the following signs present:
- fever
- weakness
- loss of appetite
- increased water intake
- increased urination
- vomiting
- enlarged abdomen

Yes → See veterinarian NOW

No ↓

Is the discharge thick and yellow or green?

Yes → See veterinarian within 24 hours

No ↓

Has a brown or red discharge persisted for more than two weeks after the birth of a litter?

Yes → Make appointment with veterinarian

No ↓

Follow home treatment

Chapter **9**

Breeding and Reproduction

Breeding, pregnancy, delivery, and nursing require a healthy mother cat. This section is provided to make your care easier and more organized before and during breeding and when the cat is pregnant. If all the steps are followed, delivery should be very easy. Most cats have no problems during delivery and nursing, but just in case, a delivery chart is provided to inform you of the general process and to let you know situations when your veterinarian's help might be needed.

BREEDING AND MATING

Once you have decided to breed your cat, the first step is to have it examined by the veterinarian. Besides updating vaccinations (see page 39) and checking for internal parasites (see page 44), your doctor will also be on the lookout for any genetic traits or diseases that might be a problem in the kittens. Your veterinarian might suggest that both cats be tested for feline leukemia and for feline infectious peritonitis. If you have picked your cat's mate, it's wise to collaborate with the other owner so that all pertinent information is available for the physical examination. If the mate hasn't been chosen, ask your veterinarian to recommend a good breeder.

Ideally, the two cats should meet at least once before they mate, preferably at the breeding site. Since male cats can be finicky about breeding away from familiar surroundings, I recommend breeding at the tom's home.

The cat has to be the most passionate creature alive—next to its "friend," the flea, that is. The flea is the champ for longest lovemaking (up to nine hours), but the cat gets the award for most vocal!

Cats have no problem finding a member of the appropriate sex for mating, but many cat owners "can't tell the players without a scorecard." To tell the sex of your pet, first lift up the tail. Below the anus is either a dot (•) or a slit (|). The dot

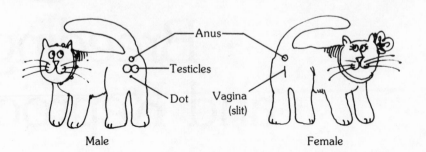

Male   Female

indicates a male cat, the slit a female. Male cats reach sexual maturity in eight months to one year; females from the age of five months to eight months. A mature male (tom) will establish its "territory"—even on another cat's "territory"—by spraying: i.e., backing up to a vertical object, lifting his tail, and squirting urine against it. It could be a neighbor's bush or your antique grandfather clock; the cat isn't particular. Howling, crying, and pacing for a "sweetheart" are also part of a male's repertoire.

For females (queens), the signs of maturity are a little more dramatic, as this scenario indicates:

"Doctor, my cat's dying! I think she was poisoned!"
"What's the matter?"
"She's screaming and rolling on the floor in pain. Now she's crouching, with her tail in the air, still screaming and treading her back feet!"
"How old is she?"
"Six months. I'm afraid she's going to die. . . ."
"She's going to die of a broken heart if she can't mate. Your cat is in heat!"

If the female is not bred, it will be in heat every two or three weeks. Queens are different from other female animals in that their eggs will not be released from the ovary (*ovulation*) until *after* intercourse.

The female selects a mate with a majestic display of vocalizing, rolling, foot treading, and crouching. (Fights may break out if more than one tom wants to mate with a single queen in heat.) The chosen partner grabs the queen by the back of the neck with its teeth. The female crouches and raises its rear end, the tail to one side. The tom thrusts its penis into the queen's vagina, ejaculates, and quickly dismounts, while the female lets out a shrill cry. The tom dismounts quickly because,

"The dating game"

to show appreciation, the female hisses and tries to scratch the mate with its front claws. The two of them may repeat the whole process a few more times.

PREGNANCY

Your female is now probably pregnant, but you should look for certain telltale signs to be sure. First of all, your cat's appetite and body weight will increase. After thirty-five days, the belly and breasts will start to enlarge. A physical exam at this time will confirm pregnancy and monitor the health and nutritional status of the cat.

Your doctor should also tell you when to expect the kittens, and he or she should help you formulate an emergency plan, in case problems arise during delivery.

The phase of pregnancy in which the uterus prepares for the development of the fetuses is called *metestrus*. The egg is released, gets fertilized, and attaches to the wall of the uterus (*implantation*) to grow. Pregnancy lasts an average of sixty-three days after conception. After fifty days milk production will begin, and a few days before your cat gives birth, the breasts may secrete a milklike substance.

BREEDING CHECKLIST

- ☐ Schedule a veterinary exam, for:
    - ☐ intestinal parasites
    - ☐ vaccinations
    - ☐ FLV and FIP
    - ☐ genetic diseases
- ☐ Choose a responsible breeder
- ☐ Introduce the cats before they mate, if possible
- ☐ Let them breed in the male's home, if possible

PREGNANCY CHECKLIST

- ☐ Feed high-quality food:
    - ☐ well-balanced commercial food
    - ☐ high protein supplements (milk products, cooked eggs)
- ☐ Divide the daily ration into 3 or 4 smaller portions
- ☐ Discuss vitamin supplements with your veterinarian
- ☐ Schedule a midgestation veterinary exam, for:
    - ☐ confirmation of pregnancy
    - ☐ health check
- ☐ Let exercise continue, but not unsupervised
- ☐ Avoid giving your cat drugs
- ☐ Arrange the nursing box
- ☐ Have this book handy, open to the Delivering the Kittens chart
- ☐ Have all utensils handy
- ☐ Have your emergency plan ready
- ☐ Stop strenuous exercise 3 days before the due date

If the pregnant queen does not seem to be in good condition, your doctor may perform a few blood tests, such as hemoglobin and serum protein, and suggest supplementing the daily balanced diet. Undernutrition is a major factor in the birth of kittens that are too small to survive the postnatal period. Also, an undernourished cat may not care for the kittens properly, and the milk production may be inadequate.

For healthy cats, a normal commercial cat food diet should provide adequate nutrients, although supplements of high-quality proteins, such as milk products and cooked eggs, certainly won't hurt. Vitamin and mineral supplements are a rather controversial topic; I suggest you discuss this with your cat's doctor.

The primary difference in the pregnant cat's diet is that the queen needs more food, more calories, and more protein during the second month of pregnancy. Divide the total daily ration into three or four smaller meals to aid digestion (see Nutrition, page 33).

Exercise is beneficial—it will keep your cat from getting too heavy and having a difficult delivery. Therefore, do not at first restrict exercise, but don't let the cat roam far without supervision. Most queens will themselves limit their exercise as the pregnancy progresses, but you should restrict all strenuous exercise three days before the expected delivery.

Drugs taken during pregnancy are potentially dangerous to the fetuses. Consult your veterinarian before giving your pregnant cat any medication. Some medications to avoid are aspirin, Tylenol®, acetaminophen, antihistamines, antibiotics (especially tetracycline, kanamycin, streptomycin, and sulfa drugs), hormones, tranquilizers, and most worming medications.

False Pregnancy

Although it is rare, some females may experience a false pregnancy: They have all the signs of the "real thing"—even labor pains—but no kittens are born. In their place, the "mother" will drag slippers, socks, or other soft objects into the "nest," wherever it is. In fact, the "babies" may even be shredded clothing or newspapers.

To check the reality of your queen's signs, palpate the abdomen very gently after thirty-five days have elapsed. If you can't feel anything, or if your cat is especially large or fat, your veterinarian can help you tell for sure. An X ray may be necessary to determine the existence of kittens.

If the pregnancy is false, hormone injections can be given to lessen or alleviate the signs, but I suggest that you just wait it out and let your cat "nurse" your slippers. The less hormone therapy, the better, because hormones can effect so many different body processes. However, I recommend spaying to prevent the almost certain recurrence of false pregnancy—probably after the very next heat.

PREPARING FOR DELIVERY

Introduce your queen to the maternity box two weeks before delivery. It should be large enough for the cat to stretch out and nurse the kittens comfortably. The sides should be high enough to keep the kittens inside, but low enough for the mother to get in and out. Line the bottom with several layers of newspaper, towels, or sheets, but whatever is used, clean the box regularly. Be sure that any material that lines the bottom goes to the edge of the box so that the newborn kittens will not get caught underneath and smother.

The temperature in the maternity box should be about 80°F, because chilling is a frequent cause of kitten mortality. Since newborn kittens have a difficult time regulating their own temperature, a 250 watt infrared (heat) bulb can be placed above the box, so that half of the box is heated. (Otherwise, a nearby radiator or electric heater may be adequate.) Attach a thermometer to the box to monitor the temperature. The "delivery room" should be a familiar area—perhaps the cat's regular sleeping area—as long as it's warm and draft-free. Place the maternity box there.

After all your preparations, the mother cat may just decide that your own bed or closet is the best choice! If this happens, gently place it back in the maternity box. If the cat still insists on delivering elsewhere, let it. You can move mother and children back to the box later.

The "delivery room" should also be supplied with:

- this book, open to the delivery section
- thread dipped in alcohol
- scissors dipped in alcohol
- warm, rough towels
- a bowl of water for the mother
- your veterinarian's phone number

After delivery, do not disturb the maternity box, especially if it's the cat's first pregnancy. Some mother cats, if they are disturbed, will attack those in the room or even eat their own young during the first few days after birth. Of course, each cat is an individual and many will be happy to have you around as long as you are quiet and gentle, so play it by ear. Clean the box after the third day.

Delivering the Kittens

First signs:
- Rectal temperature drops to 98° to 100°F.
- Restlessness, pacing, panting, loss of appetite, and nesting behavior are exhibited.
- Milk may appear at the nipples.

Lasts more than 24 hours →

Phone veterinarian for advice

Within 24 hours:
- A straw-colored liquid may appear at the vulva.
- Labor (straining and intermittent contractions) begins.

No kitten within 1 hour →

Phone veterinarian for advice

Within 1 hour:
- Kittens pass down birth canal.
- Amniotic sac breaks on delivery or the mother chews open the sac and chews off the unbilical cord.
- Kittens breathe on their own.

DELIVERING THE KITTENS

In general, your assistance won't be required, but it's a good idea to be there, if the mother cat will endure your presence, to monitor the process in case something goes wrong. Keep the area quiet, especially if this is your cat's first time; talk in whispers and avoid bright lights.

When the kitten is born, it may or may not be enclosed in the amniotic sac. The mother cat should chew open the sac immediately so that the kitten can breathe, and stimulate the kitten by licking it. The mother should then chew apart the umbilical cord. After birth, the queen may eat the placenta—that's OK.

If your cat does not chew open the sac immediately, gently tear it open yourself and clean the mucus from the kitten's mouth with your finger. Wait a few minutes to see if the mother chews the umbilical cord. If not, tie it tightly with a piece of thread that has been dipped in alcohol about one inch from the kitten's abdomen. Using scissors that have been dipped in alcohol, cut the cord on the mother's side of the thread. Rub the kitten gently with a clean, soft towel to stimulate circulation and respiration.

Kittens, like humans, may enter this world head first or feet first. If only a part of the kitten shows, wrap a clean cloth around the slippery newborn's body and, as the mother strains, pull it gently all the way out. Relax when the queen does. Call your doctor if you are not able to deliver the kitten.

If a kitten is not breathing, wrap it in a warm towel with its head down (but support the head so it doesn't wobble) and shake it downward. This should stimulate respiration and remove fluid from its breathing tubes. If a breath *still* is not taken, gently blow into the kitten's nose until its chest expands, and try rubbing it in a warm, rough towel to stimulate respiration.

The mother cat may rest anywhere from fifteen minutes to two hours between deliveries. After all the kittens are born, the mother will stop straining. Instead, your cat will comfortably lick and clean the new kittens.

Within twenty-four hours after the delivery, which in most cases occurs with no problems, the mother and kittens may be examined by your doctor. In general, however, most veterinarians don't feel that cats need to be checked or given a hormone injection after a trouble-free delivery. Be sure to keep the kittens warm if a trip to the office is necessary. A snug blanket placed in a box is perfect.

The doctor will palpate the queen's abdomen to make certain all the kittens were delivered. The mother will be given an injection of a hormone (*oxytocin*) to *involute* (shrink) the uterus and to stimulate milk flow from the breasts. Your veterinarian will determine the little ones' sexes, weigh them, and check for birth defects, such as cleft palates, harelips, heart problems, and umbilical hernias.

If there are any problems at all during delivery, *telephone your doctor*. If a kitten is stuck in the birth canal and you have tried gentle help, professional manipulation may unstick the problem. Sometimes an *episiotomy* (an incision between the upper end of the vagina and the anus that enlarges the vaginal opening and eases the birth of the kitten) is necessary.

Occasionally, *uterine inertia* (weak contractions of the uterus) will occur during delivery. If the mother is obese, old, upset by many people in the room, or has been straining for a long time, the uterus may become tired and stop squeezing the kittens out efficiently. Injections of oxytocin may help.

In some instances, a *caesarean birth* (surgical removal of the kittens through the abdominal wall) is necessary. Timing is very important, but the surgery is generally fast and safe. After recovery from the anesthesia, the mother can nurse the kittens and go home. The sutures are removed in ten days.

THE NURSING PERIOD

Usually, this is pleasant for all concerned—mother, kittens, and you. Remember not to disturb your new cat family any more than necessary for about three days. But you *do* have a few important jobs during this time: cleaning the maternity box and the mother's breasts, watching for signs of illness or malnutrition, and initiating solid foods (*weaning*).

The kittens will soil the maternity box, so on the third day, when the mother goes to relieve itself, change the newspapers or towels. Wash the queen's breasts once daily with warm water and a clean wash cloth, but do *not* use soap.

The milk produced during the first twenty-four hours is called *colostrum* and is rich in antibodies that protect the kittens from such diseases as panleukopenia for a few weeks. But if you see any signs of illness, see your veterinarian *immediately*. Most kitten illnesses need professional attention.

Appearance and milk production are the best indication of the mother's nutritional status. A well-balanced, commercial cat food is adequate for lactating queens. If necessary, supplement this with high protein foods, such as milk products and cooked eggs. A general rule is to feed an additional 100 calories per pound of kitten. By the end of the lactation period, your cat may be eating three times the prebreeding level. Vitamin and mineral and extra calcium supplements should be fed to heavy lactaters with large litters.

Using n ounce or gram scale, weigh the kittens about two weeks after birth. At that time they should be double their birth weight. Their eyes will open about ten days following birth.

Later in nursing, the kitten's teeth and nails may irritate the breasts, and their mother will lose patience and leave them for longer periods of time. Although you can help by trimming the kittens' nails, this is actually nature's way of telling the kittens to try some solid food. Now is the time to try weaning.

Hand-feeding

Hand-feeding the kittens may be necessary if the mother becomes ill or dies, if a kitten is too weak to nurse, or if the litter is unusually large. Borden's KMR is a very good commercial milk substitute. Cow's milk does not contain the level of protein, calcium, phosphorus, or calories needed by the kittens, but in an emergency, you can use one cup of homogenized milk mixed with two egg yolks, one-half teaspoon corn syrup, and a pinch of salt. The kittens should be fed six times a day at four-hour intervals. One teaspoon per day for each ounce of body weight is each kitten's daily ration. Divide this into six equal feedings.

First, warm the formula to body temperature (100°F). Feed the kittens using a doll-sized baby bottle with a nipple or a Pet-Nip®, which is sold in pet stores or by your doctor. *Note: Never* use an eye dropper for feeding. The kitten may aspirate the milk into the lungs and get pneumonia. The formula should drip out slowly when the bottle is inverted; a heated needle can enlarge the hole in the nipple, if necessary. Place the kitten on its stomach, open its mouth with your finger, and position the nipple on top of the tongue. As an extra treat, place a towel within reach so the kitten can knead. The kitten will suck vigorously and be very happy. At the end of a feeding, its abdomen should be enlarged, not bloated.

The kitten should be burped and stimulated to urinate and defecate after each feeding. Burp the kitten as you would a human baby. Hold it against your shoulder and gently pat its back. A warm, moist cotton ball washed against the anal, genital, and abdominal areas will simulate the mother's tongue (which normally would do this) to initiate urination and defecation. The bowel movements should be yellow and formed.

If the kittens are orphaned, the environmental temperature must compensate for the mother's absence. The kitten box should be kept at 85° to 90°F for the first week, 80°F for the second week, 75°F for the third and fourth weeks, and 70°F thereafter. A heating pad on "low" draped over one side of the box and covering a few inches of the bottom will suffice. This way the kitten can choose to be near the heat source or, if too warm, it can crawl away to the cooler side. The heating pad should be covered with a sheet or towel to avoid burns. Whatever external heat source is used, be sure it doesn't burn or overheat the kittens.

If you find that the kittens' skin is getting irritated from sucking on each other, separate them for a week.

Nursing Problems

There are some serious problems during nursing that require immediate cooperation between you and your doctor. Since pregnancy and milk production may demand more calcium than the mother can spare, *eclampsia* (low blood calcium) may be seen during nursing. The signs are nervousness, crying, stiffness, staggering, fever (as high as 107°F), and muscle spasms and convulsions. Eclampsia usually develops within the first three weeks of the nursing period and is a life-threatening medical emergency. Fortunately, it is rare in cats. See the veterinarian *immediately*. If the rectal temperature is 106°F or over, place ice packs between the cat's thighs to lower the fever during the ride to the doctor's office.

Intravenous calcium solutions will usually stop the signs. As the solution is injected, the convulsions cease, the muscles stop twitching, and the cat stops panting. The mother cat will not have to be hospitalized unless it does not respond to treatment (this is rare). Upon returning home, nursing should be stopped or at least restricted. If the kittens are older than three weeks, start them on solid food. Younger kittens will have to be hand-fed to prevent a recurrence of the disease. Your doctor may also prescribe a calcium supplement for the next few weeks.

A malfunction in the organ that controls calcium metabolism (the parathyroid gland) is thought to cause eclampsia. To prevent it, consult your doctor before you

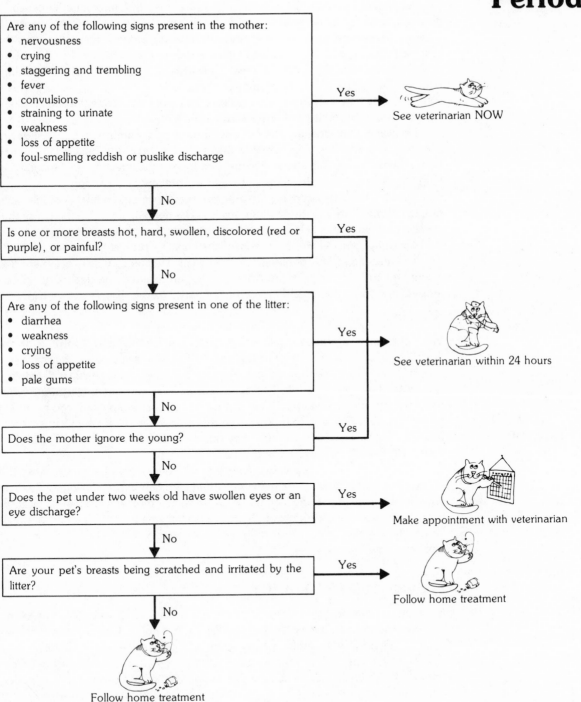

Are any of the following signs present in the mother:
- nervousness
- crying
- staggering and trembling
- fever
- convulsions
- straining to urinate
- weakness
- loss of appetite
- foul-smelling reddish or puslike discharge

Yes → See veterinarian NOW

No

Is one or more breasts hot, hard, swollen, discolored (red or purple), or painful?

Yes

No

Are any of the following signs present in one of the litter:
- diarrhea
- weakness
- crying
- loss of appetite
- pale gums

Yes → See veterinarian within 24 hours

No

Does the mother ignore the young?

Yes

No

Does the pet under two weeks old have swollen eyes or an eye discharge?

Yes → Make appointment with veterinarian

No

Are your pet's breasts being scratched and irritated by the litter?

Yes → Follow home treatment

No

Follow home treatment

breed your cat. He or she will advise you on the proper calcium, phosphorus and vitamin D supplements. Eclampsia can occur again in a female who has had it once and is re-bred. To prevent its recurrence, have your cat spayed.

A bacterial infection of the uterus called *acute metritis* is another emergency. A physical exam, blood tests, and possibly X rays may be necessary for diagnosis. If retained fetuses are seen on the X rays, an immediate ovariohysterectomy is the best treatment. If you want to breed again, a less acceptable and risky choice is to do culture and sensitivity tests and use the specific antibiotic to treat the infection. Flushing the vagina with general antibiotics may also be tried. An injection of oxytocin within twenty-four hours after delivery may prevent uterine infections. Good hygiene and appropriate care are also important.

Mastitis is a bacterial infection of one or more of the breasts. If your cat develops this, hand-feeding the kittens is necessary, because the infected milk may sicken them. In addition, the antibiotics used to treat the infection will be passed in the milk. Again, proper hygiene and care may prevent its development.

Kittens are also susceptible to some problems that can be fatal. For instance, simple diarrhea can dehydrate them quickly. Overfeeding could be the cause, but check with your doctor. Undernutrition from ineffectual nursing can make a kitten cry constantly, but so can other problems, so again—contact your doctor.

The feline infectious peritonitis (FIP) and feline leukemia viruses are suspected culprits for the "kitten mortality complex," which includes the deaths of unborn fetuses, newborn kittens, and very young kittens.

Weaning

When the kittens are three weeks of age, place a shallow saucer of formula on the floor. Dip your finger into the formula and let the kittens suck on it. Repeat this a few times until their noses get closer to the formula. They will probably walk into the saucer, but have patience; you'll be amazed at how fast the kittens will pick up your message. Moistened commercial kitten food or high protein pablum can be added to the formula to make a thin gruel. The mother cat will still let the kittens have a free lunch until they have all their baby teeth (about five weeks of age), but then their teeth will start to irritate the breasts.

The mother will be happy to cooperate with your weaning program. Keep the cat away from the kittens for a few hours during the day. After a week, let them be together just at night. At the same time, decrease the mother's food intake accordingly, to decrease milk production. If the breasts become engorged, which does occasionally happen, compresses may help. Contact your doctor if things don't improve in two or three days.

PREVENTING PREGNANCY

If you do not want to breed your cat, *please* have it neutered, for its own health and as a contribution to reducing the pet population. It is *not* true that neutering causes obesity and laziness; overeating and getting too little exercise are to blame.

The best time for the female's ovariohysterectomy is *before* the first heat (but not before five or six months of age) The estrogens secreted during the heat period may prime the breast tissue for later tumor development, and approximately 90 percent of them are malignant. Spaying early may help prevent tumors from developing.

The ovariohysterectomy is the surgical removal ("*ectomy*") of ovaries ("*ovario*") and the uterus ("*hyster*") through an abdominal incision. The size of the incision does *not* indicate your doctor's surgical skill. Some doctors make small incisions and others like to have good exposure of the surgical area. The size of the organs to be removed will vary among animals, as well.

Spaying is common surgery, but every pet is unique, and special care will be taken. A careful and thorough preoperative exam will determine your cat's ability to undergo surgery. Modern anesthesia (gas or inhalants) is very safe: an anesthetic-caused death is extremely rare in a healthy pet. Your doctor will instruct you not to feed your cat for twelve hours before surgery, which will allow the stomach to empty. If there is food in the stomach during surgery, it may be vomited and pass into the breathing tubes and lungs, and an aspiration pneumonia could occur. If the monitoring equipment (which keeps track of breathing and heart functions during surgery) indicates a potential problem, your cat can be brought out of the anesthesia in a few minutes. Many veterinary hospitals have the same heart monitors used for humans in hospital intensive care units. Emergency fluids and drugs, which are rarely needed, are readily available.

Postoperative complications (such as infection) are also very rare because of aseptic surgical techniques: The operating room is well sterilized, as are the instruments, drapes, caps, masks, and gowns. Modern anesthetics allow most cats to be on their feet minutes after surgery, which also probably lessens the postoperative discomfort. Your cat may be home the same day or the next day, depending on the veterinary hospital procedure.

Home care after surgery consists of keeping the incision clean (don't allow your pet to lie on dirt), exercise restriction (cats will normally restrict their own exercise), and checking the incision for swelling, redness, or discharge. (If any infection develops, call your doctor.) The sutures can be removed in a week.

Castration (surgical removal of the testes) is recommended to prevent or eliminate roaming, spraying, fighting, and breeding in male cats. The testicles are removed through a very small incision in each scrotal sac after the cat has been anesthetised. Most cats are sent home the same day, and surgical recovery is uneventful. In fact, when our male cat Pu was castrated, he was out of the anesthesia in five minutes. I drove him home shortly afterward, and no sooner had we arrived home than he gobbled down some cat food and briskly mounted Mitzi, our tolerant female Siamese! Now that's what I call a recovery!

It may take up to a month for the roaming, spraying, fighting, and mounting behavior to stop because it will take a few weeks for the male hormones still circulating in the body to be used up. A very small percentage of cats may still have some residual objectionable behavior. The best time for the surgery is before the behavior patterns develop, about six months of age.

Rarely, a male cat will have only one testicle (*monorchid*) or none at all (*cryptorchid*) in the sacs (*scrotum*). Although sperm will not be produced in the undescended testicle, male hormones will still be manufactured: Your cat will continue to strut around like the neighborhood lover. One problem with undescended testicles is that they frequently form a large sertoli cell tumor after seven years of age. Again, this is extremely rare in cats.

If your female cat has been *mismated* (accidentally bred), an estrogen injection followed by estrogen tablets given at home is usually successful at preventing pregnancy if given within twenty-four hours of the breeding. The injection makes the uterine environment hostile to the sperm and egg; therefore, implantation won't occur. Estrogen can have toxic side effects, however, so this treatment is discouraged. Unless you really want to breed your cat, I recommend an ovariohysterectomy.

Chapter 10

Genetics and Hereditary Diseases

The Austrian empire in the mid-1800s was *the* important center of the arts, literature, and music. At the same time that Brahms produced his brilliant *Variations on a Theme by Handel* (1861), another genius, an Austrian monk named Gregor Mendel, was making one of the most important biological discoveries ever made: An organism's traits, such as height, are regulated by two particles we now know as *genes* (Greek for "to give birth to"), one particle contributed by the female and the other by the male. Mendel performed his experiments on the garden pea plants. He noticed that when he bred tall pea plants to short pea plants, all the offspring were tall. Mendel called this characteristic the *dominant* trait, and the characteristic that "seemed to disappear" he termed *recessive*.

When Mendel bred the offspring to each other, the result was three tall pea plants for every short pea plant—a ratio of three to one. Mendel surmised that each offspring of the first breeding carried one dominant and one recessive particle and that in the breeding of the offspring, one short pea plant should be produced for every three tall pea plants.

Unfortunately, Vienna and the rest of the world neither understood nor cared about the biological sciences, which were considered antireligious. Gregor Mendel's papers were burned after his death in 1884 and his great findings were not "rediscovered" until the beginning of the twentieth century.

What is this genetic material, which determines that like shall beget like? Genes are composed of *deoxyribonucleic acid* (DNA). This DNA is found in long strands called *chromosomes* in the nucleus of the billions of cells in your pet's body. Every cell of your cat contains nineteen pairs of chromosomes.

Each gene controls the synthesis of one protein. Protein makes up about three-fourths of the body solids and is the building block of life. The majority of proteins are enzymes that regulate the chemical reactions in the cells. Blood, bone, hair, and muscle are primarily protein. Hormones such as insulin are also proteins. Structural protein called *connective tissue* gives the skin its elasticity and the hair its form.

Throughout a lifetime there is a constant turnover of cells—daily wear and tear destroys skin, hair, and blood cells, but they are constantly being replaced, thanks to the cells' ability to duplicate themselves. Before the cell divides, the chromosome forms a replica of itself (a process called *replication*). Each new cell has the exact number and order of genes as the original cell. Thousands upon thousands of activities occur and renew themselves daily in your pet's body, thanks to a biological "blueprint," called the *genetic code,* in the chromosomes.

Every part of your pet's body (and even its temperament, to a large extent) is dependent on the chromosomes that were combined when its parents mated. The fertilized egg that is a complete cell containing all the information that determines hereditary make-up. That cell divides in the mother cat's uterus, and the developing embryo contains the identical genetic make-up.

Let's suppose that you bred your pure tabby to a pure black cat. What color hair coat should you expect in the kittens? Tabby is dominant, and black is recessive. If the female has two dominant genes for a characteristic, such as tabby, the cat is called *homozygote* for that trait. Let's use the letters TT. When a dominant gene is paired with a recessive gene, the cat is called *heterozygote* (Tt) for this trait, but it still produces tabby. Since black is a recessive trait, it can appear only if two recessive hair coat genes are paired. Let's use the letters tt. Using a chart called Mendel's Checkerboard, you can predict the probability of certain genetic traits in the offspring of pea plants, dogs, cats, or any living thing.

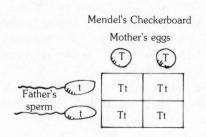

Mendel's Checkerboard

Mother's eggs

All the kittens will be heterozygote and they all will have tabby hair coats, just as Mendel's tall and short pea plants produced all tall plants in the first generation. The next generation could produce some black cats since all have at least one recessive gene.

By now, you're probably wondering what all this has to do with your cat's health. It has a *lot* to do with it! As you already know, one gene carries the message for the production of one protein. But if the DNA gets mixed up, the gene carries an abnormality known as a *mutation,* a change from the normal pattern of inheritance that appears as a new or altered characteristic.

Inbreeding (mating closely related individuals, such as mother to son, father to daughter, or brother to sister) or *linebreeding* (mating more distant relatives such as cousins) increases the chance of defects that require two recessive genes to come together or defects that require a polygenic union. Before breeding, the male and female should be checked by a veterinarian for defects or diseases that have a hereditary basis.

A disease called *globoid cell leukodystrophy* has been seen in a few kittens in which a genetic enzyme deficiency causes progressive degeneration of the nervous system and death in kittens between two and six months of age. It has a *recessive pattern of inheritance:* i.e., a kitten must receive two abnormal genes to produce the disease. A cat that has one normal gene and one abnormal gene is called a *heterozygote carrier* and will appear normal but can pass the abnormal gene to its offspring.

At the University of Pennsylvania Veterinary School, Doctors Patterson and Jezyk and their co-workers are studying the "fading puppy syndrome." In human neonates and infants, genetic enzyme defects such as *phenylketonuria* (PKU) have been identified. Newborn infants can be screened for these hereditary metabolic defects and treated before mental retardation, liver or kidney dysfunction, or death occurs. Neonatal kittens that fail to thrive (they lose weight, have problems moving, and can't maintain body temperature), may have similar disorders.

Metabolic screening is a new and important procedure in veterinary medicine. Dr. Jezyk points out, "In human medicine, 5 to 10 percent of all admissions to pediatric hospitals are for disorders which are clearly genetic, while another 10 to 15 percent are for conditions with some genetic component." The development of veterinary clinical specialties such as neurology, cardiology, dermatology, and opthalmology has increased the accuracy of diagnosis and the recognition of genetic diseases. Improved methods of both prevention and treatment of parasitic, nutritional, and infectious diseases have decreased the importance of these illnesses and has brought to light diseases that are entirely or partially genetic in origin.

Chapter **11**
Cancer–
A Chronic Disease

The improvements in the prevention and treatment of infections, parasites, and nutritional diseases have lengthened the lifespan of our pets. Consequently, a cat living into its middle and later years will develop other health problems. Probably the most dreaded disease of mid- and later life is cancer (although there are some cancers, such as lymphosarcoma [leukemia] that affect primarily younger cats). Yearly, there are almost 160 new cases of cancer per 100,000 cats.

Cancer begins as a biologically abnormal change in a single cell in one of your pet's organs. This cell divides repeatedly, producing more abnormal cells. These new cells also divide at an extremely rapid rate and cannot be stopped by your cat's normal internal monitoring system, which makes normal cells behave. These abnormal cells are biologically destructive: They form solid tumors and invade and destroy surrounding tissue. Malignant tumors produce chemical substances that aid the cellular destruction and help stimulate a blood supply (to obtain oxygen and nutrition) for the tumors. Malignant cells frequently spread throughout the body by way of veins, or lymph vessels and thus bring their destructive ways to other organs in your cat's body. This process is called *metastasis*.

WHAT IS CANCER?

Why should normal cells in your cat's body suddenly transform into malignant cells? Researchers feel that cancer is caused by one or more of the following factors:

233

contact with harmful environmental agents, heredity, viruses, immunologic factors, or body hormones.

Harmful Environmental Agents

Chemical *carcinogens* (agents that produce cancer) are being identified in our air, water, and food. Our pets share this unhealthy environment and share the carcinogens, most of which alter cellular genetic material. Asbestos workers and heavy cigarette smokers have a high incidence of lung cancer. Since cats don't smoke and don't work—especially around asbestos—they have a very low incidence of lung cancer. However, white cats that are excessively exposed to sunshine have a high incidence of skin cancer, just as do fair-skinned humans.

Heredity

Certain breeds seem to have a predisposition for and a high incidence of specific cancers.

Viruses

Tumor-causing viruses are being identified. These viruses change the genetic code in cells, transforming them into malignant cells. The most publicized cancer-inducing virus is the feline leukemia virus.

Immunologic Factors

Tumor cells have antigens (see page 39) on their surfaces. Your cat's immune system (antibodies, lymphocytes, and *macrophages*) recognizes these "foreign" cells and attempts to destroy them. It has been speculated that our pets (and our bodies) produce cancer cells quite often but the immunologic defenses in healthy humans and cats destroy these cells before they can get established. This is called *immunologic surveillance*. If the immune system fails for any reason, the cancer cells can start their destruction.

Body Hormones

Although it has not been established empirically, having an ovariohysterectomy *before* the first heat may help to avoid breast cancer in later years.

Cancer will be prevented only when we understand how and why these factors cause normal cells to transform into cancer cells. For example, if air pollution and smoking induce lung cancer in humans, why don't *all* exposed humans develop cancer?

If your pet develops cancer, don't feel that all is hopeless. In many cases, modern veterinary medicine, just like human medicine, has therapy available to help your pet. The chance for a cure or *remission* will depend on the type of tumor, its location(s), the type of therapy used, and your cat's general health (for example, whether general anesthesia or chemotherapy can be tolerated).

First, you and your doctor must be *sure* that your cat has cancer. Most types of cancer cannot be diagnosed by looking at your pet. Some of the signs, such as loss of appetite, gradual weight loss, weakness, lumps in the abdomen, and even ugly skin growths, could indicate a simpler problem. Your doctor must perform certain tests and take radiographs to verify that cancer is present, to determine the type and extent of the cancer, and to decide on the best type of treatment, if any, for the malignancy (see Laboratory Tests, page 65, and X rays, page 68). Your veterinarian may select some or all of these diagnostic tools to give you clear assessment of your cat's situation.

Once the lab tests and X rays have been studied, the doctor can determine the next step. If there is cancer and it is treatable, you should receive the following information so that you and your doctor can reach a common understanding and decision in your cat's best interests.

- What are the chances for a cure or remission?
- If we can expect a remission, how much time does this give my cat to live free of pain and discomfort?
- What type of therapy will be used?
- What are the side effects of the therapy?
- What is the cost of the therapy?
- How much of my time will be taken up by visits to the veterinary hospital for therapy and follow-up exams?
- Is there any new cancer therapy that will not cause my cat discomfort and that may benefit it and contribute to current human cancer studies?

THERAPY

At the present time, there are five modes of therapy, effective either singly or in combination, used to treat various cancers in different stages of development: surgery, chemotherapy, radiation therapy, cryosurgery, and immunotherapy.

Surgery

This is the major method to diagnose and treat cancer. The major drawback is that a microscopic number of tumor cells may be left behind, which can spread and cause a relapse. If there is a high risk of relapse, or if the entire tumor cannot be successfully removed, one or more of the other modes of therapy may also be used.

Chemotherapy

The hope of chemotherapy is in using a drug or chemical agent that will kill tumor cells while doing as little damage as possible to your cat's healthy cells. The drawbacks of chemotherapy are its expense (unless the therapy is supported by governmental grants to a university or private veterinary medical center) and the potential toxic effects on healthy tissue.

Radiation Therapy

Radiation therapy is an important and effective mode of cancer treatment in human medicine. It is now being recognized as an important form of general cancer therapy. Unfortunately, the cost of the equipment and facilities has limited its use to university and private veterinary medical centers.

The cells of certain tumors seem to be more susceptible to therapeutic doses of *ionizing radiation*. These *ions* seem to kill tumor cells by disrupting their "code of life"—the DNA and chromosomes. The cells die when their attempt at division is ineffective. Susceptible tumors are termed *radiosensitive*.

Cryosurgery

Certain tumors—especially some skin and mouth tumors—have been successfully treated with cryosurgery. This is a technique using liquid nitrogen or a compressed gas such as nitrous oxide to kill tumor cells by alternately freezing and thawing the tissue. A temporary but odorous and oozing wound is the main disadvantage until healing results.

Immunotherapy

A new form of therapy that seems to hold some promise, especially when combined with surgical treatment, is immunotherapy. Your own and your pet's immune system protects the body against "foreign" cells such as bacteria, viruses, and tumor cells. In cancer, the immune system is suppressed or blocked from destroying the tumor cells. Certain biological and chemical substances called *immune adjuvants* are being used to stimulate the immune system in hopes of getting remissions in breast cancer.

Early diagnosis and treatment are most important if therapy is to be successful. If your cat is over five years old and you suspect the presence of cancer, see your veterinarian.

Most cat owners are willing to prolong their pet's life if it will be free of pain and suffering. If you and your veterinarian reach a common understanding that this is not possible, it is in your pet's best interest to administer euthanasia (page 241). In this way, pets do not have to suffer through the pain and misery of cancer that has spread throughout the body. But please consider euthanasia only as one option. Just like heart disease, cancer can be considered a chronic illness that can, in many cases, be controlled—i.e., your cat can live free of pain and discomfort. Euthanasia should be used only if treatment has failed or if your cat has a form of cancer that is completely hopeless.

Skin cancer, lymphosarcoma, and breast cancer are three forms of cancer commonly seen in cats.

SKIN TUMORS

Any growth in or on your cat's skin should be examined by your veterinarian. Most skin tumors, such as the three shown, are benign, but any growth that increases rapidly in size and infiltrates the surrounding tissue may indicate malignancy. Early surgical removal is curative for the majority of skin tumors.

Sebaceous adenoma   Lipoma   Sebaceous cyst

Sebaceous Adenoma
This skin growth looks very much like a cauliflower: There are several small clumps of greyish matter growing from a common base. If the adenoma gets irritated, it may become red and ulcerated. You should be able to get your fingers around the growth because it does not infiltrate adjacent tissue.

Lipoma
The more common term for this growth is "fatty tumor." It grows under the skin, but you can feel it. A lipoma can get very large, although it grows slowly. Again, it should move freely because it does not spread to surrounding cells.

Sebaceous Cyst
This is similar to a lipoma in that it is a freely moving growth under the skin. However, this cyst is composed of cheeselike matter and remains fairly small, around the size of a marble. This, too, does not harm adjacent tissue.

LYMPHOSARCOMA (LEUKEMIA)

Since the early 1900s, viruses have been known to cause cancer in animals. In 1964, a virus called the feline leukemia virus (FLV) was found in a household of cats with a high percentage of leukemia cases. Since 1964, major developments have been made in understanding the nature and transmission of this virus, detecting it in the cat population, and studying leukemia and other disease states attributed to the virus. At this writing, there is no evidence that the feline leukemia virus can infect humans or other animals. A vaccine that may protect cats against the virus is currently being tested.

Lymphosarcoma is a cancer of the blood-forming cells—more specifically, the lymphoid tissue (such as the lymph nodes). The virus FLV is spread by the saliva and urine of infected cats, and it can also be transmitted in the uterus to unborn kittens and in the milk to nursing kittens. Since it is found in the blood, such blood-sucking insects as cat fleas and mosquitoes probably transmit the FLV to other cats. For some reason, not all cats that are infected with the virus get leukemia. It seems that cats that develop antibodies to the virus do *not* get the disease.

Forms of the Disease
There are three recognized forms of lymphosarcoma: chest, abdominal, and multicentric. The signs that your cat shows will depend on the lymph node or organs involved.

Chest
In this form, the enlarged chest lymph nodes compress the windpipe and esophagus, and fluid may accumulate in the chest. Your cat will experience breathing difficulties, coughing, and gagging.

Abdomen
Malignant cells may be found in the intestine, lymph nodes, liver, spleen, and kidney, causing a loss of appetite, weight loss, vomiting, diarrhea or constipation, and anemia.

Multicentric
The lymph nodes under the skin will be greatly enlarged and tumor formation can be found in many organs, including unusual locations such as the eyes or brain. The cat may or may not have a fever.

Treatment
Many of the signs of lymphosarcoma (leukemia) are also seen in other treatable diseases; therefore, your veterinarian will have to perform some or all of the following tests to reach a *definite* diagnosis of lymphosarcoma: a complete blood count, blood chemistries, X rays of the chest and/or abdomen, a bone marrow or lymph node biopsy, and an examination of the chest and/or abdominal fluids. There is also a specific blood test for the presence of FLV. This test should be done

1. on a new cat before it enters a household of cats or a cattery;
2. before you breed a tom or queen (be sure the cattery is *certified* FLV-free);
3. if your cat shows any of the signs of lymphosarcoma;
4. if your cat has a chronic disease, such as mouth ulcers or anemia that does not respond to treatment (the virus seems to suppress your cat's immunologic system and to make it difficult to fight off infections).

If in a multiple-cat household, one cat has lymphosarcoma or a positive test, *all* the cats should be tested. If this first test is negative, the cats should be retested in three months, since the virus has a long incubation period.

If your cat's illness is diagnosed as lymphosarcoma, some veterinarians will recommend treatment; others recommend euthanasia. The virus can be transmitted to other cats. FLV-positive cats should be isolated until they achieve a negative status. If they do not, the cats should be removed. Cats that are treated for lymphosarcoma with anticancer drugs or supportive therapy, such as blood transfusions, fluids, vitamins, or steroids, do not respond well. If your cat with lymphosarcoma passes away or is euthanized, discard its feeding bowls, litter pans, and bedding and clean the premises thoroughly (ordinary household cleaners suffice). *Note:* Do *not* bring another cat into the house for thirty days after removal of the infected cat.

The feline leukemia virus is also thought to play a role in a certain kidney ailment called *glomerulonephritis,* in reproduction problems such as infertility, and in the "kitten mortality complex"—the sudden and unexplained death of newborn and young kittens.

BREAST CANCER

Breast cancer is a disease of middle-aged and old female cats. Ninety percent of cat breast tumors are malignant. Any hard lump near a nipple and under the skin of a breast should be examined by your veterinarian. Early diagnosis and aggressive therapy of malignant breast tumors may prolong your cat's life.

The cause of breast cancer is not known; however, it is possible that breast cancer may be averted if your cat is spayed before the first heat. So if you do not plan to breed your cat, it may be a good idea to have the ovariohysterectomy done early.

If the lump is suspicious, your veterinarian will probably recommend two procedures—a radiograph of the chest and a biopsy of the lump. If malignancy is present, metastasis of the cancer to the lungs is a fairly common occurrence. If there is no evidence of metastasis, surgery will be recommended. The affected breast and the adjacent lymph vessels, veins, and lymph nodes will usually be removed and examined for malignancy. If the tumor is benign, breath a sigh of relief! Some benign tumors can become malignant if they are not removed. If the tumor is malignant, the surgery may increase your cat's life span and free it of discomfort or pain.

A very promising new treatment is combining surgery with immunotherapy. Immunotherapy seems to eliminate the few cancer cells that remain after surgery, and the survival time seems to increase considerably. In one study, at the veterinary cancer unit of the Animal Medical Center in New York, it increased by more than seventeen months.

As you can see, cancer is a very complex chronic disease that, in many instances, *can* be treated. Early diagnosis is *very* important, as is close cooperation with your veterinarian during treatment. The decision between euthanasia and treatment should be made only after serious consultation with your veterinarian, always keeping in mind your cat's well-being.

Chapter 12

Euthanasia: When It's Time to Say Goodbye

This is the hardest decision to make. I know, because I had to make that decision for our dear, fourteen-year-old miniature poodle, Pepe, who was suffering with pancreatic cancer. All life is precious, but euthanasia has its time and place. If your cat has an incurable disease or is vicious and dangerous, euthanasia is usually recommended. An intravenous overdose of an anesthetic that is fast and painless is used.

Many owners want to be present when their pet is "put to sleep," and most veterinarians will assent. Although the injection is fast and painless, you should be aware that there are involuntary reflexes for a few minutes after your pet has departed.

Albert Schweitzer's reverence for life was a great influence on me when I was very young. Consequently, I will not euthanize a healthy animal or an animal that has a curable disease. Most veterinarians feel the same way. If you cannot afford the necessary care, discuss it with your veterinarian. He or she may work out a long-term payment plan or may not charge you for the time.

Final arrangements for the remains should be made prior to euthanasia. Your veterinarian may suggest cremation or a pet cemetery. Many areas have public ordinances against backyard burials.

It's very hard to lose a pet that has given you love and companionship. But you'll always have the memories, and as soon as you feel ready, I recommend finding a new family member to share your love. You'll be glad you did.

Index

244